HALF SLAVE

— AND —

HALF FREE

HALF SLAVE

—— AND ——

HALF FREE

The Roots of Civil War

BRUCE LEVINE

HILL AND WANG

A division of Farrar, Straus and Giroux

New York

Published in Canada by HarperCollinsCanadaLtd
Printed in the United States of America
Designed by Victoria Wong
First published in 1992 by Hill and Wang, a division of Farrar, Straus and Giroux
Sixth printing, 1996

Library of Congress Cataloging-in-Publication Data
Levine, Bruce C.
Half slave and half free : the roots of civil war / Bruce Levine ;
consulting editor, Eric Foner.
p. cm.
Includes index.
1. United States—History—Civil War, 1861–1865—Causes.
2. United States—History—1783–1865.   3. Working class—United States—History—
19th century.   4. Slavery—United States—History—19th century.
I. Foner, Eric.   II. Title.
E459.L48   1991   973.7'11—dc20   91-10245 CIP

For sweet Madeline Augonnet

ACKNOWLEDGMENTS

Half Slave and Half Free reflects my primary intellectual interest—the resynthesis of social and political history. I first dealt with
many of the specific issues discussed here in the collaborative volume *Who Built America? Working People & The Nation's Economy, Politics, Culture & Society* (Vol. 1, Pantheon Books, 1989)
and in a monograph entitled *The Spirit of 1848: German Immigrants, Labor Conflict, and the Coming of the Civil War* (University of Illinois Press, 1992). Both projects focused my attention on
the social dimension of antebellum politics. The intellectual
creditors of *Half Slave and Half Free* thus include the long list of
individuals thanked in those earlier volumes. Ira Berlin, William
J. Cooper, Jr., David Brion Davis, Barbara J. Fields, Michael P.
Johnson, Leon Litwack, James M. McPherson, Michael Mullin,
Gary B. Nash, John Niven, James Oakes, Nell Irvin Painter,
Kenneth M. Stampp, and Stan Weir helped me find and evaluate
various documents cited in the text. None of these people, however, bears any responsibility for the use to which I have put their
counsel. Five years of teaching courses on the Civil War era at
the University of Cincinnati have considerably deepened and enriched my understanding of that period. My colleague John K.
Alexander steered me to some of the literature on colonial and

revolutionary society. The excellent staff of UC's library has made the completion of this volume immeasurably easier than it might have been. So did a fellowship from the University of Cincinnati's Charles Phelps Taft Foundation.

Eric Foner's influence on my thinking and this manuscript has been, quite simply, enormous. Arthur Wang's patient, good-humored, but persistent (!) prodding kept me going, and his sound counsel and sensitive ear for the language improved this book considerably. I am very grateful to both of them. I owe most of all to the hundreds of scholars upon whose books and articles the following synthesis draws.

CONTENTS

Were ever any people, civilized or savage, persuaded by arguments, human or divine, to surrender voluntarily two thousand millions of dollars [of property]?

JAMES HENRY HAMMOND of South Carolina
Two Letters on Slavery in the United States, 1845

That [southern] spirit which desired the peaceful extinction of slavery has itself become extinct, with the *occasion,* and the *men* of the Revolution. . . . The Autocrat of all the Russias will resign his crown, and proclaim his subjects free republicans sooner than will our American masters voluntarily give up their slaves.

Our political problem now is, "Can we, as a nation, continue together *permanently—forever*—half slave, and half free?"

ABRAHAM LINCOLN
Letter to George Robertson, August 15, 1855

Although the destruction of the oppressors God may not effect by the oppressed, yet the Lord our God will bring other destructions upon them—for not unfrequently will he cause them to rise up one against another, to be split and divided, and to oppress each other, and sometimes to open hostilities with sword and hand.

DAVID WALKER
Appeal to the Colored Citizens of the World, 1829

HALF SLAVE

—— AND ——

HALF FREE

INTRODUCTION

Freedom, Slavery, and the Legacy of the American Revolution

The American Civil War was, by general agreement, the most important event in the history of the United States. It altered the internal structure of American society more profoundly than had the Revolution. With the exception of the Haitian revolution, it was the most thoroughgoing and far-reaching assault on bound labor to occur in the Western Hemisphere. It not only dethroned the once dominant planter elite politically but eliminated it as a slaveholding class by emancipating 4 million human chattels. The war also conferred formal civic equality on the freedpeople. Indeed, as former Confederate general Richard Taylor observed in 1865, "Society has been completely changed by the war. The [French] revolution did not produce a greater change in the 'Ancien Régime' than this has in our social life." Changes introduced in the federal constitution and governmental practice have left their mark on economics, culture, politics, and law down to the present day.

Many traditional accounts of the Civil War's origins concentrate upon the thoughts and actions of the elite (and their impact on legislation and party systems) to the exclusion of other influences. But a mere glance at the massive popular mobilization that made the war possible indicates the need for a wider perspective.

Almost 3 million men donned Union blue or Confederate gray between 1861 and 1865. And though both officer corps were top-heavy with graduates of elite military institutions, planters, merchants, and professionals, the rank and file of each army was overwhelmingly composed of farmers, skilled workers, and urban and rural laborers. Of the Union forces, moreover, about half a million had been born abroad, and another 185,000 were African-Americans, nearly three-quarters of them freedmen recruited in the slave states. Although both sides eventually adopted conscription, the size and power of the Union and Confederate armies—and especially at the outset—owed far more to the voluntary service of their citizen-soldiers. Before the war had ended, one out of every five would give up his life; untold others would be maimed. No other war in the nation's history has taken so heavy a toll.

Any satisfactory analysis of the war's origins must account for this unequaled degree of popular mobilization and sacrifice. What impelled so many—rich, middling, and poor; white and black; native-born and immigrant—to risk and sacrifice so much? What brought them, their families, and the nation as a whole to that point? To answer such questions, this book reexamines antebellum political history in the light of the broader economic, social, cultural, and ideological developments that shaped the lives of the American people.

The American Revolution gave birth to a paradox, a contradiction. On the one hand, the new nation was in many respects the freest in the world. During the next two centuries, immigrants would flock to its shores by the millions to share in its political and material benefits. New nations and governments would pattern their founding documents on those of the United States.

The largest, the most populous, and politically the most important state of the new republic was Virginia, the first colony to declare its independence from Great Britain. It was home to Patrick Henry, whose defiant rhetoric in Virginia's House of Delegates helped galvanize support for independence. "Is life so dear or peace so sweet, as to be purchased at the price of chains and slavery?" he demanded memorably. "Forbid it, Almighty God! I know not what course others may take, but as for me, give me liberty or give me death!" It was the home of George Washington, the first commander-in-chief and President. And it was home to Thomas Jefferson, the new republic's first Secretary of State, third President, and author of the manifesto that best captured the nation's devotion to personal freedom. "We hold these truths to be self-evident," it declared, "that all men are created equal, that they are endowed by their Creator with certain inalienable rights, that among these are life, liberty, and the pursuit of happiness."

Jefferson's powerful language brings us to the other side of the American paradox: This new land of liberty was a great slaveholding power—the greatest, in fact, of the nineteenth-century world. And Jefferson's Virginia was the principal slaveholding state in the new federal union. Indeed, when the Constitution was ratified, about a third of all the slaves in the United States lived in that single state.

Antislavery beliefs had been spreading in the pre-revolutionary era. Patrick Henry owned slaves but in 1773 granted that to do so was "repugnant to humanity" and "inconsistent with the Bible." A revolution fought in the name of liberty inevitably stimulated such feelings. Educated in the spirit of the Enlightenment and moved by the rhetoric of revolution, some masters expressed a desire to abolish the institution. "There is not a man living," George Washington contended in 1786, "who wishes more sincerely than I do, to see a plan adopted for the gradual abolition of it." Protestant clergy and laymen (especially Quakers, Baptists, and Methodists) formed societies dedicated to that end.

Few white Virginians were more painfully conscious of this contradiction between principle and practice than Thomas Jefferson. He tried unsuccessfully to include in the Declaration of Independence a clause denouncing the British Crown for introducing slavery into the North American colonies and for preventing those colonies from outlawing the further importation of African slaves—for thereby waging "cruel war against human nature itself, violating its most sacred rights of life and liberty in the persons of a distant people who never offended him, captivating and carrying them into slavery in another hemisphere." A few years later, Jefferson observed in his *Notes on the State of Virginia*:

> The whole commerce between master and slave is a perpetual exercise of the most boisterous passions, the most unremitting despotism on the one part, and degrading submissions on the other. Our children see this, and learn to imitate it . . . The man must be a prodigy who can retain his manners and morals undepraved by such circumstances.

In private correspondence, Jefferson marveled that the same American patriot who "can endure toil, famine, stripes, imprisonment or death itself in vindication of his own liberty" could "the next moment . . . inflict on his fellow men a bondage, one hour of which is fraught with more misery than ages of that which he rose in rebellion to oppose." Even as he wrote these words, Jefferson was the owner of some two hundred slaves.

Such contradictions were most swiftly and easily resolved in the North, where slavery—never central to the region's economy—continued to decline in significance. By the revolutionary era, no powerful group of northern residents had a sizable stake in preserving bound labor there. But the Revolutionary War stimulated emancipation in the South as well, not only ideologically but practically. Both sides felt constrained to bid for the loyalty of the huge black population. In November 1775, the British governor of Virginia, Lord Dunmore, offered freedom to slaves who fought for the Crown. Other British officers did the same. Patriot officials in Maryland sought to offset these British inducements by promising freedom for slaves who would fight for the colonists. Revolutionary Virginia, Delaware, and North Carolina allowed slaves to fulfill the military obligations of their masters and often granted freedom to those who did.

Together with the humanitarian sentiment of some—leading to voluntary manumissions—and the war-spawned confusion that aided a growing number of escapes, these emergency measures swelled the ranks of free blacks in the South, and especially in Virginia and Maryland. This group numbered fewer than 10,000 before the Revolution began. Perhaps 60,000 were free by 1790, more than 100,000 by 1800, and 186,000 by 1810. The increase was dramatic and fraught with long-term significance. But it did not reduce slavery's centrality to southern society, nor did it reflect any significant weakening of the southern elite's commitment to it. Ninety percent of the region's black population remained enslaved.

Thomas Jefferson hoped that a combination of enlightened self-interest and moral awakening would induce slaveholders to embrace his own stated faith in gradual emancipation and colonization. But Jefferson consistently declined to champion that course openly. As he told a Quaker friend in 1805, "I have most carefully avoided every public act or manifestation on that subject." He thus initially opposed publication of his *Notes on the State of Virginia*, which he had prepared in 1782 for the benefit of French friends and acquaintances. "The strictures on slavery" in particular, he emphasized three years later, "I do not wish to have made public." Their appearance might "produce an irritation which would indispose people towards the . . . great objects I have in view." When Jefferson did allow publication of the *Notes* in 1787, he printed it in a small, private edition, single copies of which he circulated only within a circle of trusted friends, students, "and some estimable characters beyond that line." Further than that he was still "unwilling to expose these sheets to the public eye."

Jefferson's reticence accurately reflected the contradiction inherent in his own situation. On the one hand, he derived his political standing and influence from the support of the planters of Virginia and elsewhere in the South. On the other hand, talk of practical, statutory steps to bring about slavery's abolition was anathema to most of that constituency. Jefferson's recognition of that fact led him to abandon hope for his own generation of planters. "Nursed and educated in the daily habit of seeing the degraded condition, both bodily and mental, of these unfortunate beings," he later recalled, few of those planters "yet doubted but that [the blacks] were as legitimate subjects of property as their horses and cattle." But Jefferson continued to nurse hopes for the rising planter generation, those younger men who, shaped in the crucible of the Revolution, had "sucked in the principles of liberty as it were with their mother's milk." "It is to them I look," he wrote a friend, "to the rising generation, and not to the one now in power, for these great reformations." In fact, he asserted in 1782, "I think a change already perceptible, since the origin of the present revolution. The spirit of the master is abating, that of the slave rising from the dust, his condition is mollifying, the way I hope preparing, under the auspices of heaven, for a total emancipation, and that this is disposed . . . to be with the consent of the masters." By 1805, Jefferson even thought he saw in economic trends additional reason for optimism. It seemed to him then that "interest is really going over to the side of morality. The value of the slave is every day lessening; his burthen on his master dayly increasing. Interest is therefore preparing the disposition to be just."

In fact, however, Jefferson misread the course of economic and political development. Perhaps local trends in the tobacco culture misled him. But the American Convention of Abolition Societies had reported just a year earlier of North Carolina that "at present, the inhabitants of that state, consider the preservation of their lives, and all they hold dear on earth, as depending on the continuance of slavery; and are even now riveting more firmly the fetters of oppression." Farther south, economic developments both at home and abroad were giving slavery an even more powerful stimulus, and the rising generation of slave owners would prove, if anything, more firmly attached to their "peculiar institution" than were their antecedents. Within a few decades even Jefferson's ambivalent, hesitant, and private criticisms of slavery would become unacceptable there.

Planter intransigence could not, however, prevent others—first and foremost slaves and free blacks—from addressing the apparent contradiction between paeans to freedom and the realities of bondage. In 1791, for example, a free black resident of Maryland named Benjamin Banneker, a mathematician and astronomer, wrote Secretary of State Thomas Jefferson to chide him precisely on that subject. Citing the first sentence of the Virginian's famous Declaration, Banneker declared it "pitiable" that while white colonists

> were so fully convinced of the benevolence of the Father of Mankind and of his equal and impartial distribution of these rights and privileges . . . you should at the same time counteract his mercies in detaining by fraud and violence so numerous a part of my brethren, under groaning captivity and cruel oppression, that you should at the same time be found guilty of that most criminal act, which you professedly detested in others, with respect to yourselves.

Americans were not alone in grappling with such inconsistencies in the age of revolutions. The outbreak of revolution in France in 1789 stimulated the local elite in the French Caribbean colony of Saint-Domingue to demand expanded political privileges for itself. But that initiative, in turn, encouraged the black majority to take action in its own behalf. (It seems likely that the example of the American Revolution helped inspire that outcome, just as it had influenced others in France and Saint-Domingue. More than 500 Saint-Domingue blacks had been among the Count d'Estaing's 3,600-strong French forces that in 1779 supported North America's Continental Army at Savannah, Georgia.) In 1791, slaves under the leadership of Toussaint Louverture rose in revolt, overthrew their masters, and fought off invading armies from France, Spain, and England. In 1804, the independent black republic changed its name from Saint-Domingue to Haiti.

The international repercussions—not least of all in the United States—were tremendous. "The story of Toussaint Louverture has been told almost as often as that of Napoleon," noted patrician historian Henry Adams in 1889, "but not in connection with the history of the United States, although he exercised on their history an influence as decisive as that of any European ruler." In 1804–5, residents of Pointe Coupee Parish, Louisiana, warned the governor of the dangers confronting them there: "The news of the Revolution of St. Domingo and other Places has become common among our Blacks—and . . . a spirit of Revolt and Mutyny has Crept in amongst them—a few Days since we happyly Discovered a Plan for our Destruction."

Echoes of the Haitian drama spread quickly and rang down through the decades, inspiring slaves and free blacks elsewhere with confidence. Slave rebels organized by Denmark Vesey in 1822 drew inspiration from Haiti's example. In 1825, William Watkins reminded a meeting of fellow free blacks in the slave-state city of Baltimore that Haiti stood as "an irrefutable argument to prove that the descendants of Africa were never designed by their creator to sustain an inferiority, or even a mediocrity in the chain of being." In 1859, free black masons of St. Louis, Missouri, were still commemorating the Haitian war for independence, and Louisiana slaves were singing songs first sung during the Haitian revolution. Admiration for the Haitians' achievement even spread to some whites. "Let us be consistent, Americans," urged Connecticut's Abraham Bishop in 1792, "and if we justify our own conduct in the late glorious revolution, let us justify those who, in a cause like ours, fight with equal bravery."

The liberation standard raised in 1776, 1789, and 1791 was lofted again in Virginia in 1800, the year in which Thomas Jefferson was elected President of the United States. In accordance with an insurrectionary plan organized by a bound blacksmith named Gabriel Prosser, some one thousand slaves gathered outside the state capital of Richmond. Bad weather and a general alarm among whites forced the rebels to disband, and thirty-five of them, including Prosser, were eventually caught and hanged. The whites' relief, however, dissipated quickly when the rebels' ideological and practical orientation became apparent. Prosser, it developed, had hoped for aid from Haiti, and his chosen rallying cry would have sounded familiar to Patrick Henry. The rebels' planned banner was to proclaim: "Death or Liberty." Once again, the symbols and actual fruits of freedom were menacing the regime of bondage.

Fears of servile revolt stoked Jefferson's worries about slavery. Planters, he held, must provide for a gradual and peaceful means of emancipation or it would occur swiftly, bloodily, and "by their extirpation." Jefferson's fellow planters shared such worries but not the conclusions Jefferson drew from them. Most responded to threats against their social order by attempting to seal off the region from political contagion, by tightening their grip on their human property and the South's free black population, and by raising the level of political repression generally.

Here was one factor in the decision to outlaw the international slave trade. Commercial considerations, of course, also loomed large. By restricting the supply of slaves, those who already owned them would see their property sharply appreciate. But political motives also came into play. If memories of, contact with, or anticipations of freedom encouraged rebellion and revolt, it made good sense to exclude further importations of bound laborers who recalled an African past or were tainted by Haiti's present. The state of South Carolina forbade the introduction of all "outlandish" slaves between 1786 and 1803. The acquisition of the Louisiana Territory in the latter year created a domestic market for unfree labor that Carolina dealers could not resist; so did the westward spread of cotton cultivation. South Carolina resumed its international commerce in slaves. But by the time that the U.S. Congress finally outlawed the Atlantic slave trade in 1807–8, every other southern state had already banned that traffic on its own.

There were other ramifications as well. Planters such as John Taylor of Caroline blamed the revolt in Haiti on the agitation of that country's sizable free black population. To prevent such occurrences in the American South, they urged the exclusion from the slave states of all blacks already free and a revision of state laws to discourage any future manumissions. During the 1790s, that line of reasoning proved potent and led Virginia to repeal a 1782 law facilitating voluntary emancipation of individual slaves. Fears that free blacks would undermine slavery informed the decision to bar them from naturalization, from the state militias, and—in 1810—even from carrying the mails.

In 1802, Thomas Jefferson's Postmaster General and close adviser, Gideon Granger, laid out the thinking involved in a revealing—and for that reason highly confidential—letter sent to Senator James Jackson of Georgia, chairman of the Committee on the Posts. Granger wrote privately to raise a subject "too delicate to engraft into a report which may become public, yet too important to be omitted or passed over without full consideration." The subject's importance derived from the danger of slave rebellion. "After the scenes which St. Domingo has exhibited to the world," Granger noted, "we cannot be too cautious in attempting to prevent similar evils in the four Southern States." Especially since, he added, "in Virginia and South Carolina (as I have been informed) plans and conspiracies have already been concerted by them more than once, to rise in arms, and subjugate their masters." To reduce the danger of such events in the future required a clear-eyed appraisal of their causes, which must then be removed. Highest on Granger's list was black access to dangerous ideas and excessive freedom of action. "Every thing which tends to increase their knowledge of natural rights," he wrote, ". . . or that affords them an opportunity of associating, acquiring, and communicating sentiments, and of establishing a chain or line of intelligence, must increase your hazard, because it increases their means of effecting their object."

At last Granger had reached the immediate point of his letter—the practice of "employing negroes, or people of color, in transporting the public mails." Those free blacks employed as "post riders," he thought, were "the most active and intelligent" among their people. That is exactly what made them dangerous. "These are the most *ready* to *learn*, and the most *able* to *execute*. By travelling from day to day, and hourly mixing with people, they must, they will acquire information." Granger's fears about what they would thereby learn are particularly revealing. "They will learn that a man's rights do not depend on his color." Worse, they would then, "in time, become teachers to their brethren." Meanwhile, the unusual freedom that their occupation gave them multiplied all these dangers immeasurably.

> They become acquainted with each other on the line. Whenever the body, or a portion of them, wish to act, they are an organized corps, circulating our intelligence openly, their own privately. . . . One able man among them, perceiving the value of this machine, might lay a plan which would be communicated by your post riders from town to town, and produce a general and united operation against you.

The ideological and practical fears expressed in Granger's letter would haunt the nation throughout the antebellum era.

It became clear during the first decades of the nineteenth century that the planters of the American South were not about to follow the path of gradual emancipation that the northern states had blazed. The economies of the two regions, on the contrary, continued to evolve in opposite directions. As early as the constitutional convention of 1787, according to Virginia planter James Madison, it had been "pretty well understood that the real difference of interests lay, not between the large & small but between the N. & South'n States. The institution of slavery & its consequences formed the line of discrimination." James Wilson of Pennsylvania, for example, hoped a ban on the Atlantic slave trade would "lay the foundation for banishing slavery out of this country," would encourage southern states to adopt "the same kind, gradual change, which was pursued in Pennsylvania." Pierce Butler of South Carolina, however, declared that "the security the Southn. States want is that their negroes may not be taken from them[,] which some gentlemen within or without doors, have a very good mind to do."

Thirty years later, those differences had become considerably more marked. In 1819–20, they burst into the open in a bitter intersectional struggle over the future of slavery in the nation's expanding West. Thomas Jefferson saw in that contest the shape of things to come. Now, Jefferson anticipated, the "line of discrimination" noted by Madison would continue to widen, increasingly defining the boundaries of political loyalties and antagonisms in the country. "A geographical line," he worried, "coinciding with a marked principle, moral and political, once conceived and held up to the angry passions of men, will never be obliterated; and every new irritation will mark it deeper and deeper." Jefferson mourned for the past and despaired of the future. "I regret," he wrote in 1820, "that I am now to die in the belief, that the useless sacrifice of themselves by the generation of 1776, to acquire self-government and happiness to their country, is to be thrown away by the unwise and unworthy passions of their sons, and that my only consolation is to be, that I live not to weep over it."

The chapters that follow trace and analyze the developments anticipated by Jefferson as they actually worked themselves out between the achievement of national independence and the outbreak of civil war. Infusing the book is an argument that may be outlined briefly as follows:

1.   The Civil War was the second act of America's democratic revolution. The first, in the late eighteenth century, had freed the North American colonies from British domination and united them within a single border under a single national government.

2.   That revolution was led by an alliance, a coalition, between predominantly slave-labor and predominantly free-labor communities. Tensions existed between them, but their common interests initially prevailed. The constitution of 1788 was a product of that same coalition, and the many compromises that went into it reflected a determined and successful effort to reconcile their differences.

3.   The distinctive ways in which North and South organized their labor systems left their mark on all aspects of regional life—including family, gender, and leisure patterns and both religious

and secular ideologies. Such cultural changes, in turn, deeply influenced political life.

4. Similarly influential were forces both substantial and ideological that were not only domestic but international in scope.

5. Neither the North nor the South was economically, culturally, or politically monolithic. Important divisions existed within each section, and these helped determine the tempo and manner in which the national drama unfolded.

6. Over the seven decades following the ratification of the Constitution, the growth of both social systems progressively aggravated tensions between North and South, undermining their political cooperation. Looking back over that history, the immigrant politician Carl Schurz observed that the "slavery question" was "not a mere occasional quarrel between two sections of the country, divided by a geographic line" but a "great struggle between two antagonistic systems of social organization . . ." In a famous speech of October 1858, Senator William Seward of New York amplified on that theme, observing:

> Our country is a theater which exhibits in full operation two radically different political systems: the one resting on the basis of servile labor, the other on the basis of voluntary labor of free men . . . Increase of population, which is filling the States out of their borders, together with a new and extended network of railroads and other avenues, and an internal commerce which daily becomes more intimate, is rapidly bringing the States into a higher and more perfect social unity or consolidation. Thus, these antagonistic systems are continually coming into closer contact, and collision results.

"Shall I tell you what this collision means?" Seward continued.

> They who think it is accidental, unnecessary, the work of interested or fanatical agitators, and therefore ephemeral, mistake the case altogether. It is an irrepressible conflict between opposing and enduring forces, and it means that the United States must and will sooner or later become either entirely a slave-holding or entirely a free-labor nation.

7. The accumulating force of this central conflict finally re-organized political life; on both sides, individuals once deemed isolated fanatics (abolitionists, secessionists) became prophets and leaders.

8. At last, with the sharpening clash of outlooks and interests, the original project of the Founding Fathers—to hold together a society half slave and half free—became untenable. The result was secession, civil war, and ultimately, the irrevocable destruction of chattel slavery.

— 1 —

"Our Laborers Are Our Property": The Southern Slave Economy

In the first month of the Civil War, Confederate President Jefferson Davis reminded the Confederate Congress that in the American South slave labor had

> convert[ed] hundreds of thousands of square miles of wilderness into cultivated lands covered with a prosperous people; towns and cities had sprung into existence, and had rapidly increased in wealth and population under the social system of the South; . . . and the productions in the South of cotton, rice, sugar, and tobacco, for the full development and continuance of which the labor of African slaves was and is indispensable, had swollen to an amount which formed nearly three-quarters of the exports of the whole United States and had become absolutely necessary to the wants of civilized man. With interests of such overwhelming magnitude imperiled, the people of the Southern States were driven by the conduct of the North to the adoption of some course of action to avert the danger with which they were openly menaced.

A substantial body of literature accumulated in the antebellum South in which slave owners shared experiences with their labor system and advice on how best to manage it. In one such essay, North Carolina planter Dr. John F. Tompkins spelled out the premise of this discussion more explicitly than most bothered—

or preferred—to do. "In the first place," he asked in the *Farmers'*
Journal in 1853, "for what purpose does the master hold the servant? Is it not that by his labor he, the master, may accumulate
wealth?"

The question was rhetorical; general agreement was assumed,
as well it could be. New World slavery harnessed the ancient status of bound labor to a decidedly modern purpose—the large-
scale, profit-oriented production of commodities for a capitalist
world market.

Only by grasping this two-sided, hybrid character can the
South's slave system—and its effect on all it touched—be understood. On the one hand, the demands and rhythms of the world
market created this system and dictated much about the way it
functioned. Those who produced these commodities, on the
other hand, were themselves commodities owned by others. This
decisive fact distinguished the inner workings of the slave economy from those based on independent petty proprietorship, free
wage labor, or both. Members of an Alabama agricultural society
stressed this simple but profoundly important point in 1846:

> Our condition is quite different from that of the non-slaveholding
> section of the United States. With them their only property consists
> of lands, cattle and planting implements. Their laborers are merely
> hirelings, while with us our laborers are our property.

Slavery is among the oldest social systems on record. It existed
in ancient China, Persia, Greece, and Rome, and biblical refer-
ences to it abound. The first book of the Old Testament speaks of
it with casual approval. And "Thy bond-men and thy bond-maids
which thou shalt have," says the Book of Leviticus, "shall be of
the heathen that are round about you." Slavery survived in the
northern and southern Mediterranean well into the Middle Ages.

In the system's "patriarchal" form, the slave commonly worked
to satisfy the limited needs of a relatively small group of people—
a family or group of families—as a domestic servant, artisan,
scribe, teacher, or warrior. The arrangement thus grew out of and

expressed a very primitive division of labor. Generally regarded as subordinate members of the group to which they were attached, the slaves usually retained a variety of personal rights; their unfree status, often temporary, was rarely heritable.

As a way of organizing the production of agricultural commodities for a far-flung market, however, slavery had its own genesis and distinctive characteristics. It began to flourish in the modern era only with the expansion of world trade. During the fifteenth century, Portuguese colonists purchased tens of thousands of Africans to grow sugarcane on plantations they established on off-shore islands. The success of that venture and others paved the way for bigger slave-based colonies in the Western Hemisphere. Portugal and Spain pioneered the enterprise, followed later by France, the Netherlands, and England. From the fifteenth through the eighteenth century, fully six of every seven people who arrived in the Americas were African slaves.

In their Virginia colony, the English initially tried to raise tobacco with the labor of both slaves and indentured servants, English-born as well as African. By the late seventeenth century, trial and error had demonstrated the immense advantages of using a labor force completely and permanently unfree—and both physically and culturally distinct from other inhabitants. The founders of the South Carolina rice colony learned from the experience of their northern neighbor. "The plantations and estates of this Province," they concluded, "cannot be well and sufficiently managed and brought in to use, without the labor and service" of slaves. In 1669, a constitution drafted for the colony described the relationship deemed necessary for such an economy and society to function satisfactorily. In all dealings with "Negro slaves," it provided, "every Freeman of Carolina shall have absolute power and authority." (One of the constitution's authors, John Locke, was the most influential early philosopher of liberal capitalism. He apparently discerned no contradiction in his statements. Africans were simply written out of the community where liberal principles were meant to prevail. In this, too, Locke proved a trailblazer.)

In addition to the Indian population, just under 2 million people lived in the American South at the time of the Constitution's ratification, roughly one-third of them (nearly 700,000) black and two-thirds white. Most could be found east of the Appalachian mountain range, on the coastal plain and the adjoining piedmont region. In fact, more than a third of all Southerners still lived and worked in Virginia, more than half in Virginia and Maryland combined. Slave-based commercial agriculture still centered in Chesapeake tobacco and Carolina-Georgia low-country rice. And soon there was a growing demand for the sugarcane of Louisiana (purchased by the United States in 1803).

Some planters had also turned to a new commercial crop, cotton, and by 1791 were already producing 2 million pounds. The British textile industry seemed to have a limitless appetite for the stuff.

Until the mid-1790s, however, only "sea island" (or long-staple) cotton could be cultivated profitably in the United States, and that plant grew only along the coast of Georgia and the Carolinas. Attempts to cultivate it farther inland ended in failure. Another variety of cotton, short-staple or green-seed, would grow more widely, it is true. But this plant presented problems of its own. Its sticky seeds proved quite difficult to separate from the cotton boll, and the time required to do so manually made the whole enterprise unviable. The turning point came in 1793, when Eli Whitney (Massachusetts-born but then working in Georgia as a tutor) designed a simple mechanical device (engine, or just plain "gin") that removed these seeds quickly and cheaply.

Suddenly, cotton could be grown profitably across a vast section of southern North America. By the turn of the nineteenth century, Southerners had begun the westward migration that in the next six decades would change the face of the South. Between 1800 and 1860, southern slave states grew in number from eight (Delaware, Maryland, Virginia, North and South Carolina, Georgia, Kentucky, and Tennessee) to fifteen. (Louisiana achieved statehood in 1812, Mississippi in 1817, Alabama in 1819, Missouri in 1821, Arkansas in 1836, Florida and Texas in

1845.) The South's population multiplied more than five times. The steadily growing demand for cotton sustained this expansion. Between 1830 and 1860, world cotton consumption increased at a robust 5 percent per year.

Americans with a stake in cotton included many besides southern slave owners. Cotton exports helped balance the country's international trade and finances. By the 1830s, indeed, cotton accounted for more than half the value of all U.S. exports. Within the country, a certain division of labor appeared. Although southern farmers and planters preferred to grow their own food, the pursuit of maximum profits pushed them toward specialization in cotton, especially when cotton prices rose. That push created a southern demand for foodstuffs grown in the Old Northwest. The brisk interregional commerce that developed buoyed not only these northern farmers but also urban centers located along the route, including Pittsburgh, Cincinnati, and St. Louis. Meanwhile, commission merchants brought manufactured goods from the eastern states and Europe into the South, extended loans and offered insurance to planters, stored their cotton in port cities until it could be shipped out, and arranged its transportation and final sale. These services carried price tags, of course, and factors drew off up to 20 percent of the gross value of the cotton harvest in payment. "Cotton," concluded New York merchant and financier Philip Hone in his 1835 diary, "has enriched all through whose hands it has passed."

By 1860, the South produced two-thirds of all the cotton grown in the world. Three-quarters of this crop, some 5 million bales (1 bale = 500 pounds) in 1860, went to England. The total population of the slave states then stood at about 11 million, of whom about 7 million were white. Slave owners made up about a fourth of that white population.

The social structure of slave ownership can best be visualized as a pyramid. The broad base was composed of the great mass of small operators. The statistically "typical" slave owner was found in this group, owning five or six slaves and land valued at around $3,000. He was usually compelled to work in the fields alongside his human property. Although five times wealthier than the average Northerner and ten times richer than the average slaveless southern white, he was nonetheless particularly vulnerable to frosts, rain, parasites, and fluctuations in the marketplace (especially in prices of staples, slaves, land, and transport).

Above this group was a smaller but more prosperous layer of "middling" proprietors who owned anywhere from 15 to 50 slaves each. This group represented perhaps a fourth of all slave owners. Compared with the small owners, these people had generally been born into families of greater wealth and education, often with commercial or professional backgrounds.

At the very top of the slaveholding pyramid stood the planter "aristocracy." Three thousand families, each of which possessed at least 100 slaves, accounted for some 10 percent of the nation's slaves. The aristocracy also owned the land most suitable for the cultivation of staple crops and best served by ports or river transportation. In the hinterland of Augusta, Georgia, the wealthiest tenth of all white families in 1860 owned half of all real property.

Just under 4 million black men, women, and children—still, as in Jefferson's day, comprising about a third of the total southern population—lived and labored in slave states in 1860. Only about 6 percent (some 262,000) were legally free. Of free blacks, the great majority—two-thirds, in fact—lived in the upper South, in Maryland, Virginia, the District of Columbia, and Delaware. Most of the rest were in Louisiana and the Carolinas. Most free blacks in the South lived in the countryside. Males worked as farmers, tenants, farmhands, and casual laborers, or in occupations such as tanning, weaving, and turpentine manufacture. Their urban counterparts found work in the crafts (especially in port cities of the lower South), but much more frequently (especially in the upper South) as common laborers, peddlers, teamsters, and factory workers. Free black women worked in the fields and, in both urban and rural settings, became housekeepers and tailors ("seamstresses") and washed the clothes of better-off white neighbors.

Slaves outnumbered free blacks by more than fifteen to one.

Nine out of ten slaves dwelt in the countryside, increasingly concentrated in an arc stretching inland from coastal South Carolina
through central Georgia, Alabama, and Mississippi and then
bending southward along the lower Mississippi Valley to New Orleans.

Ten percent of all enslaved laborers in the South worked in
industry, transportation, construction, lumbering, or mining.
Another 15 percent were domestic servants or performed other
nonagricultural labor. The rest—fully three-quarters of the total
slave labor force—worked the land: 55 percent raising cotton, 10
percent tobacco, and 10 percent sugar, rice, or hemp. It was their
labor that sustained southern commercial agriculture, producing
more than half its tobacco, three-quarters of its cotton, and almost all of the sugar, rice, and hemp.

On average, agricultural production in this new and expanded
South took place on larger units worked by larger work forces than
it had in the old. In the cotton kingdom of 1860, nearly half of all
slave laborers worked on plantations boasting more than 400 acres
of cultivated land and together producing about half the cotton
output of the nation. (In contrast, the typical free farm family of
the Northwest lived and worked, usually by itself, on 50 acres of
land.) More than half of all slaves belonged to owners of at least
20 slaves each. And for every slave who worked on a farm containing fewer than 10 bound laborers there was another who
worked on a plantation boasting more than 50 slaves.

Partisans of plantation society liked to see themselves in the role
of stern but loving fathers guiding the lives of their plantation
families—and especially their slave "children"—with paternal
wisdom and justice. All members of southern society, in this view,
while enjoying different degrees of power and wealth, were nonetheless bound together by a dense web of mutual obligations.
South Carolina's John C. Calhoun articulated this vision in 1838
when he asserted that "every plantation" was "a little community,"
the various abilities and needs of whose various members were
"perfectly harmonized." Manuals on plantation management and

articles carried in southern agricultural journals ˙ repeatedly stressed the humaneness of the system, the role of noblesse oblige, and the need to honor it. Two years before Calhoun's pronouncement, another young South Carolina planter put the matter this way:

> If all men were enjoined to love one another and to contribute as much as possible to the happiness of others, how much more is it the duty of men who hold such command over others as we do our slaves. It is then indisputably our most imperious duty to treat and govern them with a view to their comfort and happiness, as is consistent with propriety, and the performance of their duties toward us.

And in 1860, a Georgian elaborated the outlook most fully. "Plantation government," he wrote, "should be eminently patriarchal," and the planter, as "the *pater-familias*, or head of the family, should, in one sense, be the father of the whole concern, negroes and all." This did not mean tolerating "undue familiarity and companionship on the part of the latter." Still, the slaves

> should yet be convinced that he cares for them—that master is their best friend and that he will, to the best of his ability, redress their grievances, settle their disputes on equitable principles, and protect them from all wrong from whatever quarter it may come.

"Wherever this is the case," he added, "peace, happiness, contentment, cheerfulness and good order reign supreme." "I manage them as my children," insisted South Carolina rice planter Edward Thomas Heriot, adding that

> there is no class of people, as far as I have seen in this country, or Europe, of the same grade, where there is so much real happiness, where the wants of nature are so abundantly supplied, where the requirements of labour are as little, and where the guaranty against poverty and distress from all conditions of existence is so great.

From Mississippi came this plea in 1849: "Let us be just and generous toward them and not be too covetous of riches—for 'the love of money is the root of all evil.' " "The master," agreed a Virginia planter, "should ever bear in mind that he is the guardian and protector of his slaves, who if well treated are the happiest laboring class in the world."

George Fitzhugh, a spokesman of the planter elite of tidewater Virginia, became one of the South's most forceful and consistent defenders of this outlook. He contrasted the paternal guardianship exercised by slave owners with the brutal individualism he saw corrupting the "free society" of the North. There, he observed, "none but the selfish virtues are in repute, because none other help a man in the race of competition. . . . Selfishness is almost the only motive of human conduct in free society, where every man is taught that it is his first duty to change and better his pecuniary situation."

The lifestyle of southern planters did differ from that of northern merchants and manufacturers. But the former were no less deeply enmeshed in the international market economy and subject to its demands than the latter. The large-scale commercial production of staples was a business run for profit, and "the truth" (according to one European traveling through the South) was that "this passion for the acquisition of money is much stronger and more universal in this country than in any other under the sun, at least that I have visited."

Satisfying this "passion" meant making the right decisions about what to grow and how and where to grow it. Thomas Jefferson worked diligently to raise the efficiency of his Monticello estate. Indeed, wrote an admiring modern biographer, he "might have qualified as an efficiency expert in another age." James Henry Hammond of South Carolina, another great landowner with rather different politics, experimented doggedly with various seeds and fertilization techniques to increase the yields on his land. "Our farms," he decided, "will be our factories." "There is no employment I am acquainted with," a young South Carolina planter declared in 1838, "that requires more constant and unremitting attention than a plantation when profitably managed. The master must have a thorough knowledge of every part of his business."

Planters who disdained such industriousness to play absentee owner did not thereby abolish market pressures; they simply unloaded them onto the shoulders of their overseers. Those who applied themselves to the South's commercial agriculture—including some white farmers who began their careers with little property—might realize substantial improvement in their fortunes. Between 1830 and 1860, thus, the slave-owning population nearly doubled in size. Many of the new additions had risen from the ranks of previously slaveless small farmers. "Among us," a typical proslavery tract boasted, "we know that there is no one, however humble his beginning, who, with persevering industry, intelligence, and orderly and virtuous habits, may not attain to considerable opulence."

Slavery was first and foremost a way of obtaining and controlling the workers whose efforts produced such wealth. But the social mobility celebrated in the passage above could operate in both directions. The slave-owning farmer or planter who ignored the requirements of profit making and labor control at the least risked substantial debts and pressures to sell some land or slaves to pay them off. At worst he flirted with the complete loss of his estate.

Despite the generally high price of cotton, most slave owners were quite mindful of such dangers in the antebellum South. Out of forty sons of Augusta-area slaveholders sampled in the 1850 census, twelve (or 30 percent) were nonslaveholders a decade later. The "proper management [of slaves] constitutes the chief success of the planter," a Carolina overseer cautioned in 1836. "If he has not a proper control of them, he had much better give up planting; for as sure as he continues they will ruin him." A Virginia planter warned in 1852 against displaying excessive leniency in setting slave work loads. "The result [of doing that] is, in many cases, the master breaks, the white family is left in poverty, and the poor negroes sold." Cotton planter Thomas B. Chaplin of

South Carolina found himself in just such circumstances early in life. In the face of sharp fluctuations in cotton prices during the 1840s, Chaplin's attempt to play the country gentleman drove him deeply into debt. He confided to his diary in the spring of 1845:

> Trouble gathers thicker and thicker around me. I will be compelled to send about ten prime negroes to Town on next Monday, to be sold. I do this rather than have them seized in Beaufort, by the Sheriff . . . I never thought that I would be driven to this very unpleasant extremity . . . to separate families[,] Mothers and daughters—Brothers and sisters—all to pay for your own extravagances.

The power of local, national, and international markets made itself felt in a variety of ways that affected both slaveholder and slave. As richer lands opened in the Southwest, the lure of greater profits and the pressure of competition from those already based there compelled comfortably settled planter families to uproot themselves, join the migration, and submit to the ruder and cruder life on the cotton frontier. Having been uprooted from North Carolina, Mary Drake found herself "discontented" in Alabama. "[T]o a female who has once been blest with every comfort, & even luxury, blest with the society of a large & respectable circle of friends . . . to such people Mis. and Ala. are but a dreary waste." Constant movement, usually from east to west, prevailed even within the new states and territories. "Nobody seems to consider himself settled," complained a New England migrant to Alabama in 1836. "They remain one, two, three or four years & must move to some other spot. Since I came here the entire population of this town, with a dozen or two exceptions has changed." During the last antebellum decade alone, this relentless westward movement displaced most of the economic elite from some of the richest counties in the state.

The impact upon the slaves was, of course, incomparably worse. Exact statistics are unavailable, but it seems some 2 million blacks were forced into this interstate slave trade between 1790 and 1860, more than a quarter million in just the final antebellum decade, most of them destined for Mississippi, Louisiana, Arkansas, or Texas. Almost 20 percent of these involuntary migrants were children under ten years of age.

Rising slave prices—and their growing value as investments—influenced the material standard of living of the slaves. In the seventeenth and eighteenth centuries, competition for bound laborers from Caribbean sugar planters had bid up the price North Americans paid for their slaves. Congress's 1808 crackdown on the further importation of slaves constricted the labor supply and boosted slave purchase prices even higher. (A field hand who cost $600 at the turn of the century would cost two to three times as much in 1860.)

High slave prices led owners to place a premium on the survival of their own chattels. "The time has been, throwing humanity aside, that the farmer could kill up and wear out one Negro and buy another," observed a planter in 1849. "But it is not so now. Negroes are too high [in price] in proportion to the price of cotton, and it behooves those who own them to make them last as long as possible." One Virginia slaveholder chose not to use his slaves in swamp drainage, paying Irish day laborers to do that work instead. "A negro's life is too valuable to be risked at it," he explained. "If a negro dies, it's a considerable loss, you know." Do "not, by attempting to do too much," warned the Alabama agricultural society report cited earlier, "over-work and consequently injure your hands. . . . Do not kill the goose to obtain the golden egg."

Rising slave prices also encouraged masters to value and encourage the birth and healthy development of slave children. Slave children were assets, representing additional laborers or valuable goods to sell. "Well treated and cared for," a planter instructed in 1857, "and moderately worked, their natural increase becomes a source of great profit to the owner. Whatever therefore tends to promote their health and render them prolific, is worthy his attention." "The rearing of slaves in Lower Virginia," reported the *Farmers' Register* in 1834, "has so generally been considered a source of profit to their owners that it has scarcely been questioned or doubted."

The rising price of slaves also played a role in reinforcing the chains of slavery over the course of the early nineteenth century. The pro-emancipationist sentiment of the 1780s and 1790s gave way to a determined campaign to foreclose chances of escaping slave status. This fact, together with northward migration, reduced the proportionate size of the South's free black population between 1810 and the Civil War.

There were limits, moreover—relative if not absolute—beyond which even material improvements rarely passed. Some slaves (especially house servants) fared better than others (especially field workers on sugar plantations). Some planters, similarly, were more humane than others. Cases certainly existed in which a planter displayed an exceptional fondness for a particular slave and acted accordingly. The fact remains: the living standards of the slave population as a whole never matched those enjoyed by free whites—or even those of free blacks. They could not do so if the system of bound labor was to serve its special purpose.

Slavery's utility lay precisely in its ability to supply profit-oriented planters and farmers with laborers who could be worked harder, longer, under more difficult conditions, and at lower cost to the owner than legally free workers would tolerate. This reality underlay Frederick Douglass's memory of "the close-fisted stinginess that fed the poor slave on coarse cornmeal and tainted meat, that clothed him in crashy tow-linen and hurried him on to toil through the field in all weathers, with wind and rain beating through his tattered garments." Twelve to fifteen hours of hard labor per day was the norm. And while most free married women worked only in the home, female as well as male slaves, children as well as adults, worked for the master. A slave owner could thus profit from the efforts of entire families in ways that a northern employer could not.

All this was possible with a labor force legally denied the right to refuse assignments, demand better conditions, bargain for higher pay, or leave the employer altogether. A South Carolina planter explained in 1833 that "any good system of management" on a plantation depended first of all upon "a perfect understanding between the master and his slave." That meant

> that the slave should know that his master is to govern absolutely, that he is to obey implicitly. That he is never for a moment to exercise his will or judgment in opposition to a positive order.

"The most important part of management of slaves," concurred a Virgina planter four years later, "is always to keep them under proper subjection. . . . Unconditional submission is the only footing upon which slavery should be placed."

To raise productivity, slave-owning farmers and planters used rewards as well as punishments. Some owners gave extra food or clothing, preferred work assignments, and (much more rarely) small quantities of cash to those slaves who picked the most cotton or bore the largest number of children. Some owners assigned slaves small plots of ground to cultivate once daily tasks were completed. Crops raised there might then be consumed, bartered, sold, or sold for them by the master.

Frederick Law Olmsted observed such a system at work on a large cotton plantation set on one of the Mississippi's tributaries. "Each [slave] family had a garden," he noted, "the products of which, together with eggs, fowls and bacon, they frequently sold, or used in addition to their regular allowance of food." Such an arrangement, one Alabama planter felt sure, must "attach the negro to his home and makes him feel that he has more than a passing interest in the things about him." "Surely," reasoned another, "if [they learn to be] industrious for themselves, they will be so for their masters."

Many masters, however, resisted material incentives (and especially cash) precisely on the grounds that these things were—in both principle and practice—inconsistent with the spirit of slavery and subversive of the "absolute submission" required of slaves. One planter (who confessed to employing them "only of a necessity" and "would gladly abandon it") considered the arrangement "frought with evil; nothing but evil, and that continually." "Negroes should in no instance be permitted to *trade*, except with their masters," another agreed. "By permitting them to leave the plantation with the view of selling or buying, more is lost by the owner than he is generally aware of." "If a negro is suffered to sell anything he chooses without an inquiry being made," a third planter added, "a spirit of trafficking is at once created. To carry this on, both means and time are necessary, neither of which is he of right possessed."

Indeed, the entire arrangement in which blacks were allotted croplands of their own compromised their status as slaves, grafting onto it aspects of freedom more consistent with serfdom or even independent proprietorship. In principle, recognizing "their" crops (or cash) as private property eroded the law of slavery; legally regarded as nothing but property themselves, slaves were not supposed to own anything. Allowing them to do so in practice weakened the master's hold over them. ("Money," as one planter commented tersely, "is power.") Specifically, it invited theft—whether in the form of goods or labor due—from the owner. Under this system, furthermore, "they will have many things in their possession under the color of purchase which we know not whether they obtained honestly." Dividing the slave's time between labor for the master and labor for himself or herself, moreover, encouraged inattention to the former. "[H]e would never go through his work carefully," warned a great South Carolinian planter, "and particularly when other engagements more interesting and pleasing are constantly passing through his mind, but would be apt to put off his [plantation] work for a future period, or slight it over."

This was no mere speculation. Already, confirmed another planter, "it is next to impossible to keep them from working their crops on the Sabbath," and "they labor [there] of nights when they should be at rest." The resulting loss of sleep translated the next day into less energetic work for the master. At present, "we have all their time and service." Let us, he urged, keep it so by directly "furnish[ing] them with such things as they ought to have."

At bottom, slaves worked for their masters—and worked hard—because they were not free to refuse, to move on, to become wage-labor bargainers or independent proprietors. Neither slave nor owner ever forgot that the fundamental basis of that system was physical, not economic ("market") coercion. It was punishment—and the fear of it—that most dramatically asserted the essence of this relationship. The Alabama agricultural society committee cited earlier contrasted disciplinary measures favored under the slave regime with those used by employers of free wage labor.

> When the laborer is dependent upon his daily income for the support of himself and family, and when the loss of wages, as is often the case, involves the starvation of his wife and children, certainly no greater force can be applied to him than the threat of turning him off to seek his bread . . . In the management of our slaves, this cannot be, as the master is bound for their support. The master must resort to other means of control. After reason and persuasion have been exhausted without producing the desired effect, punishment of some sort must be resorted to.

A South Carolina planter proceeded from the same premises when he noted that while plantation rules should be imposed "alike upon overseer and negro," violations must be dealt with quite differently. "The penalty imposed upon the overseer should be pecuniary, that upon the negro corporeal."

Nor did patriarchal principles offer much of a shield against physical punishment. The North Carolina Supreme Court demonstrated as much in 1829 when it heard a case concerning a slave, Lydia, shot by John Mann, who was then renting her. The attorney general had charged Mann with assault and battery. To justify that charge, the prosecution leaned heavily on the paternalist ideal, and (as the court noted) employed "arguments drawn from the well established principles which confer and restrain the authority of the parent over the child, the tutor over the pupil, and the master over the apprentice."

In rendering his decision, however, Judge Thomas Ruffin rejected this whole line of argument as well as the parallels on which it rested. "The Court does not recognise their application. There is no likeness between the cases," he wrote. "They are in opposition to each other, and there is an impassable gulf between them." The relationships being compared were fundamentally different in purpose.

> With slavery . . . [t]he end is the profit of the master, his security and the public safety; the subject, one doomed in his own person, and his posterity, to live without knowledge, and without the capacity to make anything his own, and to toil that others may reap the fruits.

In such a system, Ruffin added, obedience can be obtained only through "uncontrolled authority over the body. There is nothing else which can operate to produce the effect. The power of the master must be absolute, to render the submission of the slave perfect." Personally, Judge Ruffin was not happy about this state of affairs: "I most freely confess my sense of the harshness of this proposition, I feel it as deeply as any man can." But he could find no alternative consistent with the system of bound labor. "This discipline belongs to the state of slavery. They cannot be disunited, without abrogating at once the rights of the master, and absolving the slave from his subjection." The court therefore found for the defendant, John Mann, who was released.

Judge Ruffin had a reputation for unusual bluntness and for depending more on logic than legal precedent. But the core ideas expressed in his decision in *State* v. *John Mann* found echoes throughout the South. The literature of "slave management" that owners wrote for one another did repeatedly inveigh against "excessive" whipping, whipping for the pleasure of it, whipping "from mere passion and malice." But the same writers considered the use of the whip essential to enforce rules necessary to the plantation's efficient functioning and to break rebellious spirits among the slaves.

In 1851, thus, a Georgia planter won a prize for writing an

essay that encouraged the master to be "merciful and humane" toward the slaves but that also acknowledged that "when, from perverse obstinacy or culpable negligence, [the slave] repeatedly disregards and sets at naught your authority, then he should be made to know and feel that 'the rod is for the fool's back,'" and that "with the naturally obstinate and perverse, more frequent resort to corporeal punishment will become necessary." "Whipping must never be cruel or severe," the wealthy Louisiana planter Joseph Acklen advised in 1856, "but may be repeated at proper intervals, until the most entire submission is obtained." "Negroes," confided Georgia overseer S. D. Wragg in 1854, "have very little regard for anything more than to get along without being whipped." "If one is called to you or sent from you," a big planter advised in 1850, "and he does not move briskly, chastise him at once. If he does not answer, repeat the dose and double the quantity." "A great deal of whipping," Virginia planter W. W. Gilmer wrote two years later, "is not necessary; *some is.*"

Former slave Solomon Northup recalled that when a new hand

> is sent for the first time into the field, he is whipped up smartly, and made for that day to pick as fast as he can possibly. At night it is weighed, so that his capability in cotton picking is known. He must bring in the same weight each night following. If it falls short, it is considered evidence that he has been laggard, and a greater or less number of lashes is the penalty.

Dr. John Wesley Monette, a proslavery writer, related in matter-of-fact terms the way this punishment was administered. After the weighing-in procedure that Northup described,

> those who are found to have brought in less than their usual quantity, unless for good reasons, are called in the order of their names: the individual advances, and if his reasons are insufficient, he is ordered to lie down upon his face, with his back exposed; when he receives ten, twenty, or fifty stripes with the whip, according to his

deserts. In this way the overseer goes over the list, punishing only those who have idled away their time.

On the large Louisiana plantation owned by Bennett Barrow (a planter acutely mindful of the dangers of positive material incentives), one slave was flogged every four days on average in 1840–42; most could expect to be whipped more than once a year. Other Barrow slaves were imprisoned, chained, raked across the scalp, and shot. Similar practices prevailed elsewhere. Madison Jefferson was owned by a Virginia planter named George Neale. As later recorded by an interviewer, Jefferson recalled that in the fields Neale's

> drivers were allowed to inflict from twenty-five to thirty lashes on the clothes, but, when [they] complained to the overseer that they could not get any slave to do the required work, the latter would have him staked, viz., thrown down on his face with his arms and legs extended to stakes, and in that position he would receive floggings on the bare back; [Jefferson] has known from 60 to 100 lashes given in the field this way.

"Don't done your task," remembered South Carolina slave Hagar Brown, "driver wave that whip, put you over the barrel, beat you so blood run down." Nor was whipping always confined to field labor. One former slave from Alabama remembered the women who were expected to spin seven or eight cuts a day; those who did not fill their quotas were also whipped.

Such punishments were generally administered before the eyes of the other slaves to drive home the message and deepen the fear of resisting the master's demands. Solomon Northup recalled the effect. In the morning, the slave must "hurry to the field" because

> it is an offence invariably followed by a flogging to be found in the quarters after daybreak. Then the fears and labors of another day begin. . . . He fears he will be caught lagging through the day; he fears to approach the gin-house with his basket-load of cotton at

night; he fears, when he lies down, that he will oversleep himself in the morning.

The point is not that slavery was wrong only because it was brutal. "It was *slavery*, not its mere incidents that I hated," Frederick Douglass wrote of his life in bondage. "My feelings were not the result of any marked cruelty in the treatment I received . . . The feeding and clothing me well could not atone for taking my liberty from me."

"Being a slave," however, was no intellectual abstraction, no theoretical affront to one's philosophical sense of right and dignity. In the specific context of the South's profit-oriented system of commodity production, working without liberty imposed a particular way of life, living standard, labor discipline, and vulnerability to family breakup. Injunctions to treat slaves well usually took this context and the limits it imposed for granted. The master, admonished one, should "feel it his duty to make them as comfortable *as circumstances will permit.*" "*As far as practicable,*" similarly instructed a second, "families of negroes should be kept together." "Use no more force," suggested a third, "than is *absolutely necessary* to procure obedience." (Emphasis added.) This is what former slave James Pennington meant when he said, "Talk not then about kind and Christian masters. They are not masters of the system. The system is master of them." And it was the logic of that system that Frederick Douglass had in mind when he remembered being "frequently asked if I had a kind master." On such occasions, he wrote, "I do not remember ever to have given a negative reply . . . for I always measured the kindness of my master by the standard of kindness set up by the slaveholders around us." "It is not the fault of the slaveholder that he is so cruel," summarized Solomon Northup, "so much as it is the fault of the system under which he lives."

During the antebellum decades, as we have seen, the absolute number of slaveholders grew substantially. But the white population of the South increased even faster. The escalating price of slaves kept a growing share of southern whites outside slaveholder ranks. As a result, a shrinking proportion of southern whites owned slaves: 36 percent in 1830, 31 percent in 1850, and only 26 percent by 1860.

In terms of raw wealth, the chasm separating the average slaveholder and the average farm-operating nonslaveholder in the cotton kingdom was huge. The former (with assets valued at nearly $25,000) was approximately fourteen times richer than the latter (about $1,800) in 1860. But like those whites who owned slaves, the majority who did not composed a very heterogeneous population.

In 1850, about 40 percent of the South's white farmers owned no real estate at all. There was thus, worried the *Southern Cultivator* in 1856, a "large number at the South who have no legal right nor interest in the soil [and] no homes of their own." The editor of a South Carolina newspaper that year framed the matter in less sympathetic terms: "There is in this State," he wrote, "as impoverished and as ignorant a white population as can be found in any other in the Union." The propertyless included families who cultivated rented land. Ten percent of all the farms in South Carolina's Edgefield district were worked by tenants in 1860, and that proportion rose to nearly 25 percent due west in Hart County, Georgia. Still worse off were rural white laborers who worked just for room, board, and/or wages. In 1860, nearly one in six working adults in the central Georgian county of Hancock fell into this category.

For some of these Southerners, landless status was merely a temporary condition: they would acquire property as they grew older. Of the 210 residents of Hancock County who worked someone else's land in 1850, for example, 14 (or almost 7 percent) owned land there a decade later. Others probably acquired property elsewhere in the South. But the search for economic improvement may have driven some of Hancock's landless whites out of the slave states and into the free states and territories to the northwest. (Over all, twice as many Americans migrated from the slave states into the free as moved in the opposite direction.)

Among those who remained in Hancock, most seem not to have improved their situation, and a fair number may have dropped from the position of tenant to that of farm laborer or (even worse, in terms of income) textile hand.

Nonslaveholding whites who did own farms divided roughly into two components. One of these lived and worked in close proximity and cooperation with the large plantations and from an early date joined in the production of staples, especially cotton. Such marginal (and even middling) cotton producers tended to rely upon wealthy planter neighbors to gin, transport, and market their crop and to provide these services on generous terms. Large owners felt particularly comfortable doing this in years when cotton prices were high. This relationship tended to reinforce the bonds between these large and small white property owners.

A second and larger group of nonslaveholding white small farmers lived outside the plantation districts, especially in the southern hill country. In the early years of the century, few of these people produced staples or participated in the export economy. Prizing economic and social independence more than the accumulation of wealth, they ran their farms accordingly. Shunning the risks of cotton production for an unstable market, they preferred to raise crops (notably corn) that they could consume themselves and to produce with their own hands (or obtain through local exchange) most of the tools, clothing, and other items they required.

This picture changed in the 1850s, however, partly because of that decade's great and sustained surge in cotton prices. A growing number of the up-country's small farm families moved into cotton production. Other factors may also have influenced their decision. The growing population was pressing against the supply of good land, raising its price, especially in more long-settled areas. Raising some cotton for sale might bring in the cash necessary to meet such growing expenses. Those nearest to transportation facilities found it easiest to take this step. Among those whose land bordered the new Western & Atlantic Railroad in up-country Georgia, staple production doubled in the 1850s alone. This trend reinforced a sense of common interest among southern whites whose living standards and styles were otherwise very different.

Meanwhile, however, the economy of the upper South was moving in the opposite direction. The natural environment in Maryland and Virginia had never been very conducive to growing cotton, which virtually ceased there in the 1840s. Meanwhile, the center of tobacco cultivation moved inland in search of richer soil. Chesapeake cultivators responded with a shift toward mixed farming, especially of wheat and other cereals. This change of crops brought in its train transformations of much greater moment. Tobacco required a year-round work force. Wheat and other cereals needed large numbers of hands during the harvest but relatively few at other times. As farmers switched from the first crop to the second, maintaining large year-round slave labor forces (which had to be clothed and fed, even if minimally, when idle) came to be impractical.

Maryland registered this fact most clearly. In the course of seventy years, the state moved steadily toward a free-labor economy as slaveholding fell by more than half. Four out of every ten white families owned slaves in 1790. By 1850, fewer than two out of ten did so. The impact of this transformation on Maryland's African-American population was even more dramatic and sharply distinguished from the trends dominating the South as a whole. By 1860, about half of Maryland's black residents were out of slavery. Some masters transformed their slaves into either wage laborers or tenants working small parcels of land.

Issues of economic diversification and urban, commercial, and industrial growth increasingly attracted the attention of the southern elite during the final antebellum decades. The Southern Commercial Convention, founded in the 1830s to encourage and publicize regional economic development, now experienced a rebirth. One leading proponent of change was William Gregg, subsequently founder of the major South Carolina textile firm, the Graniteville Manufacturing Company. People like Gregg strove to reduce the South's economic dependence on the North, the more so as the sectional conflict deepened. "Who can look forward to the future destiny of our State," Gregg asked in 1845, "persisting, as she does, with such pertinacity, in the exclusive and exhausting system of agriculture, without dark forebodings?" Let the man who doubted the peril "only seat himself on the Charleston wharves for a few days, and behold ship after ship arrive, laden down with the various articles produced by yankee industry. Let him behold these vessels discharging their cargoes and count the cost to South Carolina." That cost, Gregg stressed, must be measured not only in dollars but also in terms of dependence. Planter and politician James Henry Hammond agreed, warning that "purely agricultural people have been in all ages the victims of rapacious tyrants grinding them down."

In fact, development did occur in the antebellum South. In the three decades after 1830, the region's urban population grew by more than three-quarters of a million. In 1860, Baltimore ranked as the fourth-largest city in the country, New Orleans was the sixth, and St. Louis the eighth. Those employed in the South's manufacturing firms grew in number by 20 percent during the 1850s alone. Capital investment in that sector increased by more than 70 percent, the value of output by more than 90 percent. On the eve of the Civil War, as a result, some 132,000 Southerners were producing manufactures valued at nearly $200 million. Commerce and transportation increased as well. Slaves, free blacks, and workers born in Ireland performed much of the unskilled and factory work involved in this growth. Free black artisans were concentrated in a handful of occupations (such as barbering and butchering) traditionally scorned by southern-born whites as too dirty, arduous, or undignified. The latter generally confined themselves to the elite trades—construction, printing, and piloting. The mass of artisan crafts in between were disproportionately filled with workers born in England and Germany.

None of this, however, qualitatively changed the basic character of the southern economy or altered its relationship with the rest of the country. Compared with the free states, the South in

1860 remained backward in both urban and industrial development. More than one out of every three Northeasterners that year lived in towns and cities; in the slave states of the Southeast, the corresponding proportion remained at only one in eight. And while 60 percent of the North's labor force was working outside agriculture by the Civil War, only 16 percent of the South's labor force was similarly occupied. Other statistics tell the same story. Whatever the measure—employment, capital investment, or total output—southern firms accounted for only about a tenth of the nation's manufacturing in 1860.

How to explain this lag in economic diversification and development? Slavery played a principal role. "The thing," mused James Henry Hammond in 1849, "is to reconcile industry with free trade, slave labour, agricultural advancement, and Southern tone." Yes, that was the thing. It was also the rub. For in a variety of ways, slavery proved antithetical to or incompatible with such changes.

First of all, access to slaves (a cheap, tractable form of labor) allowed farmers and planters to make great profits in the production of cotton. This fact tended to keep not only investment capital but also slave laborers on the land. Graniteville's William Gregg grieved that

> cotton has been to South Carolina what the mines of Mexico were to Spain—it has produced us such an abundant supply of all the luxuries and elegances of life, with so little exertion on our part, that we have become enervated, unfitted for other and more laborious pursuits.

During the 1850s, in fact, the same upward surge in cotton prices that enriched southern slave owners led them to pull slaves out of urban work just when the Southern Commercial Convention was pressing hardest for diversification.

By the same token, slavery also lessened incentives to raise the productivity of human labor technologically, the essence and driving force of real economic development and social progress.

In the Northwest, where labor was scarce and therefore relatively expensive, farmers purchased various labor-saving farm implements to boost agricultural output. The production of those tools and machines became a major regional industry that, in turn, stimulated the production of coal and iron. Slave owners bought few such implements. They maintained or expanded production by buying more slaves and placing them on richer land.

Where the South's economy did diversify, change challenged and undermined the position of slavery, a process that committed slaveholders found deeply threatening politically.

Even more than cash bonuses given to field slaves, urban industrial employment seemed to loosen a slave's bonds. This occurred in a number of ways. Compared with rural existence, life in a town or city brought the slave into closer touch with free blacks and the world outside the South. That exposure encouraged and assisted attempts to escape the bonds of slavery altogether. A Virginia owner refused to rent his slave to one manufacturer because the slave had "left no doubt on my mind but he would make an effort to reach the State of Ohio, and being placed at your Works it would greatly facilitate his Object." By passing as a free black sailor, an impersonation aided by experience in shipyard labor and the assistance of free blacks, Frederick Douglass did finally escape to the North. Employment as a slave cabinetmaker helped William Craft escape from Georgia with his wife, Ellen. Others took advantage precisely of the growing size and anonymity of southern cities and melted into the free black population resident there.

But flight was by no means the only problem posed. The greater freedom (especially freedom of movement) that generally went with nonagricultural employment tended to erode slave owners' power over their chattels. An 1822 petition to the South Carolina state legislature complained:

> By far the greater portion of negroes who work out are released in a considerable degree from the control of their masters—laboring or forebearing to labour, as their interest or inclination prompts, ren-

dering unto their owners, only a monthly account; and provided they but settle the wages with punctuality are permitted to regulate their own conduct. The consequence is, they assemble together whenever they wish, and having their time at their own disposal, can be convened at any given and fixed period, and having regular and stated meetings, can originate, prepare, and mature their own plans of insurrection. [One can almost hear the echo of Gideon Granger.] Whereas, the slaves who are kept in the yards of their masters, are immediately under their eyes.

The Carolina farmer Lemuel Reid experienced this firsthand in the summer of 1850. No sooner had he rented a slave carpenter named George from a neighbor than he chanced upon George telling his own slaves that "God was working for their deliverance, . . . would deliver them from bondage as sure as the children of Israel were delivered from the Egyptian bondage" and that "it would be soon." "It is not to be denied," a Savannah grand jury acknowledged in 1845, that such freedoms were "striking directly at the existence of our institutions, and unless broken up in time, will result in the total prostration of existing relations." As Olmsted observed, many masters resisted renting their slaves to ironmongers and other entrepreneurs because, among other things, they "had too much liberty, and were acquiring bad habits. They earned money by overwork, and spent it for whiskey, and got a habit of roaming about and *taking care of themselves.*" Industrial slaves, worried James Henry Hammond, an ardent champion of economic development, "were more than half freed" and destined to become "the most corrupt and turbulent" sector of the South's unfree labor force.

Employment in urban settings wrought the most subversive effects. "The ties which bound together the master and the slave," complained the New Orleans *Daily Picayune*, were being "gradually severed" in that city, as slave workers "become intemperate, disorderly, and lose the respect which the servant should entertain for the master." Worse still, "their example is contagious upon those [slaves] who do not possess these dangerous privileges."

But if the conditions of industrial labor weakened slave discipline, the existence of slavery itself conflicted with the formation of a free white industrial labor force, whether native- or foreign-born. The lure of slave-based southern agriculture—and its southwestern extension—helped keep rural whites out of cities and industrial employment. Competition from industrial slaves—whether direct or indirect, current or potential—tended to depress the status, conditions, and pay rates of free workers. There is no question that slave labor was cheap. It has been estimated that the cost of owning an industrial slave outright over one year was less than a third the cost (in wages and supervision) of employing a free unskilled laborer. To rent an unskilled slave for a year cost somewhere between $200 and $250; the annual wage of an unskilled white laborer was about $310.

Given the choice, therefore, most white wage earners (and about 90 percent of all immigrants) preferred to take their chances in the free states and territories. White workers who remained in the South repeatedly complained about having to compete with slaves as well as poorly paid free blacks. A convention of 400 to 500 white mechanics in Atlanta thus resolved in 1851 that "the instruction of negroes in the Mechanic Arts is a source of great dissatisfaction to the mechanical interest, prejudicial to Southern youths engaging in industrial pursuits." On the very eve of secession, a group of white mechanics in Texas wrote the state legislature to "solemnly object to being put in competition with Negro Mechanics." Such resentments frequently boiled over into assaults upon the hapless slaves themselves. A gang of angry white workers thus beat and ejected the slave caulker Frederick Douglass from a Baltimore shipyard in 1836.

Attempts by free workers to restrict the slave owners' freedom to employ human property as they wished were irritating enough. A far more ominous danger loomed, however. As urban commercial and industrial life expanded in the slave states, the planter elite grew increasingly worried that this budding resistance to the slave owners' prerogatives would flower into more generalized antislavery sentiment. Once again, Frederick Douglass's experience suggests the substance behind such fears. On the Baltimore

docks one day, a youthful Douglass helped two Irishmen unload-
ing a scow. Afterward, one of them "expressed the deepest sympathy with me, and the most decided hatred of slavery." The two
men then advised Douglass "that I ought to run away and go to
the North, that I should find friends there, and that I should then
be free as anybody." At the time, the wary young slave feigned
disinterest. But "I nevertheless remembered their words and their
advice and looked forward to an escape to the North." And in
1838, as Douglass did make his bid for freedom as a fugitive slave,
he encountered a German blacksmith he knew riding the same
northbound train. The man stared at him intently, and Douglass
was certain he'd been recognized. The blacksmith, however,
"had no heart to betray me. At any rate, he saw me escaping and
held his peace."

As the Civil War approached, slave owners saw such dangerous
attitudes spreading. Vigilantes expelled the Irish bricklayer Tom
Burch from Edgefield, South Carolina, in 1859 for using "sedi-
tious language" potentially creating "very great injury among our
negroes." A Charleston daily denounced such foreign-born free
workers as a "curse rather than a blessing to our peculiar institution." James Henry Hammond's ambition to attempt to "reconcile
industry with . . . slave labour, agricultural advancement, and
Southern tone" was evidently bearing some bitter fruit.

— 2 —

"Each Person Works for Himself": The Ideal and Reality of Free Labor

In 1782, as British and colonial negotiators wrangled over the terms of American independence, a book was published entitled *Letters from an American Farmer*. Its author, J. Hector St. John de Crèvecoeur, had years earlier emigrated from Normandy to North America, where he settled on the land. From a farm in Orange County, New York, Crèvecoeur described his adopted country. "[W]e are," he exulted, "the most perfect society now existing in the world. Here man is free as he ought to be." Our society here, he wrote,

> is not composed, as in Europe, of great lords who possess everything, and of a herd of people who have nothing. Here are no aristocratical families, no courts, no kings, no bishops, no ecclesiastical dominion . . . no great manufacturers employing thousands, no great refinements of luxury.

No, he added proudly, "we are a people of cultivators, scattered over an immense territory" in which "each person works for himself," and "a pleasing uniformity of decent competence appears throughout our habitations." If differences of wealth existed, still "the rich and the poor are not so far removed from each other as they are in Europe." Nor, he was certain, was "this pleasing equality so transitory as many others are," since "many ages will not see the shores of our great lakes replenished with inland nations, nor the unknown bounds of North America entirely peopled."

This image persisted. "The social condition of the Americans is eminently democratic," wrote another Frenchman (and Norman), Alexis de Tocqueville, after a tour through the country in 1831. "This was its character at the foundation of the colonies, and it is still more strongly marked at the present day." "Nothing," he stressed, "struck me more forcibly than the general equality of condition among the people." Indeed, he concluded, "men are there seen on a greater equality than in any other country of the world, or in any age of which history has preserved the remembrance." This was "the fundamental fact from which all others seem to be derived."

In 1790, the population of the eight northern states—Massachusetts, Connecticut, Vermont, New Jersey, New Hampshire, Rhode Island, New York, Pennsylvania—stood at 1.97 million, exactly half the national total. Like their southern contemporaries, Northerners still tended to concentrate inside a fifty-mile-wide band along the seaboard. In fact, only about one half of 1 percent of the total northern population lived beyond the Allegheny Mountains, nearly all of them in western Pennsylvania.

By no means all these people conformed to the image of freedom and independence drawn by Crèvecoeur. In 1790, eight years after his book appeared, the northern states still contained over 40,000 slaves—more than 30,000 in New Jersey and New York State alone. Of all U.S. cities, indeed, only Charleston, South Carolina, contained a larger number of slaves in 1790 than New York. And Philadelphia was the nation's largest single market for indentured servants. More than a third of the approximately 3,000 Europeans who immigrated through the city in 1771–73 paid for their passage by selling themselves into temporary servitude.

Bound labor, however, whether enslaved or indentured, was not central to the economy of the northern colonies, and both forms of servitude declined steadily during and after the Revolution. Indentured servants, accounting for about 14 percent of Philadelphia's labor force in the early 1770s, represented only 1 percent by 1800. As for American slaves generally, fewer than 6 percent of them lived in the northern states even in 1790. Thirty years later the proportion had fallen to 1 percent—and then, during the 1820s, to a tenth of 1 percent.

The decline of unfree labor across the North did not signify an equal distribution of wealth. Economic inequality was most obvious in the region's leading urban centers (Boston, New York, and Philadelphia), 5 to 10 percent of whose residents owned at least half the total wealth in the revolutionary era. This urban elite included the wealthiest merchants, professionals, and some big landowners. Its members commonly dwelt in great mansions furnished with sundry luxuries and moved about in expensive coaches and carriages imported from Britain. At the bottom of the urban scale, about a third of the urban population (mostly day laborers, mariners, domestic servants, and other wage workers) owned no property at all. Servants commonly lived in the homes of their employers. Many others of the urban poor found shelter in decaying frame houses that lined crowded streets and alleys near the docks.

But such disparities were atypical. So, for the most part, was urban life. In the revolutionary era, less than a half of 1 percent of the northern population lived in one of the region's three largest towns—the combined population of Boston, New York, and Philadelphia was less than 80,000. About eleven out of every twelve Northerners lived in rural settings, and seven in ten worked the land.

To be sure, the rural population also included examples of economic inequality. In those districts where agriculture was most commercialized by the late eighteenth century—and particularly in the hinterland of the larger towns and cities—concentration of wealth tended to be greatest. In Groton, Connecticut, and Chester County, Pennsylvania, the wealthiest 10 percent of all families owned about 30 percent of all property. In New York's river valley estate districts (some of them located directly across the Hudson River from Crèvecoeur's farm), the wealthiest tenth of all families owned about half the property. Some of these manors were immense. Cortlandt and Philipsburgh covered 86,000 and 92,000 acres, respectively. Livingston was nearly twice as big as either of them (160,000 acres), and Rensselaerwyck dwarfed them all, sprawling across one million acres of land surrounding Albany.

Concentrations of property at one pole yielded substantial propertylessness at the other. In Chester County, Pennsylvania, and Burlington County, New Jersey, approximately half the adult males in the revolutionary era owned no land at all. In 1820, more than 40 percent of all the cultivators in New York State outside New York County were tenants.

Images like these, however, must once again be placed in perspective. They were dramatic but unusual. Aggregate figures are imprecise, but down through the second decade of the nineteenth century as much as 70 percent of the northern farm population apparently owned the land they lived on. Only about 30 percent were tenants or laborers, and even this figure probably exaggerates the significance of propertylessness in early northern society. As in the South, some tenants and laborers were young men just starting out in life who could expect to acquire property in their lifetimes. Land in the North was by no means free, but compared with Europe it was still plentiful and cheap at the start of the nineteenth century.

These circumstances tended to keep agricultural labor relatively scarce and expensive in those years, forcing most farm families to rely primarily on their own efforts to cultivate the land. The limited labor supply, in turn, restricted the size of a farm that could be successfully cultivated. Under such circumstances, only about 5 to 10 percent of northern agriculturalists were able to extract much more than a modest subsistence from the soil.

The abundance of land compared to labor also exerted a downward pressure on rents. This was apparent even on the huge manors of New York State. The great landlord Oliver De Lancey complained in 1770 that it was "very difficult to settle tenants as every person can be at an easy rate a freeholder." If not "every person" truly had this option, De Lancey's general point is still well taken. In the absence of legal compulsions, landlords striving to attract—or hold—tenants had to moderate rents. And modest rents, in turn, further aided tenants trying to save enough eventually to buy land of their own.

Thus it was that almost forty years after Crèvecoeur, the New England minister Timothy Dwight could enthuse in 1821:

> Every man in this country, almost without an exception, lives on his own ground. The lands are universally held in fee-simple; and descend by law, to all children in equal shares. Every farmer . . . is the little monarch of a dominion sufficiently large to furnish all the supplies of competence.

Ten years later (1831), the *New England Farmer* found the countryside "free, flourishing, and prosperous, beyond example; there never was a country in which all men from the highest to the lowest; from the richest to the poorest, could be more independent." This cherished "independence" signified the ability to support one's own family economically and to look others squarely in the eye as a social equal.

But social independence never meant total family self-sufficiency. In fact, social independence would have been quite impossible on that basis. As the Scots-born naturalist John Bradbury observed in his travels through the western farm country in 1809–11, "A great number of things occur necessary to be done, which require the united strength of numbers to effect." To effect them, farm families fell back upon the assistance of friends, kin, and neighbors. Bradbury noted that while "money cannot purchase for the new settler the required aid," yet "that kind and generous feeling which men have for each other, who are not rendered callous by the possession of wealth, or the dread of poverty, comes to his relief: his neighbours, even unsolicited, appoint a

day when as a *frolic*, they shall, for instance, build him a house."
At such times, he added,

> no remuneration is expected, nor would it be received. It is consid-
> ered the performance of a duty, and only lays him under the obli-
> gation to discharge the debt by doing the same to subsequent set-
> tlers. But this combination of labour in numbers, for the benefit of
> one individual, is not confined to the new comer only, it occurs
> frequently in the course of a year amongst the old settlers, with
> whom it is a continued bond of amity and social intercourse, and
> in no part of the world is good neighbourship found in greater per-
> fection than in the western territory, or in America generally.

Rural independence also required at least some contact with
the world of commerce. While farm families produced most of
what they ate, wore, and used, some basic items (including salt,
sugar, coffee, tea, firearms, gunpowder, and metal products generally) could often be obtained only from peddlers, rural craftsmen, or storekeepers. Cash was also needed to pay taxes and to
buy the land on which sons could start their own farms upon
reaching manhood. In the 1830s, the price of a modest eighty-
acre farm—plus draft animals, hogs, cattle, seed, supplies, and
the first year's subsistence for the family—amounted to about
$1,000.

To meet such expenses (and to pay taxes), one needed cash.
And to raise cash, one needed something to sell—either a surplus
of the same crops raised for family consumption or some variety
of home manufactures (such as thread, yarn, cloth, brooms, butter, cheese, palm-leaf hats, suspenders, button molds).

In devoting a portion of their labors to producing such items,
most family members were evidently still striving merely to assure
or attain the traditional goal of social independence. They viewed
production for market and the accumulation of money as a means
to that end. Moreover, these market-oriented activities remained
circumscribed and subordinate aspects of life. Members of such
farm communities produced most of what they consumed or
wore; purchases were few. About two-thirds of all clothes worn in

the United States were homemade. They also consumed most of what they produced. (As late as 1820, only 20 percent of the farm crop ever reached urban markets.)

Both social-psychological and physical factors discouraged more extensive commercial ties or ambitions. Fear played a role—fear that too close involvement with the world of commerce would leave the family vulnerable to the fluctuations of the marketplace and even dispossession. "It would seem a most important rule," cautioned Rev. Henry Colman in 1821, "for every farmer to live as far as possible within his own resources; to depend upon his farm for the subsistence of his family, as far as it can be applied to this purpose."

A more stubborn barrier to extensive commercial dealings was the crude and undeveloped transportation and communications network that connected urban and rural communities. Because of roads and bridges few in number and poor in condition—and rivers running north-south rather than east-west—long-distance trade between coast and hinterland was slow and expensive. In 1817, it took nearly three weeks to move a ton of goods from Buffalo to New York City. The shipping cost was $100. That was about three times the price at which wheat was then selling in New York, six times that of corn, and twelve times that of oats. Clearly, therefore, crops raised too far inland could not be sold profitably in the East. Attempts to increase sales of imported or eastern-made manufactures in the hinterland encountered the same frustrations.

So primitive a state of commercial life helps explain the situation of the North's elite merchants in this era. Their involvement with—much less control over—the great mass of northern residents was minimal. The wealthiest traders, in fact, generally lived and conducted business at the edge of northern society in 1800, thriving off the transoceanic commerce.

This was a lucrative field of enterprise between 1793 and 1814. Intra-European wars allowed neutral American ships to command a big share of the commercial profits previously claimed by the Europeans themselves. In fact, as Philadelphia congressman and statistician Adam Seybert recalled of those bountiful days, "the brilliant prospects held out by commerce caused our citizens to neglect the mechanical and manufacturing branches of industry." The young Daniel Webster, then congressional spokesman for the merchants and shipowners of Portsmouth, New Hampshire, felt free to air his distaste for any too quick growth of manufacturing. He was, he declared in 1814, in no "haste to see Sheffields and Birminghams in America," to see the independent American yeoman transformed "in unwholesome workshops" into a stunted, dependent creature "necessarily at the mercy of the capitalist for the support of himself and his family."

But peace returned to Europe the very year that Webster voiced these hesitations—a peace that signaled renewed commercial war. American shippers found themselves driven back into a subordinate position in international trade. Many merchants, Adam Seybert noted, having grown used to "the newly acquired advantages" and regarding them "as matters of right," were now quite "confounded by the changes which were so suddenly effected." Philadelphia merchant Thomas P. Cope recalled the case of his acquaintance, the late Stephen Girard, one of the city's leading merchants and bankers:

> His mercantile operations, which were generally successful, were planned and executed when all Europe was belligerent. After the general peace & foreigners became competitors in the commerce of the world, his judgment failed, for he could not adapt his movements to this new state of things. In about one year's time he encountered losses to the extent of more than twelve hundred thousand Dollars.

To avoid such a disaster, other northern merchants began to reassess the potential profitability of domestic commerce. The first step was to improve the means of internal transportation. The energetic support of local, federal, and especially state governments soon made it possible to cover the landscape with new bridges, roads, canals, steamboats, and railroads. By 1830, the

New England and middle Atlantic states already contained more than 11,000 miles of turnpike, and by the mid-1840s, railroad investment there approached $100 million.

As a result, the time and expense involved in moving commodities across country dropped sharply. Between 1815 and the Civil War, freight rates fell more than 90 percent. By 1860, steamboats and railroads were moving cargo five times faster than was possible even on recently built canals. Parallel improvements transformed communications. Innovations in printing (such as the steam press) boosted the number of newspapers and their total circulation in the 1830s. When combined with the new telegraph system in the following decade, these papers could bring information from distant places to the attention of a mass readership in record time.

Such changes reduced the human isolation and material privation of rural life. Members of inland communities found it hard to resist the high-quality manfactures that good roads, canals, and railroads made available at unprecedented low prices. But the extra money needed to buy such items compelled them to sell still more goods and increasingly to focus their efforts on raising crops that would command the highest price in distant markets. The president of the New York Agricultural Society spelled out the logic of this evolution. The farmer seeking the maximum financial return on his labor, he explained, "cannot afford to make at home his clothes, the furniture or his farming utensils; he buys many articles for consumption for his table." Eventually, such specialization could leave farm families buying much of the food they ate.

In such ways, often imperceptibly, the involvement of farm families with commerce grew into a dependence upon the market and subordination to its rhythms. A fall in crop prices might now mean not just inconvenience but major hardship. When the price of butter fell ten cents per pound, for example, Harriet Fowler of Amherst, Massachusetts, noted that "every body is groaning with the hard times. Almost every one wears a sombre face in this village." These changes also took their toll on traditions of community cooperation. "Time and labor have become cash articles," observed the president of the New York Agricultural Society, "and [the farmer] neither lends them nor barters them." When the market economy as a whole suffered—as it did in the late 1830s and early 1840s—the decline of traditions of trust and assistance could become particularly stark. "One must now witness daily," reported the *New England Farmer* in 1843, "acts of meanness and deception among neighbors formerly expected only in companies of jockies and tavern-loungers."

The expansion of interregional commerce—and competition—initiated some of the most dramatic changes in northern economic life. Those who started farms on the virgin lands of the West increasingly shipped crops eastward, where they competed with those grown on less fertile soil. The completion of the Erie Canal in 1825 virtually wiped out grain production in much of the East and brought heavy pressure to bear on hog and cattle raising.

While change affected nearly all, some fared better than others in the changing economic scene. Those with larger farms or more fertile soil or better access to transportation tended to do well. So did farmers who had more capital to invest in improvements, such as manure, tools, and better seed. Families less blessed fared less well. Within Massachusetts, hill-country farms proved unequal to competition with farmers on the richer bottomlands. Economic historian Percy W. Bidwell captured the process admirably sixty years ago:

> As long as agriculture was self-sufficient and farm production was only for farm consumption, the superiority of one piece of land over another, and of one farm manager over his neighbor, were not obvious. But as soon as the two pieces of land and their managers were brought into business competition in producing for sale, then differences in fertility and in location resulted in differing costs of production. Thus the market acted as a selective force. Under its influence good land became more sharply differentiated from poor land.

Alarmed by the impact of this differentiation and selection, one New England farmer warned that better-off cultivators were "increasing their real estate by buying the small farms of their neighbors. By these processes, the number of land owners is diminishing and the number of dependent tenants and hired laborers is increasing." As a result, asserted another, "in many of our New England towns, two or three men own all the farms, or all the land worth having." By Lincoln's election, farm laborers constituted anywhere from 20 percent (Maine) to 38 percent (New Jersey) of those who tilled the land in the free states, and such laborer status was now evidently becoming less a temporary than a permanent condition. Northeast farming was rarely a large-scale enterprise, nor were northern financiers eyeing agriculture as a likely place to invest much capital. But Crèvecoeur's "perfect society" in which "each person works for himself" was quickly becoming a memory.

One solution lay in migration. Between 1790 and 1840, the northern population as a whole multiplied five times. But in the same years, residents of nonslave areas west of the Alleghenies multiplied in number fully forty-two times. Ohio achieved statehood in 1803, Indiana in 1816, and Illinois two years later. Michigan entered the Union in 1837, Iowa in 1846, Wisconsin in 1848, and California in 1850. Maine, a frontier region within the Northeast, became a state in 1820.

This phenomenal growth owed much to the resettlement of New Englanders. One out of every three Americans born in Connecticut and New Hampshire had left their home states by 1860 in search of a second start, mostly in the West. More than four in every ten Vermonters did the same. This population movement shifted the regional population balance fairly quickly. In 1790, only 6 percent of the North's residents had lived west of the Allegheny Mountains. Sometime during the 1850s, the Northwest and the Northeast reached population parity.

Together, the transportation revolution, commercialization of agriculture, and the growth of the West—and, for that matter, of the cotton South—created a tremendous domestic market for manufactured goods. Enterprising individuals (some of them merchants, others artisans, and still others commercial farmers) eyed these opportunities with growing interest. During the first half of the nineteenth century, they set out to claim a share of the potential profits by expanding and reorganizing northern industry. Production of thread, yarn, and then most textiles moved from home to factory. In the artisanal crafts (notably shoemaking, tailoring, and furniture production), employment and output increased and the nature of the work process changed. Grain-milling and meat-packing establishments grew into major enterprises. These sectors and others then developed expanded needs of their own. Growing firms turned out spinning, weaving, and sewing machines, farm equipment, machine tools, steam engines, locomotives, and track. Coal and iron mines and foundries expanded to meet the insistent demand for their products.

One result was a leap in the productivity of human labor. In mining and manufacturing, output per worker increased by half in real terms in just the twenty years prior to the Civil War. Frederick Douglass, having reached New England in his flight from slavery in 1838, marveled at the "striking and gratifying contrast" he observed between the productive efficiency of the North and that of the South. "Main strength—human muscle," he wrote, "unassisted by intelligent skill, was slavery's method of labor." In New Bedford, Massachusetts, Douglass discovered a greater disposition to find substitutes for (or, better, supplements to) paid labor. "In a southern port," he wrote, "twenty or thirty hands would be employed to do what five or six men with the help of one ox would do at the wharf in New Bedford." Even the maid-servant's labor in New Bedford was rendered more efficient with the help of "sinks, drains, self-shutting gates, pounding-barrels, washing-machines, wringing machines, and a hundred other contrivances for saving time and money."

The development of northern industry, commerce, and labor productivity translated into a truly staggering increase in total wealth. Between 1840 and 1860, the value added in agriculture nationwide rose by 90 percent (in fixed dollars). Over the same years, value added in manufacturing increased 350 percent—and this advance was concentrated overwhelmingly in the free states, chiefly in the Northeast. The urbanization of the North was also startling. In 1790, fewer than one in ten Northeasterners had lived in towns or cities. By 1860, the proportion had surpassed one in three in New England and in the middle Atlantic states as well. New York City boasted more than a million residents by 1860 (if one includes Brooklyn, then still formally independent), and Philadelphia was the home of half a million. These became the dominant manufacturing cities in the nation. Increasingly industrial and urban, the Northeast replaced the South as the western farmers' chief customer.

The expansion of domestic commerce and manufacturing reshaped society in the free states. The northern rich grew far wealthier. In 1860, southern planters still dominated the ranks of the United States' economic elite, comprising three-fifths of the richest 1 percent of the country's population. But concentration of wealth in the North had advanced too. The richest 5 percent of northern adults held more than half the region's total property in 1860. And this concentration was even more marked in the cities. In 1800, for example, half the taxable property in Philadelphia had belonged to the richest 10 percent of its residents. By 1850, an even larger proportion of the wealth had gravitated into the hands of the richest 1 percent. In 1820, only a hundred New Yorkers claimed personal property worth more than $20,000. By 1845, nearly a thousand individuals boasted personal assets in excess of $100,000. Twenty, in the meantime, had become "millionaires," a word that had just entered the popular vocabulary. Boston was soon claiming eighteen millionaires, and Philadelphia another twenty-five.

Still more radical and far-reaching were the changes wrought in the lives of millions of other northern residents. Between 1840 and 1860 alone, the number of people listed by the census in "mining and manufacturing" occupations tripled. These numbers signified more than just a change of occupation. They also meant a swift growth in the size of the economically "dependent" population. The widespread independent proprietorship in which so many had taken such pride in the revolutionary era was quickly giving way to a new social structure. In 1860, almost 60 percent of all adult males in the Northeast owned no real property. More than two-thirds of these individuals had less than $100 worth of property of any kind. This represented a radical shift since the days of Jefferson's presidency. In 1800, according to one estimate, less than a fifth of the nation's total free labor force had worked for someone else. By 1860, more than half did so. The proportion was even higher in the Northeast, above all in its growing towns and cities. From 60 to 65 percent of all adult males in the Northeast in 1860 may have been nonagricultural wage earners.

Where did these people come from? What had become of the earlier scarcity of available labor? One answer leads back to the transformation of northern agriculture that forced a portion of the marginal farm population to seek work, including industrial work, for wages. Another answer points abroad. Beginning in the 1830s and accelerating during the 1840s and 1850s, agricultural and industrial changes in Europe—often accompanied by social conflict and government repression—uprooted more than 4 million additional people from their native communities and drove them to seek economic, social, and political sanctuary in North America.

For the United States, the immigration that resulted represented a human tidal wave—equaling nearly a third of the country's entire free population in 1840. Nine of ten new immigrants settled in the free states—some entering agriculture but most finding employment in commerce and manufacturing. By the Civil War, more than two out of every five residents of many major northern cities had been born abroad, including New York, Chicago, Detroit, Cleveland, St. Louis, Buffalo, San Francisco, Milwaukee, and Cincinnati. A relative handful of these people were substantial merchants, manufacturers, and professionals. But among every ten immigrants reporting their occupations between 1840 and 1860, two were skilled workers, three had tilled the soil, and four more were unskilled laborers. Commenting upon this "unexampled flow" into the country from the "overstocked labor markets of Europe," a study of American manufactures in the 1860s noted with satisfaction that most "have found a market for their skill and labor in the large commercial cities and manufacturing towns, where they have supplied the drain made by steadily westward migration from the older communities." Early in the 1830s, recalled a European visitor, the United States' labor shortage was still offering real opportunities for advancement to the industrious worker. Twenty years later, however, "its seaboard—nay, three or more hundred miles inside it, is now satisfied with labor." It was this easing of the previous labor shortage that made economic growth and transformation possible.

Building and maintaining new transportation routes, towns and cities required the efforts of huge numbers of menial workers and unskilled laborers. Well-to-do urban families demanded servants and other personal attendants to increase their comfort and testify to their status. Meanwhile teamsters, carters, porters, warehousemen, dockworkers, sailors, and boatmen loaded, transported, unloaded, and stored the goods whose production and sale underpinned the era's great fortunes. Many such jobs were extremely arduous, dangerous, seasonal, and short-term—most lasting only a few weeks, some just a day or two. With diligence, the average day laborer could find employment during two-thirds of the year.

Emancipated northern slaves—and northward migration of many freed in the South—at first supplied a disproportionate share of the North's heavy, low-paid, and menial labor. Emancipation left most of them without property, skill, or formal education, and legal as well as informal restrictions imposed by white society left them (as the Pennsylvania Abolition Society reported) "excluded from most of the respectable and profitable employments of life, confined to the humblest and least gainful occupations, with strong prejudices to surmount, and labouring under every species of difficulty."

"Some of the men follow Mechanick trades," the Abolition Society noted in 1795, "and a number of them are mariners, but the greater part are employed as Day labourers." (In the early years of the century, at least one in every five of Philadelphia's mariners was black.) "The women generally, both married and single," the society's report added, "wash clothes for a livelihood." Other women found work as small traders and boardinghouse keepers. A thin stratum of professionals (doctors, ministers, undertakers, lawyers), small shopkeepers (bakers, fruit dealers, grocers), and skilled craftsmen did emerge, catering largely to other free blacks. In the 1840s and 1850s, three-fifths of Philadelphia's black families still owned no more than $60 in real and personal property combined. Nearly nine in every ten black residents of New York City in that era remained trapped in menial and/or low-paying occupations. The ex-slave Frederick Douglass discovered unexpected aspects of "free labor" as an unemployed worker in the North. "While wandering about the streets of New York, and lodging at least one night among the barrels on one of the wharves," he subsequently recalled, "I was indeed free—free from slavery, but free from food and shelter as well."

Douglass's chances of finding any work at all were further reduced because of the presence in urban centers of thousands of other would-be laborers—displaced rural people from the North's own hinterland as well as from the countryside of Europe, and especially Ireland.

Urban laborers found shelter in declining neighborhoods—the nation's first slums. Black workers were consigned to areas like Boston's "Nigger Hill" and "New Guinea" district along the docks and Cincinnati's "Little Africa." Conditions were wretched. "Thar they was," gloated a southern white traveler, "covered with rags and dirt, livin in houses and cellars without hardly any furniture; and sum of 'em without dores or winders. This, thinks I, is nigger freedom; this is the condition to which the philanthropists of the North wants to bring the happy black people of the South!"

The Irish fared little better, sometimes sharing tumbledown areas with free blacks, as in the Five Points district of New York City's Sixth Ward. In the heavily Irish Fifth Ward of Providence, Rhode Island, in 1850, two or more families commonly crowded into dwellings of just one or two rooms apiece. In Boston's North End, as a contemporary noted, "houses once fashionable" had by the 1850s "become neglected, dreary tenement houses into which the low paid and poverty-smitten . . . crowd by the dozens." Irish railroad laborers in upstate New York, according to Patrick Walsh, lived in "shanties"—"huts made of rough boards"—and shivered through the winter "with the fierce wind howling through them."

Some of the earliest and most sweeping changes in the northern economy transformed the production of textiles. Between 1800 and the Civil War, mechanization of that industry multiplied labor productivity more than fourfold.

The companies introducing these changes often combined the practical experience of an artisan or supervisor with the financial backing of long-term mercantile elements. This was the case, for example, in Pawtucket, Rhode Island. There, in 1792, a skilled worker, Samuel Slater, who had served as both an apprentice and an overseer in a major British textile firm, joined forces with prominent merchant Moses Brown to produce cotton yarn by means of an interconnected series of machines powered by the Blackstone River. The new company employed children to spin yarn inside the factory and then distributed that yarn to adults (often the children's parents) who wove it into cloth in their own homes.

Later, as the firm prepared to expand its operations, it sent agents into the countryside in search of tractable labor. One of these reported back in 1797 that the town of Marblehead seemed a likely source, since "the inhabitants appear to be very Poor their Houses very much on the decline—I apprehend it might be a good place for a Cotton Manufactory." Three years later the firm instructed its agent in Newport, Rhode Island, to seek out families "not in affluent circumstances, with children age seven to twelve," who "are dependent on daily labor for support." A widow with two children would do nicely.

A second type of textile system developed in the 1820s in Massachusetts. Another mechanic, Paul Moody, formed a partnership with merchant Francis Cabot Lowell and a circle of associates in an effort to mechanize and centralize not only spinning but weaving as well. Other differences included a much larger scale of production and a work force composed not of children or whole families but—at least at first—of single Yankee young women recruited primarily from the countryside.

By 1812, the country contained almost ninety cotton mills employing a total work force of more than 4,000. By 1840, textile companies were employing almost 100,000 people. At first, the pioneer firms' nearly desperate need to attract and hold scarce workers helped to ameliorate conditions in the factories. But after the mid-1830s, increasing competition from new firms pushed textile prices down even as a growing supply of vulnerable immigrant workers strengthened the employers' hand. As immigrants replaced native-born women in the factories, pay rates and working conditions declined.

The manner in which the early "Rhode Island" firms organized their weaving made use of already common practices among straitened New England farm families. To supplement inadequate agricultural incomes, young women and children in particular began taking in work from merchants in search of free hands at low pay. One such industry was the manufacture of hats from imported palm leaves. More than 30,000 Massachusetts residents took some part in this industry during the 1830s and 1840s.

There was an urban version of this "putting out" system too. In 1831, businessman and economist Matthew Carey estimated that 12,000 to 13,000 women in the country's four largest cities worked at home making paper boxes, hoopskirts, shirts and collars, artificial flowers, ladies' cloaks, and other light manufactures. By the 1850s, more than 16,000 female outworkers (according to the 1860 census) were providing much of the labor that made New York City the nation's principal center of men's-clothing production. The New York *Daily Tribune* described housing conditions among these women. Most rented "a single room, or perhaps two small rooms, in the upper story of some poor, ill constructed, unventilated house in a filthy street . . . In these rooms all the processes of cooking, eating, sleeping, washing and living are indiscriminately performed." Clothing workers, the *Tribune* reported, spent "every cent" of their wages on necessities but still lacked cash to "buy any other food than a scanty supply of potatoes and Indian meal and molasses for the family." The winter brought freezing temperatures to their garrets. "They are destitute of the means not only of adding comfortable clothing to their wretched wardrobes," the account concluded, "but of procuring an ounce of fuel."

The evolution of craft production involved some by now familiar influences. In the young republic, the typical urban craftsman had owned his own home, worked with his own tools in his own shop, purchased his raw materials, and made items to order for a small, localized market of his well-to-do neighbors. He made a comfortable living by the standards of the day and enjoyed a position of respect in the community. Jefferson, who considered the independent yeoman farmer the chief pillar of the new republic, praised artisans in the strongest terms known to him by dubbing them "the yeomanry of the city."

The traditional master craftsman was usually assisted by his family and sometimes by an apprentice or two, perhaps a journeyman as well. The latter typically worked in the master's shop—often enough boarding in the master's home—until he had accumulated enough money to open a shop of his own. In fact, this system was already visibly buckling by the late eighteenth century. As late as 1836, however, the national association of typesetters could "hope" that "the interests of the employer and journeymen have been assimilated and . . . rendered permanent for the time to come." By the Civil War such hopes had largely evaporated. In 1850 the organized printers resolved bitterly that

> it is useless to disguise from ourselves the fact that, under the present arrangement of things, there exists a perpetual antagonism between Labor and Capital . . . one side striving to sell their labor for as much, and the other striving to buy it for as little, as they can.

Improvements in transportation encouraged local and interregional competition and a growing scale of production. Enlarged urban and rural markets caused a shift from the custom-made production of a few commodities to larger-scale, ready-made production. As small workshops grew into larger manufactories, few journeymen could any longer expect to become independent masters. As employees, pure and simple, they worked on materials supplied by merchants and produced goods for their employers in exchange for wages. Employers, for their part, learned to convert expensive skilled work into simpler and cheaper tasks. Simplified tasks, in turn, made it possible to replace skilled journeymen with semiskilled workers, including numerous women and children. Writing in 1830, Rev. Joseph Tuckerman counted among "classes . . . who are wholly dependent upon wages" not only day laborers but a "great" number of journeymen who

> will never be anything but journeymen, in the various mechanic arts; and considerable number are also employed in the different departments of large manufactories, who possess no capital; and who know, and will continue to know, little or nothing in any other department of these establishments, except that in which they are themselves employed.

"A conscientious man in these times," wrote one Philadelphia journeyman, "can scarcely expect to earn more than a *competency*; if more than this is aimed for, a man is apt to become the oppressor of his fellows—taking advantage of their necessities and obtaining the fruits of their labor without rendering a just recompense."

In Lynn, Massachusetts, shoe production underwent such changes early and before long transformed that sleepy fishing village into the primary locus of shoe production in the United States. By the early 1830s, almost 70 percent of Lynn's journeymen household heads were without any real property. By 1850, individual firms were employing 300 to 500 hands, male and female alike. Some of these employees resided in the town; others lived elsewhere in the state and performed their labors on an outwork basis. Shoe production elsewhere—in Boston, Newark, Philadelphia, New York, Cincinnati—bent before the force of Lynn's competition. The New York *Tribune* reported in 1845 that most made-to-order footwear worn in the Empire City had been imported from New England, and since "transportation from those places [to] here amounts to a mere song," Lynn shoes could be priced low, so that "the laborer on this branch of Industry in our city is compelled to submit to the grinding competition engendered, and give all his labor, his time, and his health to earn food and clothes." In Cincinnati, businessman and booster Charles Cist proudly recounted in 1851 the cases of "a woman with three boys [who] earned in this business, three dollars a week, and each of the boys, three more" and of "an elderly man, who was out of employment when he came to Cincinnati" but who was "now earning, with [the aid of] three or four children, twenty dollars per week."

The immigration that accompanied these changes did more than ease employers' labor shortages. They also reshuffled the country's ethnic and occupational deck. Differences in experience, tradition, skill, and financial resource distinguished the various national groups from each other and from the native-born population. These differences, in turn, influenced the way each group fit (or was fitted) into the North's developing occupational and class structure.

Edward Everett Hale, no admirer of the Irish, believed their presence freed others from menial and badly compensated work. The very "inferiority" of the immigrants, he wrote in 1852, "compels them to go to the bottom; and the consequence is that we are, all of us, the higher lifted." Unskilled labor falls to the Irish, and "natives . . . are simply pushed up, into foremen of factories, superintendents of farms, railway agents, machinists, inventors, teachers, artists, etc." A British consular official similarly reported some years later that "the steady influx of immigrants" was enabling native-born Americans to turn their backs not only on the "rough toil" of "purely muscular" work but also on "skilled labour." The "chief ambition" of the "native workingman" was now "to attain the position of master workman, or, in the parlance of the country, to become a 'boss,' or to obtain a situation of clerk in an office, or of assistant in a shop."

In fact, the ethnic recomposition of the northern labor force was far from total. While many natives did find more desirable positions in these years, others stayed on at their old jobs, sharing with foreign-born co-workers the burdens of the Industrial Revolution. The trend, however, was apparent. Natives and newcomers—and among the newcomers, different nationalities—became increasingly identified with different kinds of jobs, conditions, and incomes.

Best off were immigrants from England, Scotland, and Wales. Some 40 percent of them had become farmers in the United States by 1860. Among the rest, many (like Samuel Slater) brought with them skills and experience acquired in the first industrial economy in the world. That background, combined with the inestimable advantage of speaking English, enabled British immigrants to join native-born individuals in garnering a disproportionate share of the more desirable supervisory and skilled jobs in some of the North's most technologically advanced industries. It also aided their relatively swift cultural assimilation and wide geographic dispersion. Skilled workers from the British Isles, however, also tended to bring with them greater familiarity with trade unionism and other forms of labor-reform ideas and organizations (such as cooperativism and Chartism) than many others employed in northern industry in the first decades of the nineteenth century.

Fleeing agrarian crisis, semifeudal class relations, and political inequality, tens of thousands of small farmers, tenants, and rural laborers from Sweden and Norway also made their way to North America. They settled chiefly in Illinois, Wisconsin, northern Iowa, the Minnesota Territory, and Kansas, and 40 to 50 percent entered agriculture. Many Scandinavian women became domestic servants, while men working outside agriculture gravitated toward western industries such as lumbering, furniture making, and the manufacture of farm equipment.

More than a million and a half German-speaking immigrants arrived in the antebellum era; among them, economic, religious, and political reasons for abandoning their native land were tightly interwoven. Only about a third of them had become farmers by

1860. Others took work as laborers or domestic servants. A very large number, however, entered the older, declining skilled crafts of the consumer-goods industries (notably shoemaking, tailoring, cabinetmaking). In its annual report for 1860, the New York Association for Improving the Condition of the Poor declared the Germans to be "the best portion of our immigrant population." The association was especially impressed with the newcomers' "education, industry, artistic skill, and sober, saving, accumulating habits." Germans, it noted, "can work for less wages than Americans, and live where an Irishman would starve."

These words of praise referred to the well-known fact that the Irish were the most hard-pressed immigrant group of the day. They were also the most numerous. Thousands had begun arriving even in the 1830s, driven abroad by the combined pressure of British colonial policy, landlordism, and the sheer inability of the land-tenure system to support the population. Then calamity struck. In 1845, a fungal disease appeared and devastated the potato crop, the central staple of the Irish diet. The next year, the crop was only a fifth of its 1844 size—in 1847, but a tenth. The result was devastating famine, and some 1 million people perished during the next decade from starvation or diseases bred by malnutrition. Another 1.8 million literally fled for their lives, most to the United States.

The great majority arrived virtually penniless and without any appreciable industrial skills. Barely a fourth, therefore, found their way onto the land. Young Irish women entered domestic service in great numbers, and Irish males soon performed much of the heavy labor required on canals and railroad beds and in most eastern cities. "I commenced work in digging Cellars," James Devar later recalled, "and may heaven save me from ever again being compelled to labour so severely, up before the Stars and working till darkness, nothing but driven like horses . . . a slave for the Americans as the generality of the Irish out here are." "They toil without ceasing," wrote a European observer, "for it is the only stay between them and absolute want." Despite such efforts, noted an early account, "the Irish labourer very rarely attains independence, changing only the nature of his toil, from the hackney coachman to the porter . . . or the hired drudge." A report dated 1849 from Newburyport, Massachusetts, painted the same picture:

> There is not in the town now . . . one Irishman or Catholic who is not utterly dependent for his support on his days wages . . . many cannot even find employment owing to the crowds that have come from Ireland this year, and many of the latter arrive in such a needy helpless utterly destitute state that it requires the utmost effort which their friends or countrymen can make to keep them from starving.

Poor, unskilled, desperate Irish laborers took jobs previously left to northern free blacks. "These impoverished and destitute beings," reported the *Colored American* in 1838, "are crowding themselves into every place of business and labor, and driving the poor colored citizen out." This was the case "along the wharves, where the colored man once done the whole business of shipping and unshipping—in stores where his services were once rendered, and in families where the chief places were filled by him." The shift was much more advanced by the mid-1850s, when Frederick Douglass lamented that "every hour sees us elbowed out of some employment to make room perhaps for some newly arrived immigrants," and thus "white men are becoming house-servants, cooks and stewards, common laborers and flunkeys." The immediate victims of this displacement were the northern blacks. But the sword had two edges and cut both ways; the Irish were becoming tainted not only by their impoverished and Catholic backgrounds by also by the jobs they were taking over. "In assuming our avocation," Douglass perceived, "he also has assumed our degradation." Those words shed considerable light on the significance of much anti-Irish sentiment in the antebellum era.

Between the American Revolution and the Civil War, society in the free states had undergone momentous transformation. As early as the 1830s, one immigrant likened it to "one gigantic workshop, over the entrance to which there is the blazing inscription, 'No admission here, except on business.' " Tocqueville observed admiringly that "no people in the world have made such rapid progress in trade and manufacturing." In 1847, Daniel Webster—by then a Massachusetts senator and champion of the state's business interests—had long since forgotten early misgivings about industrial development. "It is an extraordinary era in which we live," he enthused that year in a speech celebrating extension of the Northern Railroad. "Remarkable for scientific research into the heavens, the earth, and what is beneath the earth," the times were "more remarkable still for the application of this scientific research to the pursuits of life." By 1860 at the latest, the North's manufacturing sector was second only to Britain's in output and actually surpassed Britain's in degree of mechanization. A team of British investigators, reading the handwriting on the wall, concluded in the 1850s that the United States would shortly "rear up a fabric of commercial greatness, such as the world has hitherto been a stranger to" and so "enabling her soon to rival ourselves as, hitherto, the chief manufacturers of the world."

There was, however, a grimmer aspect to this impressive economic progress. One of the most visible and worrisome products of commercial development and industrialization in the North was a growing dependent population—free of slavery, yes, but free of much property as well. In this respect, the evolution of "free labor" society reminded more and more observers of the bleaker results of England's earlier industrialization. "Our good city of New York," Philip Hone noted despairingly in 1847, "has already arrived at the state of society to be found in the large cities of Europe; overburdened with population, and where the two extremes of costly luxury and living, expensive establishments, and improvident waste are presented in daily and hourly contrast with squalid misery and hopeless destitution."

— 3 —

"A Complete Revolution in Social Life": Cultural Change in the Antebellum North

Changes in the working life and social structure of the antebellum North and South brought or hastened many other important transformations. The nature of family life, the definition of gender roles (within the household and in society at large), the ways in which people entertained themselves and one another and comported themselves in public—all these aspects of social life were in flux too. These changes, in turn, helped shape the cultural values and standards with which people appraised the relative merits of two societies, slave and free.

Through most of the colonial era, the life of the free population revolved around the household and the family. The work of maintaining the family absorbed the efforts of all its members, and most of those labors were performed in or around the home. Farm males worked the fields while females cooked, cleaned, spun, wove, mended, kept the garden, tended barnyard animals, and produced items used at home or to sell or barter to neighbors or merchants. (A French traveler through the northern countryside indirectly testified to the importance of family labor by noting the "great disadvantage" confronting a bachelor farmer he encountered. "He does not have any poultry or pidgeons and makes no cheese; nor does he have any spinning done or collect goose feathers" since "these domestic farm industries . . . can be carried on well only by women.")

In the artisan household, the male family head performed the basic skilled work of his trade, perhaps assisted by sons or other apprentices. His wife, in addition to household responsibilities, might also cook and clean for apprentices and journeymen who boarded in the master's home and help her husband in the less skilled aspects of the artisanal work. Benjamin Franklin's *Autobiography* cites the advice of an old English proverb: "He that would thrive must first ask his wife." Franklin was proud and grateful that his own spouse, Deborah Read, "assisted me cheerfully in my [printing] business, folding and stitching pamphlets, tending shop, purchasing old linen rags for the papermakers, etc.," and was "as much disposed to industry and frugality as myself."

Farm women continued to produce for their families' use well into the nineteenth century, especially on the frontier. But significant changes reshaped the nature and functioning of households of well-to-do merchants, manufacturing employers, and professionals. Store-bought goods became more and more central to the family economy. Meanwhile, innovations such as piped-in gas, on cook stoves, iceboxes, and municipal water systems eased housework for those women who could afford them. Charles Dickens discovered in 1842 that Philadelphia "is most bountifully provided with fresh water, which is showered and jerked about, and turned on, and poured off, everywhere." The steadily decreasing size of the average family—from about seven in 1800 to above five in 1860—also lightened the domestic load somewhat. As a result of immigration and agricultural change at home, a growing number of women became available for domestic service. Meanwhile, economic development in the North served to break the link in many of these middle-class families between home and family life, on the one hand, and economic production, on the other. Fathers increasingly did their work outside the home—in offices, stores, workshops, and factories. This change of venue diverted male energies and attention from household matters.

While middle- and upper-class men followed business out of the home and household, their spouses generally stayed behind. For them, family and home life became a special "sphere," one strictly separated from the public sphere of business and politics. More than ever freed (and excluded) from most income-producing activities, they contributed to the economic health of their family primarily by carefully managing its budget. As the public world of commerce grew less congenial in the face of stepped-up competition and growing strain between employer and employee, writers increasingly idealized domestic life as a safe refuge. "A man's home," wrote Theodore Parker in 1843, "—it is to him the most chosen spot of the earth. It affords him a rest from the toils of life." It was the wife's responsibility, they added, to maintain the home as such a sanctuary. A magazine article gushed in 1834 over the virtues of the wife who performed this role:

> O! what a hallowed place home is when lit by the smile of such a being; and enviably happy the man who is lord of such a paradise . . . When he struggles on in the path of duty, the thought that it is for *her* in part he toils will sweeten his labors . . . Should he meet dark clouds and storms abroad, yet sunshine and peace await him at home.

The growing division and sanctification of "separate spheres" for men and women pulled in its wake an acknowledgment that mothers bore primary responsibility for rearing the children. "Oh, how solemn, how great the responsibilities of a Mother," Mary Hurlbut of New London, Connecticut, exclaimed in her diary in 1813, ". . . to teach and train these dear Children aright . . . I am in great measure responsible for their future conduct and destiny." After all, as Connecticut's Sarah Pierce put it, "most men are so entirely engrossed by business as to have but little opportunity of fully understanding the characters of their children."

The nature of middle-class child rearing also evolved. Earlier generations had stressed "breaking the will" of a child to instill automatic obedience to authority. More and more, however, mothers now sought to make their children learn self-regulation and self-discipline. Only such a rising generation would prove equal to its responsibilities in a commercial, republican society. "Governors and kings have only to enact laws and compel men to observe them," Susan Huntington, the wife of a Boston minister, confided to her diary; but "mothers have to implant ideas and cultivate dispositions which can alone make good citizens or subjects." The ideas and dispositions in question were those associated with Ben Franklin's *Poor Richard's Almanack*, which emphasized hard work, perseverance, frugality, accumulation, personal reserve, self-discipline, and temperate habits.

Stressing women's character-shaping role in the family encouraged the idea that women were the proper moral guardians for society at large. Catharine Beecher's immensely popular women's advice book, A *Treatise on Domestic Economy* (1841), made this connection quite explicit. Acting as moral exemplar, however, was not supposed to challenge the husband's ultimate power over a wife and her household; much less should it bring women into active political life. "In this country," Beecher explained, "women have an equal interest in all social and civic concerns . . . but in order to secure her more firmly in all these privileges it is decided that in the domestic relation she take a subordinate station, and that in civil and political concerns her interest be intrusted to another sex, without her taking any part in the voting, or in making or administering laws."

Many Northerners accepted these family and gender ideals as norms—or at least as goals to which to aspire. Many fewer were actually able to pattern their own lives according to it. As one journeyman printer complained in 1831, "If a workingman be married and have a family of young children, his wages cannot do more than command the mere necessities of life—impossible for him to lay by anything against the periods of sickness or old age." The same processes that transformed economically independent fathers into wage earners commonly drove other family members into the labor market to supplement the father's income. This pattern was especially obvious among hard-pressed recent immigrants, whose family arrangements reflected the pressures of poverty as well as their own struggle against it. From an early age until marriage, for example, most Irish-born young women worked for wages—some in mills and factories, far more in domestic service.

The middle-class ideal diverged from plebeian realities in other respects as well. The technological improvements that could ease housework remained available only to the prosperous. Others who had to make do without indoor plumbing hauled water several times a day from the rain barrel or public pump. Iron cook stoves and iceboxes were also rare among northern families before the Civil War. Successful housekeeping among the urban laboring poor—cooking, cleaning, mending, and procuring the family's daily requirements of water, fuel, and food—thus demanded considerable skill and expenditure of time as well as the active cooperation of both family members and neighbors.

Hard-pressed parents, thus, needed their children's active assistance. This could take a variety of forms, including participation in housework, running errands, or looking after younger sisters and brothers; buying provisions or borrowing them from neighbors; begging and scavenging for food, wood, coal, thread, cloth, or discarded items that could be pawned or sold. Such responsibilities took large numbers of children out of the home, into the streets, and away from the supervision of parents or other watchful adults. The line between scavenging and petty theft was always blurry. "Of the children brought before me for pilfering," a New York judge observed in 1830, "nine out of ten are those whose fathers are dead, and who live with their mothers, and are employed in this way. The petty plunder . . . finds a ready market at some old junk shop." "It was always very hard to send the little one out in the streets to make a living," a single German-born mother in New York's Kleindeutschland said of her twelve-year-old daughter in the 1850s. "But I couldn't help it: I must pay the rent some way." Many young women, unable to find other sources of decent income, turned to prostitution.

Privation and the cooperation needed to hold it at bay forged some families into strong units. Other households buckled or collapsed under the pressure. Parents abused or abandoned children, children ran away from home, husbands battered wives. The case of New Yorkers Patrick and Bridgett Carroll illuminates the larger pattern. One day in 1845, as Bridgett later recounted for the court, Patrick came home and "asked for his supper & what I had, I give it to him on the table—he was not well pleased at the kind of supper I had for him but I had no better—that raised words betwixt us & then he catched me by the throat and knocked me down & tramped on me & kicked me all over." Eight years later, another New York resident named Twomey flew into a rage when his wife failed to account satisfactorily for the money he'd given her for necessities. He "asked her did she think he picked this money up in the street," swearing that "if she did not give him a full account of what she got out of this money he would kill her or something like it." Twomey was as good as his word. When neighbors next saw him he was bent over her corpse, "calling her name and ask[ing] if she didn't love him and he her."

Clearly, scenes like these clashed jarringly with the era's developing ideals of proper fatherhood, motherhood, and cozy and insulated households. Numberless outside observers pointed to that divergence with mounting alarm. To upholders of the domestic ideal, the basic problem was the failure of the poor to internalize middle-class norms—the fact that (as one writer said of working women) "their ideas of domestic comfort and standards of morals are far below our own."

The changes at work in the North's economy and social structure also left their mark on leisure activities—on the ways, that is, in which people socialized and entertained themselves. One result, once again, was to widen the gulf separating different social classes.

Stressing hard work, self-discipline, personal reserve, and a social life organized around church, home, and family, the "proper" middle class of the North had little time and even less tolerance for idleness or boisterous forms of public entertainment. Respectable women were expected to observe still stricter limitations upon their activities, especially when in public. And once married, they were expected to find most sources of amusement indoors, as in music, conversation, and embroidery.

European observers frequently commented upon the relatively straitened nature of social life in polite northern society. Charles Dickens was sorry to find "no conversation, no laughter, no cheerfulness; no sociality, except in spitting." At mealtime, he noted, "every man sits down, dull and languid; swallows his fare as if breakfasts, dinners, and suppers, were necessities of nature never to be coupled with recreation or enjoyment; and having bolted his food in a gloomy silence bolts himself in the same state." Frances Trollope declared that while her British countryfolk "are by no means as gay as our lively neighbors on the other side of the Channel," still, "compared with Americans, we are whirligigs and teetotums; every day is a holiday and every night a festival."

Considerable exaggeration was at work here. Prosperous and genteel Northerners engaged in diverse cultural and leisure activities. They founded and patronized museums, libraries, theaters, opera houses, concert halls, social clubs, and summer spas. They entertained one another with dinner parties, banquets, and dances. Men went hunting, racing, horseback and sleigh riding, and enjoyed various other forms of travel (including steamboat excursions). In 1844, nautically inclined gentlemen of Gotham organized the New York Yacht Club to hold competitive sailing regattas. Counterparts soon arose in other eastern port cities.

In addition to providing sheer diversion, many of these pursuits served specific social ends. Some beckoned to those still seeking to raise their social standing. English traveler James Silk Buckingham, for example, noted in 1838 that "hundreds who, in their own towns, could not find admittance into the circles of fashionable society . . . come to [hotels] in Saratoga where . . . they may be seated at the same table, and often sit side by side, with the first families of the country." Some pastimes helped confirm and celebrate an individual's place within a certain social set. New York financier Philip Hone wrote smugly in 1848 that "this opera of ours is a refined amusement, creditable to the taste of its proprietors and patrons." There "the flowers of New York society" could bloom "under the sunshine of admiration" even as "our young men" learned "the habits and forms of elegant social intercourse" and "acquire a taste" of a "refined and elegant nature." And some of these leisure activities helped to instill respect for cherished cultural tenets of the rising northern business elite.

This last function grew in importance over time. As polite society in the North clarified its own standards of propriety and respectability, its members worked with increasing energy to discourage violations of these norms. Timothy Dwight was distressed in 1821 to see that "unhappily, in some of the larger towns, cards and dramatic exhibitions were growing in popularity," and not solely among the impoverished. John Pintard, secretary of New York's Academy of Arts and Sciences, stressed the point, warning that "the vices of polished society" increase precisely "as wealth & its consequent indulgences more & more abounds." Therefore "we must aim at giving proper direction to young minds, find out new resources for occupation & killing time, among which Theatres, Operas, Academies of Arts, Museums, &c., are to be classed as the means to attract & prevent the growth of vice & immorality." "It is upon the diffusion of sound and wholesome knowledge among the people," explained William A. Duer, merchant and president of Columbia College, "not merely of their political rights and duties, but of their religion and moral obligations—that, under Heaven, the duration of the government and prosperity of the nation depend."

People like Duer looked with particular distress upon the leisure preferences of other segments of the population. For the growing and increasingly immigrant urban work force, tightened labor discipline squeezed leisure and fraternizing out of the shop and workday and into a "sphere" of its own. There some very old forms of diversion coexisted with a growing array of newer, commercialized amusements. Among the former were cockfights, bullfights, dogfights, and bull and bear matches; card playing, billiards, foot racing, and bowling. Spirited wagering accompanied nearly all these diversions. In German districts, tamer public exhibitions—such as band concerts, theatrical productions, gymnastic exhibitions and competitions, parades, and picnics—horrified critics, partly because they commonly occurred on the Sabbath.

Before long, promoters—epitomized by P. T. Barnum—recognized the potentially huge urban market for professionally organized public entertainment. Circuses grew in number, offerings, and attendance. Racetracks proliferated, as did music halls and (by the 1850s) baseball parks.

This was the setting in which professional boxing developed and flourished. Both fighters and fans counted a disproportionate number of Irish immigrants in their number. The New York *Herald* marveled in 1849 at the "vast interest which was felt by the great floating population of this city" in one impending match. "Urchins in school could not be kept at their lessons but insisted upon their right to talk of what the whole town talked about. They became impatient of rule, were flogged for their disobedience, and returned to their seats, but to renew the forbidden conversation."

Many plebeian leisure activities took place in saloons, and public drinking played an increasing role in lower-class socializing. Many wage-earning males looked to the saloon, rather than to a crowded and tension-ridden household, for comfort and rest after a hard and oppressive day's labor. The company was familiar and congenial, and the cheap "spirits" (and, by the 1840s, lager beer) available there helped wash one's cares away. In 1855 New York City contained some 5,500 liquor establishments of various kinds. Saloons also hosted singing performances—"free and easies"—as well as boxing matches and other entertainments for the benefit of their customers. In German neighborhoods, beer and wine gardens flourished in great variety—from tiny to cavernous, from the basement saloon catering to restive single men to the quite respectable *Lokal* serving whole immigrant families, children included.

Other diversions helped bring adventure to lives that seemed increasingly dull and tedious—including carousing and brawling among rival militia companies, volunteer fire brigades, and street gangs recruited from the neighborhood. All these associations offered young wage-earning males alternative sets of personal loyalties and standards with which to locate and anchor themselves in an increasingly large, complex, heterogeneous, unpredictable, and impersonal urban world. Rowdiness expressed both youthful male exuberance and a definite intent to thumb the nose at prevalent notions of propriety and respectability.

Public holidays offered especially fine opportunities to display this mix of impulses. Independence Day was celebrated in a particularly boisterous manner. While merchants, bankers, professionals and officials staged parades, band concerts, and public speeches, other urban residents seemed to occupy their free time with gambling, drinking, fireworks, generalized revelry and irreverence. "No class of the community has so generally and constantly manifested a sense of hilarity on the Fourth of July as the working people," acknowledged Philadelphia's *Mechanics' Free Press* in 1829. "While the more wealthy classes have gradually withdrawn themselves from all public display on this national holiday as *ungenteel*, the toil worn artisan has continued to set it apart with mirth and jollity, in so much as to incur sometimes the charge of exuberant levity and small discretion from those who never knew a working day."

Probably the most popular form of commercial urban entertainment was the theater, which enjoyed an unprecedented growth during the early nineteenth century. It also showcased some of the most powerful social and political rifts and conflicts that were developing within northern society in this era. A notorious example was the protracted public rivalry between two prominent actors—Edwin Forrest, a native-born American, and the Englishman William Charles Macready—which began around 1830 and climaxed in New York City in 1849. The two thespians appealed to different social groups. A layer of prosperous businessmen and professionals (dubbed "the nabobs of the Fifteenth Ward" by detractors) liked Macready's aristocratic bearing and style; most wage earners, in contrast, preferred Forrest's outspoken democratic politics and assertive, spread-eagle patriotism.

The competition between the two men for popular favor thus tapped into deep and sharpening divisions among the populace. On Monday, May 7, 1849, hostile members of Macready's opening-night audience, seated in the lower-priced gallery, jeered and threw food, debris, and even their chairs at the stage and onto the heads of those seated in the more expensive sections below. The level of violence soon rose higher. On Thursday, May 10, an angry crowd of about 5,000 led by young journeymen craft workers, native- as well as foreign-born, gathered outside the Astor Place Opera House, where Macready was to perform. When members of the crowd hurled paving stones through the windows and tried to break through the doors, police and members of the 7th Regiment opened fire, first into the air and then into the crowd. Eighteen people fell dead, and another four died of their wounds in the following days. Nearly 150 others were wounded. The New York *Courier and Enquirer* approved the day's work:

> The promptness of authorities in calling out the armed forces and the unwaving steadiness with which the citizens obeyed the order to fire upon the assembled mob, was, in fact, an excellent advertisement to the Capitalists of the old world, that they might send their property to New York and rely upon the certainty that it would be safe from the clutches of red republicanism, or chartists, or communionists [sic] of any description.

Another reporter, however, grieved that the incident "leaves behind it a feeling to which this community has hitherto been a stranger—an opposition of classes—the rich and the poor . . . in fact, to speak right out, a feeling that there is now, in our country, in New York City, what every good patriot has hitherto felt it his duty to deny—a *high* class and a *low* class."

Revulsion against such scenes and rowdy popular culture generally helped stimulate the powerful religious revival (or "awakening") that swept through Protestant America between the birth of the republic and the Civil War. The effects of this movement (the second in a century) were profound and lasting. One measure of the change is numerical: more Americans than ever before affiliated to church institutions. Between 1800 and 1860, the combined memberships of Methodists, Baptists, and Presbyterians (the three denominations most centrally involved in the awakening) multiplied more than thirteen times. The ranks of Methodists alone swelled from fewer than 10,000 in 1780 to more than 250,000 by 1820 and to about 500,000 by 1830. By then it was the largest Protestant denomination in the land. In 1855, Methodists, Baptists, and Presbyterians together accounted for close to 80 percent of all church-affiliated Protestants in the nation.

Just as important as this explosion in numerical strength—and intimately related to it—was evangelicalism's impact upon both the form and the content of mainstream American Protestantism. Hand in hand with its proselytizing zeal went a sustained effort to render Christian beliefs easier for common people to understand and apply in daily life and to bring church members more actively, directly, and enthusiastically into religious life and church services. At the same time, the evangelical clergy was drawn increasingly from the general population. Many were itinerant, rather than full-time and well-paid, preachers.

Protestant doctrine also displayed the marks of change. According to orthodox Puritan Calvinism, God decided an individual's spiritual fate even before birth, and the nature of His decision was unknown to human beings. Furthermore, while God demanded that all His children adhere strictly to the letter of His law, nothing that any of them said or did could alter the predestined fate of their souls. Max Weber later explained how even this doctrine could be interpreted in a manner congenial with bourgeois values. Nevertheless, the fatalism implicit in predestination appealed less and less successfully to an American society that, in secular matters, increasingly prized freedom of action and especially the chance to improve one's lot. The wife of New England minister George Peck was thus by no means alone in disparaging "the repulsive force of the Calvinist doctrines." Widespread confusion and frustration caused by those doctrines popularized the following ditty:

> You can and you can't,
> You shall and you shan't;
> You will and you won't.
> You're damned if you do,
> And damned if you don't.

Popular sentiments such as these had been compelling Calvinist ministers to modify their doctrines for some time. The Second Great Awakening qualitatively strengthened and accelerated that reforming trend. To Calvinist predestination, evangelicalism counterposed belief in "free will." Anyone could achieve salvation, it held, by undergoing a profound religious rebirth (or "conversion") and then living according to a rigorously Christian code. Evangelical crusader Charles Grandison Finney entitled his best-known sermon "Sinners Bound to Change Their Own Hearts." That "God requires men to make themselves a new heart on pain of eternal death," that sermon argued, was itself "the strongest possible evidence that they are able to do it." In sum, Finney held, "a sinner under the influence of the Spirit of God is just as free as a jury under the arguments of an advocate." "I stand as a messenger of God," Rev. Albert Barnes assured a Pennsylvania congregation, "with the assurance that all that *will* may be saved."

This "Arminian" doctrine (so named after Calvin's chief sixteenth-century Protestant critic, Jacobus Arminius of the Netherlands) spoke strongly to the expectations, hopes, and habits of mind that temporal life had encouraged in many North Americans. Here, as Rev. Tobias Spice observed, was "a system that seemed to harmonise with itself, with the Scriptures, with common sense, and with experience." Rev. Alexander Blaikie, a Calvinist-minded Boston pastor, made the same point, if with considerable displeasure. "Every man," he complained, "is born an Arminian." As if in confirmation, Deborah Millet declared, "I was a Methodist in sentiment before I knew their doctrines."

Methodists pioneered many of the "new measures." Rev. Peter Cartwright later remembered that while "Calvinistic branches of the Protestant Church used to contend for an educated ministry, for pews, for instrumental music, for a congregational or stated salaried ministry," the "Methodists universally opposed these ideas; and the illiterate Methodist preachers actually set the world on fire (the American world at least) while [the Calvinists] were lighting their matches!" The interaction between evangelical preachers generally and their intended converts—and energetic interdenominational competition for such converts—reinforced these popular "new measures" and hastened their acceptance among Baptists, Presbyterians, and other evangelicals. As a writer for the *Christian Advocate* noted with satisfaction in 1853, "Revivals are no longer exhibitions of Methodist fanaticism in the estimation of our brethren of other churches. On the contrary, they too glory in them, and labor for them with great zeal and diligence."

In the North, evangelicalism's supporters embraced individuals from all social classes. In a new republic hostile to permanent, inherited class distinctions, this proved one of its chief strengths. The most fervent northern supporters of evangelicalism, however, included many successful entrepreneurs—master craftsmen, merchants, and farmers who were most quickly adapting to the new, more competitive economic order. Such people were the quickest to see the new movement and its doctrines as endorsing their own values and way of life. In particular, the Arminianist assertion that, with self-discipline and effort, individuals could influence their afterlives fit their own emphasis in this world on initiative, hard work, individualism, personal liberty, and advancement.

Evangelicalism also reinforced this group's crystallizing ideas about proper family and gender relations. Specifically, it approved the exclusion of women from commerce, their increased authority in the household, and their roles as moral teachers and exemplars in both the household and society at large. "Who can so successfully wield the instrument of influence than women?" one

Methodist tract asked in the 1850s. "By force of persuasion, how often has woman prevailed, especially when accompanied by submission and entreaty, where strength and courage and boldness would have accomplished nothing." "A sensible woman," it repeated in conclusion, "who keeps her proper place, and knows how to avail herself of her own powers, may expect, in her own sphere, almost any degree of influence that she pleases." Everywhere in the free states, women composed the clear majority of church attendees. The replacement of will breaking and of corporal punishment as the chosen methods of child rearing similarly received religious approval. In 1835, a father who proudly described his adherence to older techniques in a religious journal saw himself angrily denounced by other letter writers for showing such "brutality toward his own offspring," an offense that "should gain for him the anathema of the public and the indignation of every parent."

But the appeal of evangelicalism was not limited to the already prosperous. The same features that attracted well-to-do individuals also touched people of lesser means but high hopes. The promise of personal advancement in the future, if only one lived right and worked hard, spoke to the dreams of many middling shopkeepers and farmers. It also captured the hearts of certain skilled workers, especially but not only those less hurt by economic change (such as native-born building tradesmen). Also attracted were some struggling to avoid falling into the pit of poverty and wage labor—and still others struggling to clamber up out of that pit. In evangelicalism, such people believed, they had found a faith and code of personal behavior that could rescue them from a life of hopelessness and misery, "idleness and dissipation."

Evangelicals felt themselves flanked—literally, on both right and left—by "papists" (whom they considered corrupt and profoundly antirepublican) and infidels ("freethinkers" or "religious liberals"). These two groups could hardly have shared less, and indeed heartily despised one another. In evangelical eyes, however, they represented symmetrical threats to freedom and order.

Roman Catholics were by midcentury the nation's largest non-

Protestant group and the largest single religious denomination of any kind. American Catholics numbered only some 30,000 in 1790. By 1830, their ranks had swollen to 600,000 and by the early 1850s to some 1.6 million. Natural increase accounted for some small proportion of this phenomenal growth; so did the acquisition of Louisiana's Creole population. Many others arrived from Germany. But the greater part represented the impact of the Irish immigration.

Though nominally identified as Catholics, however, a great proportion of the Irish and Irish-American populations were actually barely conversant with the sacraments and doctrines of their church. No more than half of New York City's Catholic population evidently attended mandatory Sunday mass. Many, one priest discovered, "had no clear explicit knowledge of Catholic doctrines." A priest in Ohio agreed that "scarcely one out of ten of our Irish on the railroad goes to his duty" and "one half are grown up to 20–25 years & never made their first communion [and] know nothing of their catechism."

Much Irish-American loyalty to Catholicism derived from other sources. One of the most important was the link between religion and national identity. Protestantism, after all, was the religion of Ireland's hated English conquerors and their Scots-Irish allies; the Irish majority clung all the more fiercely to its religion. "Half our Irish population here," affirmed the New York priest quoted above, "is Catholic merely because Catholicity was the religion of the land of their birth." For a great many Irish-Americans, noted one of them, "fidelity to their faith and loyalty to their country" were "so closely interwoven, so thoroughly identified. The English Government, by banning both, made religion dearer and patriotism more noble; by placing the love of God and the love of country in the same category, it made martyr and patriot synonymous terms." Hostility and discrimination in the New World strengthened that link. As New York's Archbishop John Hughes observed, persecution "tended powerfully to unite Catholics."

This church was republican in neither structure nor philosophy. As elsewhere, its clerical structure in North America was large, hierarchical, and clearly distinguished from parishioners in dress, lifestyle, training, and function. Only members of the priesthood could perform church ceremonies. For the community the priest was, therefore (in the words of one church publication), "the center of . . . religion" and "the means of their sanctification." The sacraments, moreover, were conducted largely in Latin and were considerably more elaborate and traditional in form than in any American Protestant denomination.

The central role that Catholicism accorded its distinctive clergy complemented its view of the parishioners. Where members of evangelical congregations aspired to perfection, Catholicism held that original sin made such a goal unattainable (and, indeed, blasphemous). Frail human beings would inevitably and repeatedly relapse into sin. To pretend otherwise was vain (in both senses) and led either to hypocrisy or to abandoning salvageable souls to Satan. Salvation therefore led not through a single, apocalyptic conversion but through a lifetime of steady faith, an earnest attempt to abide by God's laws, and fidelity to the church and observance of its sacraments—including regular repentance before God's clerical deputies.

The Vatican's explicit political philosophy reflected the church's loyalty to the remnants of autocratic and aristocratic power in Europe. In an 1832 encyclical, Pope Gregory XVI rejected the doctrines of both press freedom and separation of church and state and condemned "the senseless and erroneous idea, better still, absurdity, that freedom of conscience is to be claimed and defended for all men"; "complete and unrestrained freedom of opinion which is spreading everywhere to the harm of both Church and State"; and all attempts to rebel against "our dearest sons in Jesus, the princes." His successor, Pius IX, later continued that tradition, most clearly in an encyclical called "The Syllabus of Errors." Among the errors excoriated there was the belief that "the Roman Pontiff can and should reconcile himself to and agree with progress, liberalism, and modern civilization."

In the eyes of its opponents, these characteristics and others marked Catholicism simultaneously as "the most dangerous enemy of freedom" and "the most dangerous enemy of order." Concerning the latter charge, one critic wrote, "Instead of toiling to elevate human nature to the noble standard fixed by divine precept and example," the Catholic Church "had lowered the standard till it was beneath the average level of human nature." It boasted "an immense dispensary of anodynes for wounded consciences" and "doctrines consolatory of transgressors of every class."

At the far end of the religious and political continuum from Catholicism stood freethinkers, rationalists, or "religious liberals." Some were outright atheists. Others believed in a God, but one who played so small a role in the day-to-day life of human beings as to be almost irrelevant. Virtually all were deeply suspicious of organized religion and church hierarchies, viewing them as bastions of superstition, privilege, and tyranny. While never very numerous, freethinkers attracted attention by virtue of their sheer iconoclasm and by their association (often enough in leadership positions) with movements demanding radical changes in economic, social, or political life.

In the late eighteenth century, Enlightenment-inspired religious rationalism had attracted many educated members of the colonial and early national upper class, in the South as well as the North. Soon, however, fears that such heterodox thought might spread to the mass and there encourage social and political radicalism helped to discredit religious skepticism among the elite. During the first half of the nineteenth century, indeed, organized free thought did seem to find its strongest support among certain groups of urban craft workers and sympathetic members of the intelligentsia.

In the early decades of the century, these plebeian rationalists tended to be either native- or British-born. The ethnic recomposition of the labor force changed this too. By the 1840s and 1850s, as German immigrants streamed into many of the most crisis-ridden trades, free thought in the United States was also becoming increasingly German in leadership and support. One meeting of a German rationalist organization in New York City in 1858 reportedly attracted an audience of about 2,000. More than seventy rationalist-influenced German "free congregations" sprouted in the Ohio Valley alone. Though most German immigrants probably identified with Reformed, Lutheran, or Catholic churches, conservative-minded German clergy were deeply distressed by the spread of "infidelity" among their immigrant countryfolk. Lutheran theologian Philip Schaff returned to Germany in the mid-1850s after a decade spent in America. Speaking to audiences in his homeland, Schaff complained of "the modern European heroes of liberty, or rather licentiousness—too many of whom have unfortunately been sent adrift upon [America] by the abortive revolutions of 1848." They included "the very worst forces of irreligion and infidelity, which, as far as their influence extends, cover the German name in the New World with shame and disgrace." Native-born and Anglo-American clergymen commonly employed more pointed language. New York Episcopalian minister Stephen H. Tyng warned in 1848 that Germans and other foreigners were bringing with them the spirit of infidelity and dissipation, "spreading its poison into every dark spot and fetid kennel of our cities, groping along in every sly place."

The growing visibility of both Catholics and freethinkers only added to evangelical certainty that a spiritual and moral regeneration was urgently required.

In general, evangelicalism spoke simultaneously to popular hopes and fears, at once consecrating business-oriented values while focusing anxieties about some of the by-products of economic change. A profound ambivalence was evident here. The North's urban, commercial, and manufacturing development was, on the one hand, essential to prosperity and to individual hopes of attaining it. On the other hand, however, these same phenomena seemed to carry within them the seeds of moral corruption. "We are becoming another people," Presbyterian Lyman Beecher grieved. "Our habits have held us long after those moral causes that formed them have ceased to operate. These habits, at length, are giving way." Now, he observed, "drunkards reel through the streets . . . with entire impunity. Profane swearing is heard . . . The Sabbath is trodden down by a host of men whom shame alone in better days would have deterred entirely from this sin." A Congregationalist minister "fear[ed] the facilities of [commercial] intercourse in this Country—while increasing the business and moneyed interests in the Nation . . . will by spreading vice and irreligion prove its ruin. Those very things which all regard as improvements will be our destruction."

Commercial amusements—the theater, the circus, and even the concert hall—called forth especially strong denunciations from churchmen. Racing and especially betting—but dancing too—deeply offended evangelicals, as did "disorderly" public conduct of any kind. To see the city's public spaces marred by such behavior affronted them personally and seemed to augur the kind of general moral backsliding and decay that they associated with the end of republican societies.

Evangelicals discovered corrupt behavior at all levels of northern society, including among the well-to-do. A religious tract of the era warned that "the spirit of enterprise and of change" easily spawned "lawless ambition" that seduced the weak-willed into "the abandonment of all moral principle." A minister quoted earlier feared that "the passion for prosperity" was about to obtain "tenfold more activity & power."

But sin seemed to find a special haven among the urban poor. A group of New York Federalists expressed this concern early in the century when they asserted that "the annals of history attest that almost every free state of antiquity lost its liberty in the corruption of the lower classes of its citizens." Lyman Beecher too warned that "our vices are digging the grave of our liberties and preparing to entomb our glory." And in this undertaking, Beecher felt sure, it was the "ruff-scruff" of society who most energetically applied shovel and spade. Young people new to urban life, such evangelicals believed, "thrown out upon the open bosom of our city," were soon "reduced to penury, stript of character, and corrupted by sensuality," moving rapidly from "the dram-shop [and] the brothel" to "the prison, the gallows, or some other miserable end." Apprehension mounted in the 1840s and 1850s as industrialization proceeded and more and more immigrants crowded into low-income occupations and declining neighborhoods. Particularly offensive were the Irish and German fondness for liquor and lager beer and the readiness of many of them to observe the Sabbath with public celebration rather than solemn contemplation.

Northern evangelicals approached social ills in the same spirit that they did personal ones. "As saints [i.e., the converted] supremely value the highest good of being," Finney said, "they will and must take a deep interest in whatever is promotive of that end. Hence their spirit is necessarily that of the reformer." Evangelical reform proceeded along three fronts—exhortation, charity, and prohibitory legislation. The first front was the most heavily fortified. Most social ills, it was assumed, sprang from the moral disorientation of individuals rather than from problems in the design or functioning of society. Improvement was achieved by "perfecting" those individuals—converting them and drawing them into the true Christian community. Thus, to combat prostitution a group of evangelical reformers in New York stationed themselves outside brothels in the city's most impoverished neighborhoods, read aloud from the Bible, and called upon those within earshot to abandon and repent of their sinful ways.

To aid good Christians suffering through no fault of their own—such as orphans, industrious widows, the infirm, and others of the "deserving poor"—the saints offered some direct material support. And finally, to mend the ways of citizens deaf to religious entreaties, northern evangelicals were ready to back up moral law with the force of civil legislation. Primarily as a result of their efforts, the state of Maine passed laws restricting the manufacture and sale of alcohol in 1846 and 1851. That campaign was led by Neal Dow, a Maine resident grown wealthy in leather tanning, speculation, finance, and railroading and since 1848 vice president of the American Temperance Union. By the middle of the 1850s, similar legislation had been enacted in at least thirteen other states and territories.

To spearhead such multi-tiered campaigns of social reform,

evangelicals created an imposing network of church-linked but interdenominational organizations—a veritable united evangelical front. These bodies trained ministers and founded missions and Sunday schools; spoke out against dueling, war, and violence generally; printed and distributed Bibles and religious tracts; campaigned for a "puritan" Sabbath (opposing, for example, mail delivery on Sundays); distributed food, clothing, and money to destitute people; and (as noted) fought against prostitution and alcohol consumption.

Women provided most of the reform societies' shock troops, but leadership normally fell to men, especially to prominent businessmen and professionals. The chief sponsors of the American Tract Society, for example, included merchant Arthur Tappan and banker Moses Allen. Rev. Franklin Y. Vail, an agent of the Tract Society, appealed directly to the wealthy for financial support, assuring them that the spread of religion would "dry up the sources of crime and taxation." Then "there would be flowing back to them a hundred-fold reward for all their benefactions in the safety and success of their business operations and the general prosperity of our common country." Nor did ambivalence about economic development and concern for the poor mean encouraging the latter to organize collectively against the prosperous. On the contrary, explained Rev. James W. Alexander, a prominent member of both the Bible and Tract societies. A pamphlet he produced in 1847 specifically for the "American Mechanic and Workingman" advised that whatever "tends to set the rich against the poor, or marshals these two classes into conflicting hosts," was completely "disorganizing and ruinous" in God's eyes.

Northern evangelical church leaders were not disposed to lead a concerted campaign against slavery. Charles Grandison Finney, for example, opposed the political agitation of the abolitionists, arguing that it would only "roll a wave of blood over the land." More conservative evangelicals expressed considerably greater hostility. The Bible and Tract societies remained in the hands of men who firmly supported "colonization" of free blacks abroad—

a program anathema to abolitionists. A week after the founding of New York City's abolition society, a public meeting in support of the Colonization Society attracted many well-to-do evangelical reformers, including Moses Allen, Jasper Corning, Samuel Ward, and Richard T. Haines.

The important fact remains, however, that in both spirit and principle northern evangelical Protestantism clashed with slavery. Finney detested the peculiar institution, bracketing it with war and "licentiousness" as "evils and abominations." The true Christian, he said, "longs for their complete and final overthrow."

One wing of the antislavery movement arose from evangelical ranks and framed its critique of bound labor in religious terms. Slavery, it pointed out, denied one group of human beings the freedom of action necessary to "free will"—and, therefore, moral responsibility for their own behavior. Meanwhile, it assigned to other humans a degree of temporal power that virtually guaranteed their moral corruption. Both master and slave were thus trapped in a relationship that inevitably led both down the path of sin and depravity. "Does not its essence lie in the counteraction of the human will?" asked evangelical abolitionist James G. Birney. "Man is justly subjected to moral law," wrote George Bourne, "but property, a slave who has no will, cannot be the proper object of rewards and punishments." Moreover, he went on, it "causes and nourishes pride, laziness, haughtiness, cruelty, oppression, deceit, fraud, theft, lying, Sabbath-breaking, drunkenness, adultery, fornication, and all uncleanness, murder, and everything that is hateful and abominable in the sight of God!"

Just as objectionably, asserted one of Bourne's co-thinkers, slavery encouraged sexual indulgence and the consequent corruption of both master and slave, thereby "undermining the foundations of moral and consequently political virtue." Henry C. Wright saw parallels between the debauchery of slaveholders and the moral atmosphere of the impoverished Irish Five Points section of New York—and declared he preferred even the latter to the former. In fact, Thomas Wentworth Higginson asserted, compared to the slave South, "a Turkish harem is a cradle of virgin purity." "Insist principally on the SIN OF SLAVERY," the American Antislavery Society instructed its advocates.

The economic development of the free states had tremendous cultural consequences. A northern farmer said as much in the 1850s when observing that "the transition from mother-daughter power [in the home] to water and steam power" in the mill and factory brought about "a complete revolution in social life and domestic manners." This revolution laid hands on the nature of family life, definitions of gender roles, standards of public behavior, forms of popular entertainment, and—by no means least of all—the form and content of popular religion. No more uniform in their impact on Northerners than were the economic changes with which they were linked, these social-cultural changes profoundly affected the ways in which residents of the free states regarded and related to one another. They also deeply influenced the ways diverse groups of Northerners perceived and responded to the nature of life in the slave states.

— 4 —

"The Anointed Lords of Creation": Culture and Society in the Antebellum South

The hybrid nature of the South's slave-labor system lodged a powerful contradiction at the core of antebellum southern culture. The most obvious tension characterized relations between whites and blacks. The spirit of Jeffersonian and Jacksonian democracy and ideals of free commerce coexisted uneasily with the palpable centrality of unfree labor. Neither master nor slave could miss the contradiction or its manifold expressions in all aspects of life. But ambivalence was almost as apparent among whites themselves and in the family, leisure, and religious lives they led. Traditions of hierarchy and deference squared poorly with promises of civic equality, popular government, and upward mobility. Aristocratic gentility and condescension, cavalier pride and swagger, libertine indulgence and gaming rubbed against evangelical tenets of equality, humility, austerity, sobriety, and propriety.

Southern family life and gender roles changed least during the antebellum era in those areas where slave labor and market forces mattered least—notably in the southern highlands. As in semi-subsistence farming areas of the North, small family-run farms predominated, producing primarily for their own use; the patriarchal family unit and ties of kinship remained at the center of cultural as well as economic life.

The picture was quite different in the plantation society of the "black belt" (so called because of the rich, "black" quality of the soil). For one thing, a sharper division of labor prevailed among whites resident on commercial plantations. To some degree, indeed, the assignment of tasks recalled the pattern then crystallizing in the urban North. The patriarch governed the farm's moneymaking activities—the production of staple crops—as well as dealings most directly linked to them. The plantation mistress supervised the domestic sphere, excluded from that of business and politics.

But the basis of the family's fortune, slave labor, left its distinctive mark on planter families. The plantation regime shaped a "domestic sphere" that could be quite extensive. Especially on a large estate, the domain of the planter's wife commonly included not only the white family's actual residence but also the smokehouse, storehouse, dairy, and separate kitchen. The cultivation and preparation of foodstuffs for the slave population might also proceed under her direction, as could the provision of medical care and the production and repair of clothing. Purchases associated with these tasks also fell within her purview. The temporary absence or death of her husband further enlarged both her responsibilities and her legal rights.

Other things distinguished plantation existence from life among the North's business elite. In the former, most obviously, home and workplace were physically joined. The master thus remained in greater physical proximity to—and exercised greater control over—family life and the household, which reduced the effective power of his wife in equal measure. Plantation families experienced the realities of rural isolation. Emily Burke described one of Georgia's principal plantations as "a township of itself," boasting "so many resources of convenience, that setting aside those things that can only be termed the luxuries of life, it could be quite independent of any foreign aid or article of merchandize." This substantial self-sufficiency was an aspect of the comparative underdevelopment of commercial exchange in the South. At the personal level, it also limited female friendships other than those between kin. "I seldom see any person aside from our own family, and those employed upon the plantation," Mary Kendall complained to her sister in 1853. "For about three weeks I did not have the pleasure of seeing one white female face, there being no white family except our own upon the plantation."

On the plane of norm and ideology, slavery and its defense re-inforced the patriarch's supremacy within his own home and em-phasized even more than in the North the wife's subordinate station. Bound labor, as the foundation of planter culture, strengthened patterns of thought and behavior rooted in the prin-ciples of hierarchy and deference, not those of individualism and equality. Implicitly or explicitly, planters considered their chil-dren, wives, poor white neighbors and employees, and their slaves to be all—albeit to different degrees—inferior to them-selves in social status and personal rights. Planters justified their power over their laborers partly by invoking other examples of hierarchy, especially those associated with the family (or, in George Fitzhugh's approving phrase, "family despotism"). "Wives and apprentices are slaves," Fitzhugh commented, "not in theory only, but often in fact." "Do you say," inquired another planter spokesman addressing an antislavery critic, "that the slave is held to involuntary service? So," he countered triumphantly, "is the wife," whose "relation to her husband, in the immense majority of cases, is made for her and not by her." It was in this sense that many planters referred to slaves as their "people," as their "black family."

In other ways too the fact of slavery distinguished the condition and status of the mistress from that of northern bourgeois women. On the one hand, the mistress exercised a degree of power over house servants incomparably greater than that wielded by well-to-do wives over domestics in New York, Philadelphia, or Boston. On the other hand, the mistress often watched helplessly while the planter's sexual access to female slaves eroded her self-respect, marriage, and moral authority on the plantation.

The case of "Mrs. N.," a plantation mistress in antebellum Vir-ginia, testifies eloquently to the pattern. According to a divorce petition filed in 1848, the planter (Mr. N.) regularly flaunted his "strong dislike and aversion to the company" of his own wife by sleeping with his favorite female slave "on a pallet in his wife's room." One morning, Mr. N. told this female slave to join his family at the breakfast table, "to which Mrs. N. objected, saying that she (Mrs. N.) would have her severely punished." "In that event," her husband responded, "he would visit her (Mrs. N.) with a like punishment. Mrs. N. then burst into tears and asked if it was not too much for her to stand." Mr. N. "told her that if she did not like his course, to leave his house and take herself to some place she liked better." The humiliation was doubtless magnified by the fact that Mrs. N.'s wedding dowry in "land and negroes" constituted a significant portion of Mr. N.'s estate.

Scenes like this disgusted the more pious planters and embarrassed slavery's apologists. Their stubborn recurrence in the face of condemnation points back to the two souls at war within nineteenth-century American slavery. That conflict expressed itself at work, in the home, and in the way planters took their entertainment, morality, and religion.

At one extreme, the most sober-minded among them sometimes seemed as skeptical of frivolity and diversions as Ben Franklin. One prominent North Carolinian announced in 1802 his "plan . . . to amuse myself with improvements in agriculture." Another advised his son some forty years later that "a plantation to be well managed should never be left but at very short intervals." Yes, he conceded, "if it is a matter of life and death, and the owner is of any use[,] then he should go away, but not otherwise." The greater number who allowed themselves more leeway, moreover, entertained themselves in a manner familiar to the northern mercantile elite. Yachting was a favorite of wellborn southern males, especially those who owned residences in coastal towns or cities. Planters especially loved horse racing, organized jockey clubs, and built private racetracks to accommodate the sport. (The slave quarters supplied many of the jockeys.) Indeed, owning a string of expensive thoroughbreds quickly became a cherished status symbol. The sharing of leisure-time diversions with

Northerners at first brought members of the regional elites together. At the beginning of the nineteenth century, New York City was horse racing's chief national center, and visiting planters delighted in attending races there. Many also passed their summers at the northern resorts described in the previous chapter.

But in leisure activities as in other matters, the differences between northern merchants and manufacturers and southern planters and their associates made themselves felt—and more heavily with the passage of time. Many planters referred to themselves as "the chivalry" (or "Southrons," a term borrowed from Sir Walter Scott) and regarded themselves as the cultural heirs of Europe's feudal aristocracy. Although deeply dependent upon the world of commerce and commodity production, the most romantic of these men publicly disdained hard work as the province of slaves and overseers, priding themselves instead on being men of breeding, generosity, flair, and daring. An old Alabaman lovingly described Mississippi's Seargent Prentiss in such terms:

> When he treated, it was a mass entertainment. On one occasion he chartered the theatre for the special gratification of his friends— the public generally. He bet thousands on the turn of a card and witnessed the success or failure of the wager with the nonchalance of a Mexican monte-player, or, as was most usual, with the light humor of a Spanish muleteer. He broke a faro-bank by the nerve with which he laid large bets, and by exciting the passions of the veteran dealer, or awed him into honesty by the flame of his strong and steady eye. His confidence knew no bounds . . . scorned all considerations of prudence and policy. He made his friends' quarrels his own . . . [and] would put his name on the back of their paper, without looking at the face of it, and gave it his *carte blanche*, if needed, by the quire.

The evident idealization of this portrait is as valuable to our understanding of the type as the actual details of Prentiss's makeup.

Men of this mind-set did their best to reproduce elements of what they thought of (based on heavy doses of Sir Walter Scott) as the aristocratic lifestyle. The results included lavish plantation parties and balls, deer and fox hunts, and even—in the late ante-bellum era—jousting tournaments. In the latter, rival champions took the names of medieval knights (encountered in the works of Scott or other European authors) and competed for prize money and the right to designate "the queen of his heart." Having been crowned with a wreath of flowers, the queen took her place on a throne as the other knights and their ladies paid her court.

Fittingly, the dominant image of the plantation female de-picted her as the chivalric male's perfect romantic and then mar-ital object. She was the very embodiment of leisurely grace, gen-tility, and refinement, and the ideal recipient of male attentions and beneficiary of male efforts. "Maidenly delicacy," affirmed the president of one southern university in 1810, is "the very foun-dation of society." During the 1830s, Georgia's centennial cele-bration featured the following toast: "Woman!!! The center and circumference, diameter and periphery, sine, tangent and secant of all our affections." The audience responded with twenty cheers. Women of the planter class were expected to steer clear of strenuous physical activity. At southern resorts, accordingly, re-called one woman, "there was no golf or tennis, not even the innocent croquet, to tempt the demoiselles to athletics, so they drifted more to the 'Lydia Languish' style."

The puritanical cultural standards that gained strength in the North during the Second Great Awakening struck many male devotees of the chivalric tradition as unworthy—shameful, bloodless, unmanly. As religious attacks upon drinking, gam-bling, public dancing, secular theater, and idleness and frivolity generally gained strength in the North, planters began to seek their entertainments closer to home. By the 1840s, more and more of them were frequenting local and Gulf Coast watering places such as Pascagoula, Biloxi, Bay St. Louis, and Ocean Springs. So did Northerners who shared the southern view of lei-sure. Explaining the growing preference for southern resorts, *De Bow's Review* pointed to the "contrast" between the "hollow-heartedness" and hubbub it found characteristic of northern spas (as of northern society generally) and "the quiet ease, the careless abandon, and the habits of home-life" of those in the South. When disapproval of gambling began to cramp New York's horse-racing style, New Orleans became the national horse-racing capital—and, more generally, a magnet for members of the southern elite seeking relaxation of various kinds. "From all the neighboring States," reported one visitor in the 1850s, "the planters come with their wives and daughters and spend one or more weeks, or even months, in dancing, fiddling, flirting, smoking cigars, and abusing Abolitionists."

Blood sports also retained their appeal through the antebellum era. Cockfights attracted wagerers, and cheering spectators included both planter and yeoman "without regard to status" (as Elkanah Watson of North Carolina noted). They continued to draw long after being driven underground or (at least nominally) outside city limits. In the spring of 1852, a disapproving New Orleans *Picayune* reported that 5,000 spectators had come to watch a grizzly bear and a bull "tear and mangle each other" and "to incite, provoke, and drive them into a fight, for which their natural instincts were not sufficiently savage." As these accounts suggest, attempts by southern evangelicals to modify planter conduct were respected more often in appearance than in reality.

George Fitzhugh sturdily denied that slavery eroded family ties. "The sanctity and purity of the family circle," he asserted, benefited greatly from the existence of human bondage. "Slavery, marriage, religion"—these were "the pillars of the social fabric [and existed in] intimate connexion and dependence." "The Slave Institution at the South," insisted another slaveholder intellectual, C. G. Memminger, "increases the tendency to dignify the family." Indeed, asserted Fitzhugh, the master's power over his slaves shored up and improved the quality of family life among the latter.

Others more concerned with pecuniary than paternalist considerations also saw advantages in stable slave marriages. "As far as practicable," wrote Georgia's Nathan Bass, "families of negroes should be kept together . . . With a family of children around them, they feel more attached to home and do not form the habit of running about the neighborhood at night, when they should be asleep." "Servants ought, as far as possible, to be divided into families," Rev. H. N. McTyeire of Tennessee wrote in *De Bow's Review* in 1860. In this way, he explained, "the home feeling of the servant" is strengthened:

Local as well as family connections, thus cast about him, are strong yet pleasing cords binding him to his master. His welfare is so involved in the order of things that he would not for any consideration have it disturbed. He is made happier and safer, put beyond discontent, or the temptations to rebellion and abduction, for he gains nothing in comparison with what he loses. His comforts cannot be removed from him, and he will stay with them.

Some masters did try to abide by such injunctions. But few who sanctioned—or even encouraged—slave marriages had the same concept in mind as their slaves. The relative of one plantation master described the way he paired off newly purchased slaves. The man would simply

arrange the men in one row and the women in another and make signs to them to choose each man a wife and would read the marriage service to them and thus save time by settling their matrimonial affairs. The young people of the family would select names from novels they had read and other sources, and sew these names into the clothes of each.

However created, moreover, slave families had no external guarantee of survival. The law accorded them no force at all; much less did it protect them against dissolution at the pleasure of the master. Once again, some masters—Thomas Jefferson among them—tried to keep slave families intact. But the structure and exigencies of the larger system commonly frustrated such efforts. Owners with economic problems often sold off individual members of slave families, separating husbands from wives, children from parents. A slave owner's death was often the occasion for distributing slave family members among the deceased's various creditors and heirs. Masters also sold slaves away from their families as a punishment for various infractions of the rules. Nor was sale the only cause of such calamities. Marriages linking slaves owned by different masters were shattered when one of those masters decided to move (along with his human property) deeper into the cotton kingdom. In these and other ways, masters forcibly broke up somewhere between a fifth and a third of all slave marriages.

The human toll of family destruction was incalculable, but a scene played out in Charleston, South Carolina, in March 1865 hints at the torments involved. A month after Union troops captured this spiritual capital of the Confederacy, the city's black population celebrated the end of bondage with a mass procession through the streets. As a reporter for the New York *Daily Tribune* noted, the march included "a large cart, drawn by dilapidated horses," upon which stood "an auctioneer's block, and a black man with a bell represented a [slave] trader. This man had himself been sold several times[,] and two women and children who sat on the block had also been knocked down at auction at Charleston. As the cart moved along, the mock-auctioneer rang his bell and cried out: 'How much am I offered for this good cook? She is an excellent cook, gentlemen. She can make four kinds of mock turtle soup—from beef, fish, or fowl. Who bids?' " Onlookers called out, "Two hundred's bid! Two fifty. Three hundred." "Who bids? Who bids?" intoned the auctioneer again. At this point, the journalist observed, black women lining the streets "burst into tears as they saw this tableau—and forgetting that it was a mimic scene, shouted wildly: 'Give me back my children! Give me back my children!' "

By far the most important initiative for creating and protecting families came from the slaves themselves. The burdens, deprivations, and oppression that defined their work lives and legal status made family and kinship ties extraordinarily precious. Where else could they turn for personal assistance, human respect, warmth and intimacy, and whatever protection could be found against their master's exactions? Parents thus strove to nurture children, spouses looked after one another, children tried to shield their parents. Frank Bell remembered how at harvesttime he and his brothers would position themselves behind their parents as the slaves worked their way up the furrows. "In that way one could help the other when they got behind. All of us would pitch in and help Momma, who warn't very strong." Bell also noted that the black driver, his uncle, "always looked out for his kinfolk, especially my mother."

Beyond such immediate forms of assistance, the slave family served to incubate the unfree population's distinctive outlook and set of standards and values. The same family unit was also the primary means of transmitting that culture from one generation to another. A Louisiana planter's complaint about the slave he called Big Lucy—that she "corrupts every young negro in her power"—unintentionally captured something of the transmission process. Cultural prohibitions against marrying blood cousins (evidently of West African origin) encouraged slaves to marry outward, thereby linking many different families. This practice created networks of practical help and communication that could extend deeply into the countryside.

The irreplaceable nature of these relationships helps explain why slaves struggled, with or without the consent of their masters, to establish, maintain, and protect their family and kinship bonds. Slave men and women went through regular marriage rituals in order to stabilize and formalize their relations. The fugitive slave John Warren reported that "in regard to marriage" the slaves "try to make it as near lawful as they can." Most of these marriages survived until one partner died, and the average child grew up knowing both father and mother. Slave parents named their children in ways that would link them to ancestors and kin.

Within the typical slave family a basic division of labor did prevail. Women cooked, sewed, knitted, cleaned, and raised the children. Pregnant women and nursing mothers were normally expected to do somewhat less work than others. Fathers supplemented meager food rations by fishing, hunting, and trapping, at night, on Sundays, and at other opportunities. They also gathered firewood and built furniture for the cabins. Especially on larger plantations, the heaviest field labor—such as plowing, land clearing, and wood chopping and hauling—fell primarily to men. So did assignments as artisans and drivers.

Here again, however, the nature of the labor system intervened. The master's drive to obtain the maximum amount of labor from his chattels limited the sexual division of labor. Both male and female slaves tended livestock, cleaned cotton, milled flour, and shelled corn and peas. Women as well as men generally labored in the fields, although the labor gangs themselves were normally sex-segregated. As a slave in Alabama, for example, Sara Colquitt had "worked in the fields every day from before daylight to almost plumb dark." And not even childbearing and its promise of enhancing the master's wealth guaranteed safety from physical punishment. Masters determined to discipline a pregnant slave simply "made [her] lie face down in a specially dug depression in the ground" before laying on the whip.

Slaves confronted to the obstacles placed in their way as best they could. They evolved a range of attitudes and practices distinct from those prevalent under freedom. Such was the case, for example, when husbands and wives belonged to different owners. Spouses thus separated pressed for the right to visit one another. "Father lived on one side of the river," recalled Daniel Dowdy of Georgia, "and my mother on the other side. My father would come over every week to visit us." The difficulties here were palpable, compelling family members to reassign to other kin or community members some daily responsibilities otherwise undertaken within a nuclear family. Slave husbands and wives separated by too great a distance (as by sale or migration) tacitly freed one another to take another mate. The slave community did not stigmatize unwed mothers or children born out of wedlock. But women were expected eventually to marry, after which point promiscuity was frowned upon. Most slave women could take up spousal and maternal labors only after field work was done. As a result, many mothers had little time to tend to their children. This fact, coupled with others, took its toll. Henry Bibb reported of the children that their "mothers have not time to take care of them—and they are often found dead . . . for want of care." Infant mortality among slaves was high indeed. Between 1850 and 1860, more than one in every three black children died before reaching ten years of age. A white child's chance of reaching adolescence was twice as good.

Slavery denied to black men and women many of the rights and responsibilities that defined parenthood in free families. Whether as spouses or as parents, their power and authority were consistently denied, in matters both large and small. The humiliation, abuse, and corporal punishment of husbands and fathers, wives and mothers—as well as their children—before the eyes of other family members starkly reminded all present where ultimate power resided. As one child recalled, "Many a day my old mama has stood by and watched massa beat her children 'til they bled, and she couldn't open her mouth." Slaves challenged the rape of black women by owners and overseers only at terrible risk. Minnie Fulkes remembered what happened when her own mother resisted a Virginia overseer. The woman was stripped naked, hung from a rafter, and whipped "'til the blood run down her back to her heels." A white man in Louisiana regularly strode into the cabin of one slave family and ordered the husband "to go outside and wait 'til he do what he want to do" with the man's wife. The husband "had to do it and couldn't do nothing about it." "What we saw," another ex-slave remembered, we "couldn't do nothing about it. My blood is boiling now at the thoughts of them times."

"If only the abolitionists could see how happy our people are," mused slave owner Hiram B. Tibbetts to his brother in 1848. "The idea of unhappiness would never enter the mind of any one witnessing their enjoyments." In fact, the manifold burdens and brutalities of slave life made opportunities to relax and socialize especially precious. Most gatherings occurred when slaves were not compelled to labor—that is, on occasional Saturday nights, Sundays, holidays, and rain days. Those times were seized upon eagerly and celebrated with food, drink, games, makeshift instruments, dancing, and elaborate storytelling. They were oases of relief from labor and discipline. They also offered the chance to assert common cultural values and practices that united the slave community and expressed its distinctive view of life and how it should be lived.

The folk tales related at such slave celebrations played an especially important role, given the centrality of an oral tradition to a people denied access to the printed word. Many stories centered on a physically small but clever creature (often an animal) who outwitted stronger but dull-witted enemies. Br'er Rabbit, the best known of these, explained, "The rabbit is the slickest of all the animals the Lord ever made. He ain't the biggest, and he ain't the loudest, but he sure is the slickest." Other tales were more straightforwardly populated by human slaves and masters and taught the measures necessary for human beings to survive in bondage.

However the protagonists were defined, these tales shared a number of themes. Many drove home the cruel unpredictability of life and the perils of trusting the sincerity of the powerful. (The Br'er Rabbit stories commonly begin with Br'er Fox and Br'er Bear exchanging hypocritical greetings with Br'er Rabbit—sometimes Sabbath greetings—just before the two predators attempt to devour him.) They also illustrate the importance of concealment and deception.

In one such tale, a slave couple has just stolen the leg of a slaughtered hog from their master and hidden it under their bed. Into the cabin promptly strolls the master, wishing to hear the husband play his fiddle. The man complies, singing as he plays, "Ding-Ding a Dingy—Old Lady put the pig's foot further [under] the bed." His wife, humming in unison, casually glides over to the bed and tugs the cover smartly down over the protruding loot. "Yessir, that's a new one," the oblivious master notes of the song dreamily. "Yessir, that's a new one." In a similar story, underfed slaves sadly inform their master that a bunch of his hogs have died from the disease "malitis," which has rendered the flesh unfit to eat. The master, unwilling to see so much meat go completely to waste, orders the dead animals butchered and fed to the slaves themselves. The story ends with the teller explaining the origin of the dreaded disease to the listeners. "Don't you all know what is malitis? One of the strongest Negroes got up early in the morning, long before the rising horn called the slaves from their cabins. He skitted to the hog pen with a heavy mallet in his hand. When he tapped Mister Hog between the eyes with that mallet, 'malitis' set in mighty quick."

Rejection of the status quo could also take religious form. Southern whites who resented the planter elite (as well as the elite's culture, pretensions, and Anglican Church and clergy) provided an important early source of recruits for both Methodist and Baptist denominations. Most evangelical converts in the mid-eighteenth century were middling farmers. (For example, the average Baptist identified in Lunenburg County, Virginia, in the 1760s owned 190 acres of land and 2.4 slaves—a level of property ownership lower than the county average.) In evangelical congregations, such people could find personal sanctuary, emotional release, communal self-discipline, spiritual egalitarianism, and reinforcement for their own sense of worth, dignity, and independence. Membership in these churches helped them reject—and gave them an alternative to—the condescension, ostentation, frivolity, and self-indulgence ascribed to the planter elite. Such "prideful" conduct was unworthy of God's own children, and those who engaged in it lost the right to set the spiritual tone for the population at large.

The evangelical message and practice proved compelling, and the movement spread beyond its original circle of adherents. By the 1790s, in fact, most southern Protestants had joined the fold. The Second Great Awakening signified a new burst of spiritual energy. It began in the trans-Appalachian river valleys—especially in the Cumberland region—of Kentucky and Tennessee and radiated outward from there. Camp meetings attracted scores, hundreds, and even thousands to prayer sessions that often continued around the clock over a number of days. Bishop Thomas Coke reported that when Methodists convened their quarterly conferences, "the brethren for twenty miles around, and sometimes for thirty or forty, meet together. The meeting always lasts two days. All the traveling preachers in the circuit are present, and they, with perhaps a local preacher or two, give the people a sermon one after another." By the Civil War, nine out of ten southern Protestants were either Methodists or Baptists.

Not surprisingly, the evangelical outlook initially affronted and alarmed many—at both the top and the bottom of southern white society—content with the traditional, familiar, hierarchical, deference-based society and religion. More objectionable still was the readiness of some ministers—Methodists in particular—to speak openly and sympathetically of the "poor distressed Africans," the "sons and daughters of oppression." At stake was much more than a rhetorical formula. The evangelical affirmation of a universal Christian brotherhood led some preachers to stretch out their hands toward African-Americans, both free and slave, and invite them into the church.

Black Southerners responded as enthusiastically as did whites. As Maryland slave John Thompson noted, "This new doctrine . . . brought glad tidings to the poor bondman; it bound up the broken hearted; it opened the prison doors to them that were bound, and let the captive go free. As soon as it got among the slaves, it spread from plantation to plantation, where there were but few who did not experience religion." As early as the turn of the nineteenth century, blacks may have constituted 25 percent of the membership of both the Methodist and Baptist denominations. Until the 1830s, in fact, most Methodist congregations in southern cities were overwhelmingly black. Some free blacks, principally in cities of the upper South, were able to form independent congregations of their own early in the nineteenth century. The Baptist belief in the autonomy of each congregation particularly assisted such black Christians to shape their religious lives. By the 1820s, it is true, these churches were supervised by white ministers, but they remained the first and only formal institutions that catered to the black community as a whole. During the fifteen years preceding the Civil War, the number of black Baptists doubled—from 200,000 to 400,000.

Since the colonial era, slave owners had generally discouraged Christian proselytizing among their chattels. Bishop Thomas Secker regretted in 1741 that "some . . . have been averse to their slaves becoming Christians, because, after that, no Pretence will remain for not treating them like Men." The Anglican clergy had tried repeatedly to allay such fears. But, especially in the late eighteenth century, more than a few evangelicals gave them substance. If Africans also had mortal souls, they wondered, did they not belong to the same human community as whites? And could one Christian enslave another and still retain God's grace? Doubts reached into slaveholder ranks. "When I consider that . . . their forefathers were born as free as my Self," wrote the slaveholding farmer Daniel Grant to his son-in-law in 1790, "& that they are held in bondage by compulsion only . . . when I consider that they are human creatures Indeed with Immortal Souls capable of Everlasting happiness or liable to Everlasting misery as well as ourselves . . . It fills my mind with horror and detestation."

Although southern evangelicalism did not label slave owning as sinful, individual ministers—especially in the upper South— did help found societies dedicated to ending slavery gradually through moral suasion and pressure. In 1780, a conference of seventeen Methodist ministers in Baltimore declared slavery "contrary to the laws of God, man, and nature—hurtful to society; contrary to the dictates of conscience and pure religion, and doing that which we would not [wish] others should do to us and ours." In 1789, a Baptist body declared slavery "a violent deprivation of the rights of nature and inconsistent with a republican government." Five years later, Methodist preachers determined definitively "to extirpate this abomination from amongst us," threatening excommunication for all congregants who failed to emancipate their chattels within two years at most. In 1818, the

General Assembly of the Presbyterian Church labeled slavery as "utterly inconsistent with the law of God."

It was not surprising, therefore, that (as former slave John Thompson related) the spread of evangelical religion "produced great consternation among the slaveholders. It was something which they could not understand." Perhaps they understood it too well. In either case, they resisted. Rev. Thomas Coke preached against slavery in Virginia in 1785 and promptly found himself menaced by an angry crowd and formally charged with criminal activities. Evangelicals encountered violent opposition elsewhere in the South as well. Chastened, the Methodists withdrew their ban on slavery just six months after imposing it. As Rev. Coke explained, the church leaders "thought it prudent to suspend the minute concerning slavery, on account of the great opposition that has been given to it, our work being in too infantile a state to push things to an extremity." In 1816, the Methodist General Conference resolved that "little can be done to abolish the practice." Two years afterward, the Presbyterian General Assembly coupled a formal condemnation of slavery with a declaration judging "hasty emancipation to be a greater curse" than bondage itself. It also decided to uphold the decision by the Lexington, Kentucky, presbytery to depose Rev. George Bourne for making antislavery pronouncements.

This equivocal response made possible a new departure in relations between evangelicalism and major slaveholders. By the late 1830s, growing numbers had themselves entered the ranks of reborn Christians. Probably their most aggressive representative was James Henry Thornwell of South Carolina. Starting life as an overseer's son, he later became proprietor of Dryburgh Abbey plantation and assumed leadership of the southern Presbyterian Church. At Mississippi's 1861 secession convention, thus, some 80 percent of the churched delegates belonged to the Methodist, Baptist, or Presbyterian denominations.

By and large, evangelical churches were happy to welcome such "enlightened and refined people" into their fold. They, in turn, continued to back away from emancipationist notions.

True, some evangelicals, particularly in the southern hill country, continued to doubt the compatibility of slaveholding with Christianity. In a number of piedmont counties of North Carolina, for example, antislavery Wesleyan Methodists remained dug in through the 1850s. In general, however, those preachers who openly resisted southern evangelicals' accommodation with slavery found themselves silenced or driven out of the South. Such was the fate, for example, of Rev. Adam Crooks, forced to leave North Carolina in 1851 after four years in the ministry there. Still more telling was the case of the near-legendary Methodist circuit rider Peter Cartwright. An organizer of the early southern revivals, Cartwright had by the 1830s been dissuaded from mentioning slavery in his sermons; eventually he was compelled to leave the pulpit altogether.

Thus tamed and tested, southern evangelicalism increasingly commended itself as a medium through which to reconcile slaves to their servitude. Georgia planter Nathan Bass, for one, reasoned that "in proportion as the moral character of the slave is elevated, and imbued with correct opinions in reference to his moral obligation faithfully to discharge his duty as a servant, and to respect and venerate the authority of his owner, you make him a more faithful and obedient servant." James Henry Hammond of South Carolina was, like Jefferson and others of the revolutionary generation, something of a rationalist and skeptic. Those personal doubts, however, did not prevent him from erecting two churches on his plantation. "Something supernatural . . . appears to be indispensable in the government of man in all his relations," Hammond explained. Attempting to do without such beliefs, he thought, would bring only "endless revolutions in the political and social systems." Therefore "let Priests reign a while yet over those who require hell & devils to restrain them."

Southern evangelical missions began to issue pamphlets that spelled out the acceptable position on slavery for the benefit of preachers and congregants alike. This literature was designed (in the words of one publication) "to show from the Scriptures of the Old and New Testament, that slavery is not forbidden by the Divine Law." An injunction from Ephesians was especially prized for use among slaves: "Servants, be obedient to them that are your masters according to the flesh, with fear and trembling, in single-ness of your heart, as unto Christ." Charles Colcock Jones, the principal champion of missionary work among the slaves, in 1834 published his *Catechism for Colored Persons*. It instructed slaves "to count their Masters 'worthy of all honour,' as those whom God has placed over them in this world; 'with all fear,' they are to be subject to them and obey them in all things, possible and lawful, with good will and endeavor to please them well." "What did God make you for?" asked the catechism's 1844 edition. The approved answer was: "To make a crop." To ensure that this was, indeed, the version of Christianity observed by African-Americans, south-ern whites moved against the existing independence of black congregations. In the countryside, where African-American churches were rare, planters sought to outlaw separate black "praise meetings."

At the national level, the accommodation between slavehold-ing and the southern evangelical churches eventually triggered crises in the major Protestant denominations, whose northern congregants were developing very different attitudes toward the peculiar institution. By 1850, John C. Calhoun could accurately recall that "already three great evangelical churches have been torn asunder" by the slavery conflict. The chastening collision with chattel slavery—and the assertive and even skeptical spirit in which more than a few influential planters entered the fold—cooled the ambition of southern evangelical reform generally. Much more than in the North, the churches fought shy of trans-lating calls for individual regeneration into demands for political action. Whatever moral reform was desired was to occur on an individual basis, within the individual's heart, and without under-mining existing social relations.

As in the North, evangelical churches celebrated the family household as a moral refuge and cornerstone of society. They also extolled the mother's central position within that household and applauded her abstention from "male" activities. Also as in the North, women took an active part in church affairs and made up a majority of church members. Those churches sponsored female educational societies, prayer groups, missionary bodies, and other institutions for women, which developed organizational and other skills and provided additional opportunities for participation in community life.

But the explicit goal of southern evangelicalism was to keep the religious role of white women within narrow and carefully policed bounds. Evangelical Southerners clearly designated men as society's (and women's) rightful rulers and ultimate authorities. They were, in the 1830 words of southern writer Virginia Carey, "the anointed lords of creation"; St. Paul's injunction that wives "submit yourselves to your own husbands as to the Lord" provided the text for many a Sunday sermon. As noted, northern evangelicalism also subscribed to a doctrine of "separate spheres." In the South, however, far more than in the urbanizing and industrializing North, that doctrine and its prescribed limits were successfully enforced. No movement for women's rights—much less for slavery's abolition—ever took root in the antebellum South. Those unable to abide such restrictions—like Angelina and Sarah Grimké, daughters and sisters of substantial South Carolina planters, who rejected both slavery and the subordination of women—commonly left the South in despair.

Slaves resisted religious indoctrination and control in various ways. Usually they sat through approved sermons silently, if often sullenly. Later that day or night, however, without the master's knowledge, they would often gather in their quarters or nearby woods to hold the "real meeting." Sometimes, however, enslaved Christians manifested their real religious beliefs openly. An old Virginia slave named Silas, evidently unable to sit mutely any longer, demanded of the white preacher, "Is us slaves gonna be free in Heaven?" When the startled minister tried to ignore the question, Silas repeated it. Another slave subsequently recalled what then transpired:

> Old white preacher pulled out his handkerchief and wiped the sweat from his face. "Jesus says come unto me ye who are free from sin and I will give you salvation." "Gonna give us freedom along

with salvation?" asked Uncle Silas. "The Lord gives and the Lord takes away, and he that is without sin is going to have life everlasting," preached the preacher. Then he went ahead preaching, fast-like, without paying no attention to Uncle Silas.

Similarly, Charles Colcock Jones noted the way in which a congregation of slaves responded to a sermon he delivered in 1833:

[W]hen I insisted upon fidelity and obedience as Christian virtues in servants and upon the authority of Paul, condemned the practice of *running away*, one half my audience deliberately rose up and walked off with themselves, and those that remained looked anything but satisfied, either with the preacher or his doctrine. After dismission, there was no small stir among them; some solemnly declared "that there was no such an Epistle in the Bible"; others, "that they did not care if they ever heard me preach again!" . . . There were some, too, who had strong objections against me as a Preacher, because I was a *master*, and said, "his people have to work as well as we."

"My father," remembered former slave Lucretia Alexander, "would have church in dwelling houses and they had to whisper . . . Sometimes they would have church at his house . . . They used to sing their songs in a whisper and pray in a whisper." Such meetings, she added, occurred "once or twice a week." Participants risked a great deal. "The white folks would come in when the colored people used to have prayer meeting," recorded one former slave, "and whip every one of them." The former slave Wash Wilson recalled, "When the niggers went around singing 'Steal Away to Jesus,' that meant there was going to be a religious meeting that night . . . down in the bottoms or somewhere. Sometimes us sing and pray all night." A common feature of these meetings was the "ring shout," in which participants danced slowly in a circle, the hand of each on the shoulder of the next.

The tenacity with which slaves defended their independent religious life confounded the plans of their masters. James Henry Hammond's plantation journals testify eloquently on this score.

The year 1831 found Hammond recording his definitive decision to stamp out all clandestine religious gatherings among his slaves. After the passage of twenty years, he was still chronicling his campaign to "have . . . all church meetings . . . be broken up except at the Church with a white preacher."

The slave owners' hostility to independent black churches and attacks upon clandestine rural prayer meetings were not arbitrary. They reflected their assumption (as one Mississippi slave put it) "that when colored people were praying [by themselves] it was against them." That assumption, in turn, was hardly unfounded. Peter Randolph, a Virginia slave, reported that at these meetings "the slave forgets all his sufferings . . . exclaiming 'Thank God, I shall not live here always!' " Mingo White recalled that "when the day's work was done the slaves would be found . . . in their cabins praying for the Lord to free them like he did [the] children of Israel." Jacob Stroyer remembered his father praying that "the time which he predicted would come, that is, the time of freedom when . . . the children would be [their] own masters and mistresses."

Some slaves apparently did accept the omnipresent, constantly reiterated tenets of planter-sponsored Christianity. "I have met, at the South," Frederick Douglass later wrote, "many good, religious colored people who were under the delusion that God required them to submit to slavery and to wear their chains with meekness and humility." At least one black Baptist congregation—in Petersburg, Virginia—repeatedly expelled from its midst slave congregants who had run away from their owners.

But most slaves, Douglass added, rejected the message urged upon them by white preachers. For this black majority, Douglass noted, "it was in vain that we had been taught from the pulpit at St. Michael's the duty of obedience to our masters—to recognize God as the author of our enslavement—to regard running away as an offense, alike against God and man—to deem our enslavement a merciful and beneficial arrangement—to esteem our condition in this country a paradise [in contrast] to that from which we had been snatched in Africa—to consider our hard hands and dark color as God's displeasure, and as pointing us out as the proper subjects of slavery—that the relation of master and slave was one of reciprocal benefits."

The content of black Christianity thus remained a terrain of struggle down through the Civil War and even afterward. Although generally unable to read, slaves became acquainted with—and proved disquietingly attached to—certain passages in the Bible that seemed to document their own understanding of Christianity. These included: "God is no respecter of persons"; "Thou shalt love thy neighbor as thyself"; "Whoso stoppeth his ears at the cry of the poor, he also shall cry, and shall not be heard"; "Do justice to the afflicted and needy, rid them out of the hand of the wicked"; "Call no man master, neither be ye called master"; "Let the oppressed go free." Slaves similarly identified with the agonies of Old Testament prophets, with little David, who slew huge Goliath, with Samson, who brought the temple crashing down upon his tormentors, and with Jesus, God's innocent child, who suffered for the sins of others. They especially treasured and repeated the story of Exodus, cherishing the tale of the Israelite slaves' liberation as well as the punishments God inflicted upon Pharaoh and his minions.

In these and other ways, slaves formulated a vocabulary in which they could express their own pain and anguish at their condition and bolster one another's morale without immediately incurring punishment for open defiance or rebelliousness. Jacob Stroyer remembered the departure from the plantation of one group of fellow slaves sold into the Deep South. "Those who were going did not expect to see their friends again. While passing along many of the negroes left their master's fields and joined us . . . [Some] were yelling and wringing their hands, while others were singing little hymns that they had been accustomed to for the consolation of those that were going away, such as:

> When we all meet in heaven,
> There is no parting there;
> When we all meet in heaven,
> There is parting no more."

In their own brand of Christianity, slaves were also able to formulate a common standard of proper behavior. They used it to evaluate their treatment by whites; against this standard all were found wanting. A northern visitor could thus hear one slave tell her mistress, "You no holy. We be holy. You in no state of salvation." Thus it was that (as one former slave noted) "when the white folks would die the slaves would all stand around and pretend like they was crying but they would say, 'They going on to hell like a damn barrel full of nails.'"

Slaves also used their own understanding of Christianity to promulgate an agreed-upon code of rights and responsibilities among themselves. In the process, they asserted and reinforced a sense of group identity, mutual ties, and readiness and determination to govern themselves. Perhaps the clearest manifestation of their distinct views here dealt with the definition of theft. They distinguished sharply between taking the property of the master and stealing from another slave. As for the former, recalled ex-slave Henry Bibb, "I did not regard it as stealing then, I do not regard it as such now. I hold that a slave has a moral right to eat and drink and wear all that he needs, and that it would be a sin on his part to suffer and starve in a country where there is plenty to eat and wear within his reach. I consider that I had a just right to what I took, because it was the labor of my hands."

The same rules, however, did not govern relations within the slave community. "They think it wrong to take from a neighbor but not from the masters," reported Benjamin Drew, adding that "a slave that will steal from a slave is called *mean as a master*. This is the lowest comparison slaves know how to use: 'just as mean as white folks.'" "They didn't half feed us either," recounted the former slave Robert Falls of North Carolina. "They fed the animals better. They give the mules the roughage and such, to chaw on all night. But they didn't give us nothing to chaw on. Learned us to steal, that's what they done. Why, we would take anything we could lay our hands on, when we was hungry. Then they'd whip us for lying when we said we don't know nothing about it. But it was easier to stand [bear] when the stomach was full."

But black Protestantism was not merely an aid to survival under slavery. It expressed an ardent desire for—and expectation of— freedom. As one of their "spiritual" songs put it:

> O my Lord delivered Daniel,
>> O why not deliver me too?
> He delivered Daniel from the lion's den,
>> Jonah from the belly of the whale,
> And the Hebrew children from the fiery furnace,
>> And why not every man?

Among slave evangelicals, a particular form of "pre-millennialist" interpretation of the gospel found broad support. It held that the Second Coming of Christ would inaugurate an apocalyptic, revolutionary transformation of human society. God would reward His long-suffering children and exact heavy payment from their tormentors. Emily Burke was not alone in noting of the slaves that "they all believe in a future retribution for their masters, from the hand of a just God." "The idea of a revolution in the conditions of the whites and blacks," recalled former slave Charles Ball, "is the corner-stone of the religion of the latter." "The God I serve is a man of war," they sang. Only after His martial work was done would there begin the anticipated thousand years of earthly peace and justice.

The hot core of this outlook was normally concealed in the antebellum era with indirection and biblical allusions. "We used to have to employ our dark symbols and obscure figures," a former North Carolina slave recalled after the war, "to cover our real meaning." As conditions changed, southern blacks grew bolder in expressing their beliefs; the veil of ambiguity began to lift. In the spring of 1861, slave owners in Georgetown, South Carolina, grew alarmed when they discovered their slaves singing a spiritual that promised:

> We'll soon be free,
> We'll soon be free,
> We'll soon be free,

When the Lord will call us home.
My brother, how long,
My brother, how long,
My brother, how long,
 Before we done suffering here?
It won't be long,
It won't be long,
It won't be long,
 Before the Lord will call us home. . . .
We'll soon be free,
We'll soon be free,
We'll soon be free,
 When Jesus sets me free.
We'll fight for liberty,
We'll fight for liberty,
We'll fight for liberty,
 When the Lord will call us home.

By war's end, southern blacks were singing,

Oh! Father Abraham,
Go down into Dixie's Land,
Tell Jeff Davis
To let my people go.

— 5 —

"Called by the Same Name":
The Many Meanings of Liberty

Faith that the New World would witness humanity's spiritual rebirth took root in the earliest New England settlement. By the late eighteenth century, that religious ideal had become firmly intertwined with a temporal one—that the New World must become a citadel of human liberty. The Connecticut Baptist Elias Lee exulted in 1794 that victory over monarchical Britain had raised "the standard of liberty and republicanism" internationally. Thomas Paine anticipated Lee by almost twenty years, arguing in *Common Sense* in 1776 that, since "every spot of the old world is overrun with oppression," "the cause of America is in great measure the cause of all mankind." Paine reminded his compatriots that "freedom hath been hunted round the globe" and urged them to "receive the fugitive, and prepare in time an asylum for mankind." Decades later, novelist Herman Melville deftly joined biblical to secular imagery in affirming that "we Americans are the peculiar, chosen people—the Israel of our time; we bear the ark of the liberties of the world." (The protection of the American Union against all threats, internal or external, thus became directly linked in the popular mind with the defense of these liberties.)

But this libertarian vision—of the United States as a beacon of freedom and of its people as destined to bring freedom's light to the world—grew clouded over time. Americans found themselves increasingly caught up in heated disputes among themselves concerning the true meaning of liberty. No one put this problem more clearly or perceptively than Abraham Lincoln in a speech he delivered in the spring of 1864. "The world," he began, "has never had a good definition of the word liberty," and this unclarity was especially evident among Americans. "We all declare for liberty," Lincoln noted, but

> in using the same *word* we do not all mean the same *thing*. With some the word liberty may mean for each man to do as he pleases with himself and the product of his labor; while with others the same word may mean for some men to do as they please with other men and the product of other men's labor.

"Here," Lincoln observed, "are two, not only different, but incompatible things, called by the same name—liberty."

With these words, Lincoln identified the crux of much public discussion, debate, and conflict in the new nation during its first seventy years of life. In the midst of the national celebration of the American Revolution and the achievement of republican freedom, the very meaning of those achievements became controversial. Deepening differences in the economic and social lives of North and South led spokesmen of their elites to conceptualize liberty and democracy in increasingly different ways and to grant them in different degrees to different classes of people. Simultaneously, certain divisions *within* each region grew in significance, and intraregional conflicts both complicated and aggravated the national political crisis.

In the North, differences over the meaning of political republicanism asserted themselves early. Many state constitutions drafted during or immediately following the War of Independence contained important limits on popular self-government, even by adult white males. Property or taxpaying requirements restricted the right to vote and—still more commonly—to hold public office. Newly settled and less wealthy areas were frequently badly underrepresented in state legislatures, and many government officials were appointed rather than elected. The most extreme case was Rhode Island, where in 1840 fewer than half of all adult white males could vote. By steadfastly resisting demands for change, that state's political elite provoked an abortive armed insurrection in 1842 (the so-called Dorr War, after rebel leader Thomas W. Dorr).

Elsewhere, demands for political reform succeeded—beginning at the turn of the nineteenth century and continuing through the 1830s—in broadening the franchise, reducing disproportions in representation, and placing growing numbers of public offices under electoral control. Just between 1824 and 1840, the proportion of all adult white males who actually cast ballots rose from about 27 percent to 80 percent.

The drastic expansion of the electorate introduced important changes in the structure, content, and rhetoric of political life. Most obviously, it further democratized American politics, increasing popular participation in government and compelling party leaders to respond. It was in this era that Tocqueville observed that for the average American male, "to take a hand in the regulation of society and to discuss it is his biggest concern and, so to speak, the only pleasure an American knows." And though denied the vote, women could also be swept up in—and affect— politicial enthusiasms of the time. As one northern woman wrote, "If Ladies cannot *vote*, they can at least influence others" who could. The principles of popular democracy, still strange and threatening to the old Federalists, became the lingua franca. "No party," observed the *Ohio State Journal* in the 1850s, "dared to go before the people upon any other avowed object." Especially after 1840, politicians vied with each other to appear the most authentically "common" in background, habits, and principles. "If there is any thing in this country fixed," wrote Boston merchant John Murray Forbes in 1856, "it is the prejudice against aught which has the appearance even of aristocracy."

Alongside this process of political reform there developed a running public debate concerning the proper nature of economic rights and the demands of community welfare. On one side of this dispute stood supporters of the free-trade doctrines that Adam Smith developed in 1776 in *The Wealth of Nations*. Smith regarded unrestricted commerce as "the natural system of perfect liberty and justice." He and his disciples rejected traditions legitimating government (or spontaneous, popular) regulation of economic activity. They held that both the principle of liberty and the interests of the community were best served when all could buy and sell freely, without interference, at whatever prices prevailed on an open market.

In fact, the ideas that Smith systematized had already gained a substantial following by the late eighteenth century. By the outbreak of the Revolution, most Patriot leaders already took much of Smith's creed for granted. "It is contrary to the nature of commerce," Benjamin Franklin asserted in 1766, "for government to interfere in the prices of commodities. Trade is a voluntary thing between buyer and seller[,] in every article of which each exercises his own judgment, and is to please himself. . . . Where there are a number of different traders, the separate desire of each to get more custom[ers] will operate in bringing their goods down to a reasonable price. . . . Therefore . . . trade will best find and make its own rates."

Over the following decades, such ideas came into even greater currency, propounded in the nation's institutions of higher learning and propagated in its literature on political economy. Rev. Samuel Stanhope Smith, president of New Jersey's Presbyterian College (which later became Princeton University), argued in 1812 that prices were naturally set by the balancing of goods and money, that "this constant ratio of things no law or authority of the state could alter without violence to liberty and manifest injury to the interests of trade."

Those who found themselves on the other side of these debates included many who shared—all other things being equal—a belief in the principle of free commerce. They refused, however, to allow that principle to eclipse other rights and liberties they considered at least equally compelling. Some of these people found alternative standards of economic justice in tradition, some in religion, and some in the ideals of political democracy. Many appealed to all three. Adhering to such customary, spiritual, and civic standards, they maintained, sometimes required qualifying or setting aside the verdict of the marketplace and substituting the judgment of the people, their government, or other popular institutions.

Advocates of these two contending outlooks clashed dramatically in revolutionary Philadelphia. A convention there charged with drafting a democratic state constitution only narrowly rejected a proposed article that warned that "an enormous Proportion of Property vested in a few Individuals is dangerous to the Rights of and destructive of the Common Happiness of Mankind" and that endorsed governmental attempts to "discourage the Possession of such Property." When the war with Britain spurred severe inflation after 1777, some of the city's laboring poor blamed greedy and unpatriotic merchants for the rising cost of living and threatened to take matters into their own hands. In the process, they asserted a basic human right to survive and the community's responsibility to protect itself and its members against the greedy actions of a few.

These principles were soon made explicit. A mammoth public meeting in May 1779 formed a committee to bring about a reduction in food prices. That committee justified its charge by asserting that, in general,

> the social compact or state of civil society, by which men are united and incorporated, requires that every right or power claimed or exercised by any man or set of men should be in subordination to the common good, and that whatever is incompatible therewith must, by some rule or regulation, be brought into subjection thereto.

Property, the committee added, was the fruit of "the collected efforts of the community," the populace. In return for obtaining the "advantage of their service," the merchant "owes them his [ser-vices] in return, at a price proportioned to what he gave." In a meeting of their own, leading Philadelphia merchants flatly re-jected all such reasoning, repeating that the laws of free exchange "have their foundation in the laws of nature, and no artifice or force of man can prevent, elude, or avoid their effects."

The attempt to regulate food prices in revolutionary Philadel-phia failed, but the impulse behind it survived and reasserted it-self in New York City more than half a century later. In 1837, a financial panic that robbed thousands of work and income coin-cided with sharp increases in the price of some basic necessities. In the sixteen months after August 1835, the price of flour ap-proximately doubled. A call addressed "to all friends of humanity, determined to resist Monopolists and Extortionists" brought thou-sands of New Yorkers to a public meeting in February 1837. "Bread, Meat, Rent, Fuel—Their Prices Must Come Down," that call insisted. "The Voice of the People Shall be Heard, and Will Prevail." After listening to a number of speakers, hundreds of housewives and workers, skilled and unskilled alike, left the larger meeting, marched upon and broke into some merchants' warehouses. They then confiscated or destroyed hundreds of bar-rels of flour and fought off a combined force of police and state militia. Whig leader Philip Hone denounced "the unlicensed fury of a mob"; rioters found their license in an unwritten popular right to obtain food at reasonable prices.

The polarization of wealth and the attendant growth of agrarian tenancy and wage labor (described in Chapter 2) bred consider-able strife. Craft workers put down their tools in Philadelphia and New York as early as the 1780s and 1790s. Over the decades, such strikes became steadily more numerous and common (the 1830s and 1850s were especially turbulent) and gave rise to increasingly durable trade union organizations. These initially embraced in-dividuals with the same skills in a single workshop. Later they began to unite workers employed in various establishments. By the Civil War, a handful of trades had created the nuclei of national unions. Simultaneously, federations of unions began to cohere, first on a citywide and then on an intercity basis as well.

These practical struggles over pay rates, working conditions, and the like fostered equally heated ideological disputes over basic matters of economic right and justice.

For most free-market enthusiasts, an expanding market in human labor power posed no insurmountable problems, whether theoretical or ethical. Wage labor had nothing in common with exploitation. Unlike the slave or serf, the legally free worker labored voluntarily for an employer of his or her choosing in exchange for a compensation agreed upon in advance and in an atmosphere free of physical coercion. A world of difference, similarly, distinguished selling other human beings outright and selling discrete units of one's own productive energies. The latter transaction was the logical extension of legitimate commercial principles and must be undertaken free of outside interference.

As wage labor grew in economic importance, its defenders gained in self-confidence. The New York Society of Master Leather Curriers explained in 1836 that "labour, like every other commodity, will seek its own level, and its true value, in an open and unfettered market." "The true regulator of prices, whether of labor, goods, real estate, or any thing else, is demand," agreed the New York *Journal of Commerce*. Philadelphia merchant and journalist Condy Raguet condemned all attempts to regulate the price or length of a working day by collective or government action as contrary to "the great principle of nature, called the law of competition." "Wages," wrote Professor Francis Lieber in 1841, "are no more an invention than property itself. They are the natural and necessary effect of the state of things—of the relation of man to the things around him."

This form of society was not only natural but beneficial to all involved in it. "The interests of the capitalist and the laborer," wrote Henry C. Carey in 1837, "are . . . in perfect harmony with each other, as each derives advantages from every measure that tends to facilitate the growth of capital." Blessed with personal freedom in a nation of civic freedom, labor scarcity, and land aplenty, Raguet asserted, workers who displayed "industry, sobriety and economy" would one day become property owners and employers themselves. Most of those who fared poorly, it was widely held, reaped only what they had sown in indolence, inertia, or indulgence. "Poverty in this country," Philadelphia merchant Thomas P. Cope wrote in his diary, "that is extreme poverty, is generally occasioned by intemperance and idle habits."

Not everyone was as sanguine. The labor movement and its well-wishers observed the expansion of wage labor with a jaundiced eye. Plebeian radical democrats sought to make the free market serve a cohesive community of economically independent citizens. Growing extremes of wealth and poverty and a growing pool of propertyless producers were unacceptable. In Boston, a committee of the Mechanics' and Laborers' Association protested in 1845 that "monopoly has laid its ruthless hands upon labor itself, and forced the sale of the muscles and skill of the toiling many, and under the specious name of 'wages' is robbing them of the fruits of their industry." Was nothing above the power of the marketplace? Must everything, then, go up for sale? "Is the work of creation to be let out on hire?" asked the New York City machinist Thomas Skidmore in 1829. "And are the great mass of mankind to be hirelings to those who undertake to set up a claim . . . that the world was made for them?" If so, then "why not sell the winds of heaven, that man might not breathe without a price? Why not sell the light of the sun, that a man should not see without making another rich?"

Critics of the new order often based their arguments on a premise of classical political economy that Adam Smith endorsed— the belief that all wealth was the product of human labor. From this premise, however, they drew different conclusions. In their eyes, the enrichment of those who employed rather than performed manual labor was unjust and illegitimate. At its founding in 1827, thus, Philadelphia's Mechanics' Union of Trade Associations asserted that "all who toil have a natural and inalienable right to reap the fruits of their own industry; and that they who . . . labour (the only source) are the authors of every comfort, convenience, and luxury." "In justice," they were "entitled to an equal participation, not only in the meanest and the coarsest, but likewise the richest and the choicest of them all." Instead, they watched helplessly as the wealth they produced was "emptied into and absorbed by the coffers of the unproductive . . . In return for which, exclusive of a bare subsistence (which likewise is the product of their own industry), they receive—not a thing!"

This arrangement was not merely unjust but antithetical to American ideals of liberty and self-government. In 1827, founders of Philadelphia's labor federation criticized economic developments from the standpoint of "freemen and republicans." Others struck the same chord. In August 1834, delegates representing upward of 25,000 workers in the Northeast founded the National Trades Union (NTU), declaring that "the accumulation of the wealth of society in the hands of a few individuals . . . is subversive of the rights of man." It was also, said New York City's labor federation the same year, "hostile to the best interests of the community at large, as well as to the spirit and genius of our government," for "as the line of *distinction* between employer and employed is widened, the condition of the latter inevitably verges toward a state of vassalage while that of the former as certainly [is] approximated towards supremacy." Universal respect for republican norms and values was thereby subverted. The people must demand that "all social institutions" prove their "utility" and compatibility "with the principle of moral justice."

Those dedicated to improving the condition of free labor pursued a variety of practical strategies. Most sought legitimacy in appeals to customary standards, religious precepts, and republican liberties. This was true, for example, of the antebellum struggle for shorter working hours. In 1828–29, New York journeymen rejected an eleven-hour working day, holding that "those who undertake to exact an excessive number of hours of toil for a day's work are aggressors upon the rights of their fellow citizens." A few weeks later, journeymen bakers in the same city refused to work on Sundays any longer. That refusal, they contended, was "in accordance with the customs of man [and] sanctioned by the laws of God." Wage earners repeatedly justified a shortening of the working day in the name of their rights and duties as citizens of a democratic republic. "We have rights, and we have duties to perform as American Citizens and members of society," declared a circular printed in Boston in 1835, "duties to God, our country, and ourselves . . . which forbid us to dispose of more than Ten Hours for a day's work."

Some more visionary reformers sought explicitly to transform the nature of property holding. One such proposal came in 1829 from New York machinist Thomas Skidmore. He urged "the friends of equal rights" to gain control of government and then redistribute property on a more equitable basis. "As long as property is unequal," he argued in 1829, "then those who possess it *will* live on the labor of others." Upon each individual's death, Skidmore continued, his or her property should revert to the community for redistribution among the rising generation. The New England iconoclast Orestes Brownson revived the essence of this proposal about a decade later.

More popular, however, were attempts to achieve economic equality without laying hands on the property of anyone—by founding entirely new and voluntary communities whose participants lived according to egalitarian principles. A religious movement called the Shakers founded the largest of these communities; by the 1830s, it claimed more than 6,000 members. Cooperative communities like Hopedale and Brook Farm drew inspiration from the Protestant revivals of the period. Industrialist Robert Owen applied ideas about social reform developed in his native England to cooperative colonies such as New Harmony, Indiana, in the 1820s. A similar movement, called Associationism, based itself on the vision of Frenchman Charles Fourier and gained a following during the 1840s and 1850s. Altogether, the decades between the Revolution and the Civil War witnessed the establishment of more than a hundred such experimental communities in the free states.

More modestly conceived producer and consumer cooperatives also grew in number. Owned by their own employees and subscribers, these attempted to enforce mutualist principles *within* existing society, rather than alongside it. A committee of the National Trades Union recommended in the mid-1830s the establishment of such cooperative enterprises to "enable the mechanic to have the sole and absolute control over the disposal of his labor." A committee constituted by Boston's Mechanics' and Laborers' Association asserted in 1845:

> The direction and profits of industry must be kept in the hands of the producers. Laborers must own their own shops and factories; work their own stock, sell their own merchandise, and enjoy the fruits of their own toil. Our Lowells must be owned by the artisans who build them, and the operatives who run the machinery and do all the work. And the dividend, instead of being given to the idle parasites of a distant city, should be shared among those who perform the labor. Our Lynns must give the fortunes made by the dealer and employer, to those who use the awl and work the material.

During the 1840s and 1850s, such establishments appeared in virtually every major town and city of the North and West.

In the meantime, the organized labor movement and its supporters called upon the government to take certain specific initiatives on behalf of wage earners. Prominent among these—in the 1830s and 1840s—were laws reducing the length of the working day. Mass unemployment produced calls for other types of government action. Groups of unemployed northern workers demanded municipal relief or public employment during the panic of 1854–55 and even more widely during the crisis two years later. It was "the duty of the government," resolved a meeting organized in New York in 1855, to "secure to us our right to labor."

Particularly persistent, from the 1820s through the Civil War, in periods of prosperity and crisis alike, was the call to distribute uncultivated government land among would-be homesteaders. The federal government owned vast quantities of land in the West. Some of it went to war veterans. More went in the form of subsidy to private railroad companies. Much of the remainder was sold in large tracts on the open market, a policy that suited well-heeled speculators eager to purchase and resell it in smaller parcels but at higher unit prices. Land reformers protested these government policies and the landlordism and landlessness they reinforced. "If these public lands were left open to actual settlers" rather than to speculators, asserted the National Trades Union during the 1830s, then surplus workers would be "drained off" from the cities and funneled into agriculture, where they would add to the rural "demand for the produce of mechanical labor."

In 1844, individuals from diverse national, social, and political backgrounds came together to form the National Reform Association. The new body based its platform on now familiar interpretations of economic and political rights and their proper interrelation. "If any man has a right on the earth," the National Reformers contended, "he has a right to land enough to raise a habitation on. If he has *a right to live*, he has a right to land enough for his subsistence. Deprive anyone of these rights, and you place him at the mercy of those who possess them."

To guarantee an adequate supply of land for all and to prevent the future re-creation of "land monopoly," National Reformers put forward a three-point program. First, public land must be made available free of charge, and then only to those prepared actually to settle on it. Second, none must be allowed to accumulate more land than was necessary for the subsistence of their family. Third, no one must be evicted from their land on account of debt. The first of these demands received by far the most broad-based and fervent support, particularly in the crowded cities of the East. It was not long before residents of the new West began to raise the land-reform banner too.

The idea of land reform had broad appeal and attracted individuals previously active in other democratic causes. Among them were Chartists exiled from England, Scotland, and Ireland; veterans of the Dorr War; native- and foreign-born labor journalists and leaders of various labor associations in the United States; and advocates and residents of cooperative communities. Each industrial crisis seemed to impart new strength to the land-reform cause. During the hard times of 1854–55, a crowd of 5,000 New Yorkers—native, Irish-, and German-born alike—demanded that "lands belonging to the state be set apart and distributed, free of charge," in equalized plots to all in need; that the federal government pass "a homestead bill that will secure the actual settler the unrestricted use of 160 acres of land"; and that Congress pay the costs of transportation, farm equipment, and subsistence for all those wishing to establish such homesteads in the West.

All of these reform projects aroused considerable controversy. The organization of trade unions and strikes was called a form of unjustifiable collective coercion. The New York *Journal of Commerce* in the 1830s declared that "all combinations to compel others to give a higher price or take a lower one, are not only inexpedient, but at war with the order of things which the Creator has established for the general good, and therefore wicked." Some twenty years later, Cincinnati furniture manufacturers rebuffed the demands of the cabinetmakers' union with assurances that "no wrong, much less suffering, exists except when incapability or intemperance is the cause" and that only "the law of Supply and Demand will regulate the scale of [labor] prices, and fix it on an equitable basis."

Land-reform proposals for many years received similarly cold receptions. For one thing, selling public land instead of giving it away to homesteaders yielded government revenues with which Whigs like Henry Clay wished to finance roads, canals, railroads, and other improvements in the infrastructure. Demanding payment for that land, moreover, also avoided the outcome explicitly sought by trade unions but dreaded by many eastern employers—reducing the supply of wage labor in eastern cities. Give the land away, warned the New York *Herald* as late as 1852, and "Lowell and other manufacturing towns will be essentially injured by the delusion drawning off their operatives and increasing the price of labor."

Other reform proposals provoked other objections. Rev. Francis Wayland (a leading evangelical reformer and president of Brown University, a Baptist institution) opposed both public assistance and private charity for the able-bodied poor on the grounds that all such aid lessened the incentive to work. Better to leave such people to their own resources alone. In that way, "labor will be applied to capital in proportion as every man suffers the inconvenience of idleness." Calls for government employment of the jobless triggered expressions of outrage. The New York *Herald*, once again, was shocked in January 1855 to discover that "the crowds who assemble in the Park and parade [up] Broadway . . . demand present relief, not as a favor or as charity, but as a right." That demand was "at war with reason, sound policy, and the law . . . [and] based on the grand fallacy that it is the business of the State to care for them, to give them work when they want it, and generally to relieve them of the responsibility of looking after themselves."

To be sure, northern politicians differed among themselves over important aspects of government economic policy. Such differences, indeed, were at the heart of party cleavages and affinities from the 1830s through the early 1850s. Northern leaders of the Whig party urged government to play a relatively interventionist role—enacting tariff protection for manufacturing, chartering a national bank, and providing generous support for internal improvements. This platform appealed most strongly to northern voters best served by economic growth and development. Democrats, in contrast, tended to oppose most of these measures. That stance attracted many northern voters uneasy about the nature or pace of economic change and fearful that a powerful national government would accelerate the concentration of economic power ("monopoly").

Despite these differences, most Whigs and Democrats agreed that government must never interpose itself between employer and employee, must never assume that the latter required or deserved protection against the former. Condy Raguet denounced "the erroneous notion that capital gets more than its just share." "If this doctrine is permitted to gain strength," he believed, ". . . incalculable mischief will be done to the country." "Every disturbance of property," Francis Lieber warned, "is a proportional blow to industry," resulting in "no farther increase of capital . . . , no increase of property, no advance in civilization" "Let *all* men, therefore, rejoice whenever they see that one of their fellow creatures has succeeded in honestly accumulating a substantial fortune."

Debates over the nature and merits of the free-labor system took place simultaneously with a deepening national dispute about chattel slavery. The way in which Americans framed that dispute changed significantly over time.

In the early nineteenth century, much of the white South discussed its peculiar institution in the terms favored by Thomas Jefferson. Unfree labor was a dangerous social "evil," troubling to Enlightenment-trained consciences and menacing to society's security. William Broadnax expressed this outlook in 1831 when he asked, "Is there one man in Virginia who does not lament that there was ever a slave in the State? . . . Does any man doubt that Slavery is an evil?" Unfortunately, he and others continued, the actions of earlier generations had left slavery central to the South's economy and necessary to its prosperity. It could not, therefore, be easily or immediately dislodged now. Still, its decline—at some unspecified point in the future—was surely inevitable. A majority of Virginia's state legislature thus insisted in 1832 that they "look forward" to "final abolition of slavery" and promised to "go on, step by step, to that great end."

Looking back on those years in the late 1850s, James Henry Hammond of South Carolina recalled that the white South then "believed slavery to be an evil" and "shrank from the discussion of it . . . and in fear and trembling she awaited a doom that she deemed inevitable." That state of affairs changed, however, when "a few bold spirits took the question up" and "compelled the South to investigate it anew and thoroughly, and what is the result? Why, it would be difficult to find a Southern man who feels the system to be the slightest burden on his conscience." If Hammond exaggerated the completeness of this ideological transformation, he certainly grasped its basic nature and trajectory.

A number of developments conspired to reorient the white South's view of slavery between Jefferson's day and Hammond's.

Among the most important was the powerful economic stimulus given to plantation agriculture beginning around the turn of the nineteenth century by the dramatic expansion of the English cotton-textile industry and the invention of the cotton gin. At least equally significant, however, were a range of ideological and practical challenges to bondage. Some of these originated among the slaves themselves. Others arose within the free white population, chiefly those of the free states but also in the South. And some threats to slavery's stability came from outside the country altogether.

Strengthening the ideological defense of slavery seemed increasingly urgent as the free-labor system developed and grew in assertiveness. In the late eighteenth century, slavery still flourished in all of Europe's principal overseas colonies and in most states of the new North American union. In 1790, thus, more than 40,000 slaves still lived in the states of the North. In political power, northern and southern states enjoyed rough parity; the population of the two regions were about equal, as was their representation in Congress.

That situation, however, soon began to change. By 1820, even with the assistance of the Constitution's three-fifths clause, the South found itself with just 42 percent of the votes in the U.S. House of Representatives; only in the Senate did it still hold its own. This was the more ominous because northern interests and values were diverging from those of the South even as its population and political representation in Washington grew. By 1805, every northern state had begun the process of dismantling slavery within its own borders. In the meantime, as noted in Chapter 1, the revitalization of slavery via its migration into the Deep South went hand in hand with its visible decay in the Chesapeake and elsewhere in the upper South.

The political import of these changes became evident in 1819. The House of Representatives that year barely rejected an attempt to expel slavery from the Arkansas Territory (composed of those still unorganized lands south of Missouri acquired in the 1803

Louisiana Purchase—i.e., the area later organized into the states of Arkansas and Oklahoma). In that same year, the Missouri Territory—straddling the same latitudes as parts of the free Midwest but containing some 10,000 slaves—applied for statehood.

What followed confirmed planter apprehensions about the power and inclination of the North. Representative James Tallmadge, Jr., of New York, proposed two conditions for Missouri's statehood. One would bar any additional slaves from entering Missouri. The other would emancipate all slave children born in Missouri following statehood once those children reached the age of twenty-five. "The right to hold human beings in perpetual and hopeless slavery," declared one Massachusetts congressman, "is only found in the codes of barbarians and despots." The moral evil of slavery, asserted Tallmadge and his allies, should not be permitted to expand beyond its existing confines. Tallmadge modeled his proposal for Missouri on the formula for gradual emancipation that he had helped enact in his home state just two years earlier.

Behind this northern initiative lay more than ethical considerations. To permit slavery's limitless expansion, explained Tallmadge's fellow New Yorker Rufus King, would deny to the North all "political power or influence in the Union. The slave region will parcel out the great offices, will determine all questions [and] . . . remain our Masters." (In fact, Virginians occupied the White House for thirty-two of the first thirty-six years of the republic's existence.)

Tallmadge's proposal was all the more worrisome for coming not from a diehard Federalist (like Rufus King) but from a member of Thomas Jefferson's own Democratic-Republican party. More alarming still was the support his initiative received. Mass meetings in New York, Boston, Philadelphia, Trenton, New Jersey, and Newport, Rhode Island, inveighed against Missouri's admission as a slave state. The legislatures of New Hampshire, Vermont, Massachusetts, New York, New Jersey, Pennsylvania, Ohio, and Indiana passed similar resolutions. And although 14 northern members of the House of Representatives voted against

Tallmadge's measure, fully 80 voted in its favor. Even more alarmingly, two votes from upper South representatives gave Tallmadge a majority in the House. The Senate, where the slave owners were stronger, voted (22 to 16) to impose no restrictions on slavery in Missouri.

The resulting stalemate was broken by a compromise narrowly passed in 1820 over the protests of a large northern minority. Under its terms, Missouri would obtain statehood without Congress imposing any restrictions upon slavery therein. No further slave states, however, would ever after be admitted from the old Louisiana Purchase north of Missouri's southern border—36 degrees 30 minutes latitude. (Maine, whose application for statehood had in the interim been blocked by southern senators, would now also enter the Union.)

Northern hostility to slave society expressed during the Missouri crisis reverberated throughout the South. Responding to it—and to the Vesey revolt of 1822 and the impending (1833) end of slavery in the British West Indies—South Carolina political leaders began blazing an ideological trail that led in a new direction. It was time, they said, to cease replying to attacks upon the southern way of life with an "apologetical whine" that betrayed "the false compunctions of an uninformed conscience." To bolster the self-confidence of slavery's partisans, wrote influential pro-Calhoun journalist Duff Green, "we must satisfy the consciences, we must allay the fears of our people. We must satisfy them that slavery is of itself right—that it is not a sin against God—that it is not an evil moral or political force. . . . In this way, and this way only, can we prepare our people to defend their own institutions." Accordingly, such men set about elaborating a doctrine that justified the indefinite servitude and enforced labor of some on behalf of the prosperity and liberty of others and in the fundamental interests of all.

An early attempt to enunciate such a view came from South Carolina governor Stephen D. Miller, whose message to the state legislature in 1829 argued that slavery was "not a national evil; on the contrary, it is a national benefit," and insisted that "upon this subject it does not become us to speak in a whisper, betray fear, or feign philanthropy." During the next decade, a few Virginians experimented with kindred ideas. Thomas Roderick Dew lauded the system of bound labor as being in all important respects superior to alternative forms of society. Unlike northern wage earners, Dew wrote, slaves were cared for year-round, and "a merrier being does not exist on the face of the globe." Indeed, he went on, "at this very moment, in every densely populated country, hundreds would be willing to sell themselves" into bondage "if the laws would permit." In any case, someone had to do society's hard, menial, and poorly compensated work; prudence dictated that those who did so be denied the right to protest and rebel. The social conflicts then erupting in free-labor societies (in the North as in Europe) and the spread of plebeian radicalism in those places already suggested the perils of granting legal freedom to those whose labors satisfied society's material needs. The only way to "ward off the evil of this agrarian spirit" was to deprive the drones of civil rights.

But it was in South Carolina, once again, that planters earliest and most energetically rallied around such aggressive proslavery doctrines—South Carolina, with its unusually high concentration of slaves and its fabulously wealthy aristocracy of absentee masters along the swampy rice-growing coast. In a famous speech in February 1837, John C. Calhoun termed slavery "a good—a positive good," and "the existing relations between the two races . . . indispensable to the peace and happiness of both." "There never has yet existed a wealthy and civilized society," he said, "in which one portion of the community did not, in point of fact, live on the labor of the other." Nor, he added, would it be "difficult to trace the various devices by which the wealth of all civilized communities has been so unequally divided, and to show by what means so small a share has been allotted to those by whose labor it was produced, and so large a share given to the non-producing classes." If in "ancient times" these means involved "brute force and gross superstition," equivalent results were achieved in "modern" times by "subtle and artificial contrivances."

Given this fact, Calhoun continued, "I fearlessly assert that the existing relation between the two races in the South . . . forms the most solid and durable foundation upon which to rear free and stable political institutions." This, said Calhoun (here echoing Dew), was because only slavery completely deprived the direct producers of the ability to cause trouble. "There is and has always been, in an advanced stage of wealth and civilization," the Carolinian declared, "a conflict between labor and capital," but "the condition of society in the South exempts us from the disorders and dangers resulting from this conflict." This fact demonstrated, he asserted, "how vastly more favorable our condition of society is to that of other sections for free and stable institutions."

During the final antebellum decade, George Fitzhugh of eastern Virginia fashioned what was probably the most philosophically complete and seamless version of this proslavery apologia. Attempts to base societies and governments on supreme and sacrosanct individual rights, wrote Fitzhugh, were absurd. All forms of society, he argued, were based on principles of *group* organization. And since society's members always display varying degrees of intellectual and physical capabilities, their responsibilities and rights must vary as well. "The doctrine of Human Equality," he wrote in 1856, "is practically impossible, and directly conflicts with all government, all separate property, and all social existence." The mutual dependence of individuals with varying merits and abilities grounded society not in abstractions about "individual liberty" but in relations of strict domination and subordination. Successful societies were those whose members acknowledged and accepted their places within that hierarchy, honored their specific and distinct obligations to one another, and thereby made possible a regime of prosperity, security, and order.

Fitzhugh caustically spelled out the implications of this philosophy:

> We conclude that about nineteen out of every twenty individuals have "a natural and inalienable right" to be taken care of and protected, to have guardians, trustees, husbands, or masters; in other words, they have a natural and inalienable right to be slaves. The one in twenty are as clearly born or educated or some way fitted for command and liberty.

This conclusion Fitzhugh summarized even more pithily in the words: "Liberty for the few—Slavery, in every form, for the mass!"

The consistency of this aristocratic worldview might impress a logician. But musing about enslaving all who toiled with their hands generated little popular enthusiasm among the great mass of hardworking, nonslaveholding southern whites. That was a signal problem at a time when challenges to slavery from both within and without the South made such support crucial. And a defense of slavery that appealed to—rather than antagonized—southern whites of small means was all the more vital because such people were at that very moment obtaining unprecedented political rights.

In the South as in the North, many state constitutions drafted by planters and their representatives in the revolutionary era had effectively excluded from political life most white male Southerners of little or no property. In subsequent decades, those plebeians demanded the same kind of political reforms then taking place in the North—equal rights to vote and hold office and a more equal system of legislative apportionment. In 1829, thus, landless (and therefore disenfranchised) citizens of Richmond, Virginia, submitted a petition that asserted that "virtue [and] intelligence are not among the products of the soil. Attachment to property, often a sordid sentiment, is not to be confounded with the sacred flame of patriotism."

Political change occurred unevenly. In general, states that entered the Union following the Revolution contained less entrenched aristocratic rulers and imposed relatively fewer restrictions on the political rights of propertyless whites. Some older southern states moved in the same liberalizing direction without too much friction. Elsewhere, a mass popular movement had to raise the level of confrontation before the existing political elite relented. Only in 1845 did Louisiana withdraw its stipulation that only taxpayers could vote. Virginia's 1776 constitution left nearly half its adult white male taxpayers disenfranchised through the 1820s. The reforms enacted there in 1829–30 still left one-third of those taxpayers without the vote. Universal white male suffrage came to the Old Dominion only in 1851. Even then, aristocratic eastern Virginia—with a minority of the population—retained firm control of the malapportioned state senate. Tennessee, Georgia, and North Carolina dropped substantial property qualifications on the right to hold office only in 1835; Louisiana hesitated an additional decade. South Carolina enacted universal white manhood suffrage in 1810 but required substantial property ownership as a condition of holding office right down through 1861. How did this requirement affect the distribution of power? "The people," approved James Henry Hammond in 1845, "have none beyond electing members of the legislature." That arrangement was quite satisfactory to Calhoun supporter George McDuffie, who believed that "an unmixed democracy, without . . . a check to secure property against numbers, will prove I fear to be a disastrous experiment."

Some planters who nursed such qualms about the political power of propertyless whites gravitated toward the Whig party, whose conservative wing maintained a distinctly aristocratic air. But southern Whigs also appealed to urban workers, professionals, and merchants as well as to slave owners interested in their region's commercial and industrial development. Southern Democrats, meanwhile, presented themselves as the most consistent opponents of all the economically monopolizing and politically centralizing tendencies that their constituents identified with the North generally and with northern Whigs in particular. Just as important, southern Democrats claimed to be the most consistent upholders of slavery and the most enthusiastic advocates of equal rights for all men with white skins.

It was the Democrats who here felt the winds of history in their sails. The growing electoral power of the mass of white male citizens was a fact, one that increasingly shaped political life, in the South as in the North. (Representative James Graham of North Carolina characteristically noted in 1840 that "I have always accomodated [sic] my habits and Dress to the People when electioneering . . . I have always dressed chiefly in Home spun when among the people.")

In this political setting, the more politically astute and effective defense of chattel slavery rested heavily upon arguments from racial inequality. Genetic and cultural facts, it held, suited all Africans but no whites for economic and legal subordination. Calhoun thus professed not to champion "slavery in the abstract, but . . . slavery as existing where two races of men, of different colors and a thousand other particulars, were placed in immediate juxtaposition."

Of course, Calhoun's formulation neatly upended both historical chronology and causation, implying (as the Jeffersonians were wont to do) that biracial "juxtaposition" preceded and necessitated the decision to enslave. But lest anyone assume that the Carolinian also shared Jefferson's longing to undo both "juxtaposition" and slavery—say, by colonization—Calhoun quickly added that since "a mysterious Providence had brought the black and the white people together from different parts of the globe . . . no human power could now separate them." The more so because the providential enslavement of blacks now underpinned the status and ensured the prosperity and liberties of the "white race" as a whole. "Domestic slavery," George McDuffie assured the South Carolina legislators in 1835, "instead of being a political evil, is the cornerstone of our republican edifice." In 1850, Arkansas senator Solon Borland lauded slavery for "underlying as a sort of substratum," and being "inseparably connected with, the structure of all our institutions." Its future, he explained, thus "affects the personal interest of every white man."

It was in this this pointedly race-conscious form that the "positive good" defense of slavery finally triumphed in the white South. Southern politicians, editors, academics, physicians, and clergymen defended and "documented" race-based proslavery ideology. By 1861, even Fitzhugh ("Slavery, in every form, for the mass!") had come to embrace the "new and fruitful idea" that "the negro is physically, morally, and intellectually a different being (by necessity) from the white man, and must ever remain so."

Racism, of course, was by no means peculiar to the South; northern society was riddled with it. The South put racial doctrine to a special use—to shore up a form of economy and society that most Northerners found increasingly repugnant and threatening. As we have seen, however, a common antipathy to slavery did not imply universal satisfaction with the direction in which northern society was developing. Deepening differences about the legitimacy and justice of the free-labor system undermined northern unity in the face of the planter challenge.

— 6 —

To *"Fight Against the Serpent"*: Antislavery and Its Early Progress

It is in the nature of slavery that its victims may not openly reject the demands made upon them or the ideological claims of their masters. Survival in bondage often depended upon hiding real feelings behind indirection and deception. "Persons live and die in the midst of Negroes," complained evangelical leader Charles Colcock Jones in 1842, "and know comparatively little of their real character. They are one thing before the whites, and another before their own color. Deception towards the former is characteristic of them." "The white folks made us lie," a former slave later explained. "We had to lie to live."

Day-to-day resistance to the slave regime thus took covert form. Slaves feigned stupidity, forcing masters or overseers repeatedly to explain the simplest task, thereby creating a precious pause for the laborer. With deliberate clumsiness, slaves destroyed tools and injured livestock, once again slowing the pace of work and reducing the expectations of their owners. A feigned pregnancy might for a time spare a slave woman some of the heavier field chores. Theft supplemented a meager diet and personal possessions. "So deceitful is the Negro," agreed one Georgia planter, "that as far as my own experience extends I could never in a single instant decipher his character. . . . We planters could never get at the truth."

The religious life of the slave population (as discussed in Chapter 4) revealed, at least to those able and willing to see, more about the slaves' real attitudes toward bondage. And slave revolts, though ultimately doomed, necessarily thrust aside the veil of secrecy and pretense, exposing explosive sentiments and beliefs. Particularly striking is the way in which African-Americans appropriated both the democratic-republican and evangelical Christian doctrines of the nation that held them captive and reshaped those materials into weapons of liberation. Denying the legitimacy of the slave regime, they claimed the right to share in civic freedom and equality, and they asserted divine support for that claim. Slave rebellions also asserted the right to achieve liberation through violence. For this claim too, rebels found ample justification in both modern and biblical history. The record of slave revolts also reveals some of the conditions that encouraged overt action. Slave rebels displayed acute sensitivity to developments that distracted, demoralized, or divided the captor nation. Such sought-for developments ranged from expressions of antislavery sentiments (by free blacks or whites, North or South, domestic or foreign) through involvement in international war.

As already noted, Gabriel Prosser's conspiracy of 1800 evidently drew confidence from the American Revolution and its rhetoric. It also bristled with evidence of religion's influence. Recruitment and planning had taken place during praise meetings. Martin Prosser, Gabriel's brother, was a preacher and invoked biblical precedent to reassure others that God would smile upon their plans. "Their cause was similar to the Israelites'," Martin reportedly declared, and accordingly promised that "five of you shall conquer an hundred & a hundred thousand of our enemies."

The next major attempt came in 1822 in Charleston, South Carolina, at the initiative of a free black carpenter named Denmark Vesey. Like most of his supporters, Vesey attended the city's African Methodist Church, which was affiliated to the Philadelphia-based African Methodist Society, and there preached the legitimacy of insurrection and vengeance. "His general conversation was about religion," according to one deposition, "which Vesey would apply to slavery, as for instance, he would speak of the creation of the world, in which he would say all men had equal rights, blacks as well as whites." Leaders of this revolt evidently sent letters (via free black seamen encountered in Charleston) to Haitian president Jean Pierre Boyer seeking aid in their insurrectionary plans. Had the insurrection itself proved successful, Vesey and his lieutenants evidently planned to sail for Haiti.

Nine years later, in late August 1831, the slave Nat Turner led a rising that killed approximately sixty white residents of Southampton, Virginia, before being suppressed. Turner was a religious leader, a self-made Baptist preacher who learned of his revolutionary mission through revelations. In the first, "white spirits and black spirits engaged in battle, and the sun was darkened, and thunder rolled in the Heavens, and blood flowed in streams." In the second, the Holy Ghost bade Turner to "fight against the Serpent, for the time was approaching when the first should be the last and the last should be the first."

Perhaps the fullest, clearest, and most direct exposition of southern black antislavery principles came from David Walker. Born free in 1785 in North Carolina, Walker lived there for forty years before resettling in Boston in 1825. In 1829, Walker published and distributed his *Appeal to the Colored Citizens of the World*. Within a year it had gone through three editions.

The pamphlet's inflammatory nature was clear in its very form; Walker's "appeal" was directed not only—and not primarily—to masters but "to my much afflicted and suffering brethren." The appeal itself endorsed and justified open revolt and provided specific advice about when and how to undertake it. "Never make an attempt to gain our freedom or natural right, from under cruel oppressors and murderers, until you see your way clear," Walker counseled. But "if you commence, make sure work—do not trifle, for they will not trifle with you—they want us for their slaves and think nothing of murdering us in order to subject us to that wretched condition—therefore, if there is an attempt made by us, kill or be killed." That it could be done had been proved in

Haiti, that "glory of the blacks and the terror of tyrants." (Despite all the Haitians' subsequent ordeals, "they are men who would be cut off to a man before they would yield to the combined forces of the whole world." Walker therefore encouraged those who escaped from American masters to seek sanctuary in Haiti, which "is bound to protect and comfort us.")

A violent end for American slavery, however, was ordained only if whites refused to "repent," to liberate their chattels, and to acknowledge the African's right to enjoy the liberties espoused in the Declaration of Independence. "Tell us no more about colonization," Walker wrote, but simply "treat us like men, and there is no danger[,] but we will all live in peace and happiness together. For we are not like you, hard hearted, unmerciful, and unforgiving. What a happy country this will be, if the whites will listen."

Eventually, some did listen, but the militant spirit that infused Walker's pamphlet was alien to the Enlightenment-inspired northern merchants and professionals who headed the white anti-slavery movement of the first post-revolutionary years. John Jay, Alexander Hamilton, and Benjamin Franklin led the Pennsylvania Society for the Abolition of Slavery (founded in 1784) and the New York Manumission Society (founded the following year). Those bodies, in turn, sponsored the creation in 1794 of the American Convention for Promoting the Abolition of Slavery and Improving the Condition of the African Race, which launched an educational campaign in support of gradual emancipation throughout the United States.

The perspectives of these organizations were grounded in a rather mechanistic optimism—a general assumption that slavery was an anachronism destined for extinction by the inexorable advance of economic development, spiritual cultivation, intellectual illumination, and moral suasion. As New York financier and philanthropist Thomas J. Eddy phrased it, "The light with which Providence has been pleased to enlighten the minds of men, as it regards moral or religious truths, is gradual—as was the commencement of the abolition of slavery" in the North.

Much seemed to justify this optimistic, gradualist outlook. The experience of the northeastern states and the Northwest Territory (in which the Continental Congress outlawed slavery in 1787) encouraged confidence that slavery was well on its way to extinction. So did Congress's ban on the Atlantic slave trade in 1808 and the apparently declining fortunes of Britain's slave-based West Indian sugar plantations. Exceptions to this trend—such as Congress's refusal (in 1798) to ban slavery in the Mississippi Territory or (in 1804) in the Louisiana Purchase—could still appear mere anomalies. Gradualism also commended itself to members and friends of the northern elite because of the presumed "unreadiness" of the slaves for immediate freedom. Paternalist traditions and assumptions left them skeptical of the ability of slaves to assume the rights and responsibilities of freedom without an extended period of benevolent guidance and preparation. (The New York Manumission Society thus refused to exclude slaveholders from membership and even conferred its presidency upon the slave owner John Jay.)

This gradualist bias informed all the efforts of the American Convention for Promoting the Abolition of Slavery. In 1812, Rev. Samuel Stanhope Smith, president of New Jersey's Presbyterian College, had proposed an arrangement whereby slaves would be permitted to purchase their liberty by hard work over a stipulated period of time. The American Convention promulgated a similar proposal in 1821. It provided that, during a period of "tutelage" prior to complete emancipation, former slaves would continue to work for their old masters, though now formally in exchange for wages, while being educated in the meaning and requirements of liberty. The same spirit dictated the Convention's advice to southern chattels. Until gradual emancipation became law, it wished to "impress upon [slaves] . . . the necessity of contentment with their situations," the better to win the sympathy of their masters. As for blacks already out of bondage, they should "cultivate feelings of piety and gratitude to your Heavenly Father for the many blessings you enjoy."

Before long, the Convention took a further step in a conservative direction. The American Colonization Society had been launched in 1817 to promote the transportation of emancipated slaves to its African colony, Liberia. Prominent upper South slave owners—including John Marshall, James Madison, James Monroe, and Henry Clay—applauded colonization. In 1820, Thomas Jefferson expressed himself eager to see a "general emancipation and *expatriation . . .* effected" and believed that "gradually, and with due sacrifices, I think it might be." In part to win the favor of such men, the American Convention reversed its previous stand and endorsed colonization too.

The assumptions and expectations animating the American Convention were slow to die. For decades, Northerners like Philadelphia's Thomas Cope continued to believe that "if slavery is ever to be extinguished in these United States, it must be by the cooperation of men who hold others in bondage," that "a commencement has been made . . . & if our fierce, rash, anti-slavery men will keep hands off, this germ will grow & ripen into wholesome fruit." After all, Cope opined, "more is gained by moderation, charity & persuasion than by acrimony, intemperate zeal and splenetic personal abuse."

But such arguments began to lose their potency during the 1820s. A patient, patrician gradualism had proved sufficient for extinguishing bondage in the North, where slavery had never been central to the general economy or to the prosperity of any influential, distinct section of the elite. It was otherwise in the South, as the Missouri dispute had suggested. And in that confrontation, the forces demanding not slavery's extirpation but its expansion had prevailed.

Hopes that the planter elite could be talked out of its human property were put to a practical test early in the 1830s; the Nat Turner revolt of 1831 precipitated an extended debate in the Virginia state assembly over bondage and its future. A number of the legislators—including those from districts where planters were fewest and small farmers, fishermen, and urban dwellers most numerous—expressed unhappiness with the slave-labor system. (One important source of that displeasure was the fact that slave property was counted in apportioning representation in the state legislature. Large eastern planters thereby retained control and exercised it to frustrate the developmental projects of farmers in the western counties.) Much of the debate revolved around a proposal from Thomas Jefferson Randolph (Thomas Jefferson's grandson) to make all slaves born after Independence Day 1840 property of the state once they reached maturity. Virginia would then hire them out in order to fund their "removal beyond the limits of the United States." Until such slaves came of age, their masters would retain all ownership rights, including the freedom to sell their chattels into the Deep South—beyond, that is, the reach of the state's emancipation law. And those slaves born prior to 1840 would remain slaves until they died.

When the proposal finally came to a vote, the representatives decided by a margin of 73–58 against the "expediency" of taking any legal action against slavery in Virginia. The affair had thus demonstrated two salient facts. First, that opposition to slavery and hopes for its demise still existed among a section of the Upper South's white population. But second, that most planters even of that region (unlike the old slave owners of the northern states) remained adamantly opposed to any practical steps toward emancipation. The second revelation further deflated hopes for voluntary, gradual abolition in the South.

This development combined with the maturing secular and religious values nourished by the North's free-labor system to inspire a more radical form of antislavery doctrine and movement, one that demanded the immediate end of slavery, rejected colonization, and sought full civil equality for free blacks.

In January 1831, the first edition of *The Liberator* appeared in Boston. Its editor, William Lloyd Garrison, a former Baptist temperance advocate, had been converted to emancipation two years earlier by the antislavery Quaker editor Benjamin Lundy. In 1832, Garrison and eleven other white men founded the New England Anti-Slavery Society in Boston. In New York City, meanwhile, the wealthy evangelical-minded merchant Arthur Tappan was working toward the establishment of a national abolition organization. At the end of 1833, sixty-two people (most of them white male Quakers and evangelical Protestants but also including Congregationalists, Unitarians, four white women, and three black men) from eleven free states gathered in Philadelphia to found the American Anti-Slavery Society (AAS). Garrison drafted its declaration of principles, which labeled slavery a sin "unequalled by any other on the face of the earth," which rejected colonization, and which demanded that everyone, regardless of race, be made "secure in his own right to his own body—to the products of his own labor—to the protections of the law—to the common advantages of society." These words perfectly summarized the essence of free-labor ideology.

The size of the free black representation at this conference severely understated the importance of that group to the rise of immediatist abolition. In fact, initiatives taken by various free blacks living in the North had preceded these events by a number of years. We have already noted the example of Benjamin Banneker and his correspondence with Thomas Jefferson. A year prior to Gabriel Prosser's rebellion, a group of free blacks living in Philadelphia petitioned Congress for "justice and equity to all classes," urging a national program of emancipation. "As we are men," they held, "we should be admitted to partake of the liberties and unalienable rights . . . held forth" in the Constitution.

Another portent was an 1813 speech that George Lawrence delivered in a New York City African Methodist Episcopal (AME) church. Celebration of the fifth anniversary of the ban on the Atlantic slave trade provided the occasion. As in most such messages, Lawrence devoted much of his time to thanksgiving, to optimistic hopes of "melting" the cold hearts of slave owners with "good works" and "examples," and to enjoining "Fathers, Brethren, and Friends" to "let malice and hatred be far from your doors." Evidently, however, there were limits to so much pacific patience and goodwill. "The iron hand of oppression must cease to tyrannize over injured innocence," Lawrence told his listeners, and "the time is fast approaching." By the end of his address, the speaker was calling upon the "father of the universe and disposer of events" to "crush that power that still holds thousands of our brethren in bondage."

Three years later, Rev. Richard Allen of Philadelphia became the first bishop of the new national AME denomination. It was in his Bethel Church that 3,000 black residents of Philadelphia gathered in 1817 to protest colonization plans on the grounds that they "will stay the cause of the entire abolition of slavery in the United States" and "must insure to the multitudes . . . misery, sufferings, and perpetual slavery." To colonize free blacks, Allen declared on another occasion, was the dream of masters who feared to let their human property "see free men of colour enjoying liberty." But "this land which we have watered with our *tears* and *our blood* is now our *mother country*," Allen declared, "and we are well satisfied to stay."

Ideas current in northern black society also expressed themselves through Walker's *Appeal*. It was in Boston, after all, that David Walker learned to read and write, joined the Methodist Church, made a living by selling used clothes, and gained prominence as an intellectual leader in the growing black community. He belonged to and spoke before the Massachusetts General Colored Association, which had been founded in 1826 to pursue abolition and community elevation. In 1827, John Russwurm and Rev. Samuel E. Cornish launched the first newspaper ever published by African-Americans, the New York *Freedom's Journal*, partly to combat colonization. "We wish to plead our own cause. Too long have others spoken for us," the paper declared. "Too long has the publick been deceived by misrepresentations, in things which concern us dearly." David Walker wrote for and distributed the *Journal* in Boston.

Walker's *Appeal* created a sensation in both the North and the South. It signaled a new stage in the development of antislavery generally and in the bearing and conduct of its free black partisans. Savannah's mayor called on his Boston counterpart to arrest Walker. Southern state governments moved immediately to prevent the *Appeal*'s circulation—though not, it seems, before free blacks in Virginia, Georgia, Louisiana, and perhaps elsewhere had obtained copies. William Lloyd Garrison, as a committed pacifist, disliked the *Appeal's* "general spirit" and regretted the appearance of this "most injudicious publication." He conceded, however, that it spoke "many valuable truths and seasonal warnings." Garrison had picked up his own hostility to colonization from free blacks like David Walker. Three years after its founding, Garrison noted, "of the whole number of subscribers to *The Liberator*, only about one-fourth are white. The paper, then, belongs emphatically to the people of color. It is their organ."

The founding of the American Anti-Slavery Society made possible the expansion of immediatist abolitionism. During its first three years of life, the new organization distributed more than a million pieces of antislavery literature, mostly by mail, some of it in the South. In mid-1835, the AAS reported the existence of about two hundred local antislavery organizations. Within a year that number surpassed five hundred; by 1837 it stood at a thousand. The total membership of these organizations had probably reached 200,000 by 1840.

For specific purposes, the abolitionists found they could enlist the support of significantly larger numbers of Americans. Antislavery petitions of various kinds had been submitted in modest numbers to Congress since the 1790s. In the 1830s, the AAS decided to transform this trickle into a flood. An unprecedented number of petitions—directed especially against the continuation of slavery in the District of Columbia—were now circulated through the free states. The campaign would have multiple benefits. It would provide a useful way to engage citizens in discussing the merits of slavery. It would force Congress to address the same subject "and turn it into a vast Anti Slavery Debating Society, with the whole country as an audience." It might even achieve its immediate goal. During the first year and a half of the campaign, according to the AAS, the number of petitions reaching Congress soared from a mere 23 to some 300,000—and to some 600,000 in 1837–38. AAS officer Henry B. Stanton calculated that in 1838 and 1839, the society obtained 2 million signatures on such petitions. Many of those who signed were female, and women were prominent in many abolition societies. Some were Quakers, others belonged to one or another evangelical Protestant denomination. Future leaders of the movement for women's rights (including Susan B. Anthony, Elizabeth Cady Stanton, Lucretia Mott, and Lydia Maria Child) obtained some of their first political experience in the abolitionist cause. Black women such as Susan Paul, Grace and Sarah M. Douglass, Harriet Purvis, Sarah and Margaretta Forten, and Maria W. Stewart played key roles in mobilizing abolitionist opinion.

Women, of course, could not vote. In 1840, nevertheless, abolitionists committed to political action decided that a large enough number of antislavery voters now existed to sustain an independent political party dedicated to abolition. The new Liberty party's national platform accepted the federalist premises of the Constitution, according to which Washington had no power to ban slavery within the states. It did hold, however, "that slavery should never be extended beyond its then existing limits; but should be gradually, and yet, at no distant day, wholly abolished by state authority."

In the meantime, Liberty candidates would fight discrimination against free blacks in the free states and seek "the denationalization of slavery"—the removal of all federal approval of or support for bondage. "The political dominion which slavery has gained" over the nation, abolitionists held, is "a main pillar of support and tower of defence to the system of slavery itself. Shorn of political power, slavery would fall by its own weight, and die of its own imbecility." Accordingly, the Liberty party demanded the end of slavery in the District of Columbia, in all territories, on the high seas, and in interstate commerce and opposed the admission of any additional slave states. Thus isolated and deprived of all external props, slavery would be undermined in practice, compelling masters to accede to voluntary emancipation.

Support for organized abolition proved strongest in New England (where slavery had never been important) and in the lands to the west into which emigrants from New England were pouring during the first half of the nineteenth century—in New York's upstate "Burned-Over District," Ohio's Western Reserve, and northern Illinois and Indiana. Liberty party leaders included disproportionate numbers of middling entrepreneurs, especially those resident in prospering small towns and cities, who were convinced of the virtues of the free-labor system. Although a handful of wealthy Northerners were active abolitionists (the Tappan brothers and Gerrit Smith are outstanding examples), most of the economic elite took a far more conservative position. Personally repelled by slavery, they felt at least as threatened by attempts to push that issue to the center of national politics. Doing so would antagonize the planters (with whom many maintained old and cherished business ties) and threaten the survival of both the Democratic and Whig organizations nationally and ultimately the federal Union. The abolitionist *Philanthropist* denounced "capitalists at the North who own slave property at the South" or "who from business, social connections, or otherwise, are interested in perpetuating the supremacy of the slave-interest."

The North's free white workers generally detested the institution of chattel slavery on principle. It embodied all the evils that they strove to avoid—the loss of personal independence, mutual respect, political equality, the right to the fruits of one's labor. When they sought the most powerful ways to denounce their employers, Lynn shoemakers, Lowell mill operatives, and other working people compared them to slave owners. Protesting their own condition, they referred to themselves as "wage slaves." Labor reformers, freethinkers, and communitarians (such as Thomas Skidmore, Frances Wright, and Robert Dale Owen) expressed their hostility to slavery in particularly blistering terms. Substantial numbers of those who signed antislavery petitions during the 1830s were craft workers who owned little or no real property. In 1846, a convention of New England wage earners protested the fact that "there are at the present time three millions of our brethren and sisters groaning in chains on the Southern plantations." Wishing "not only to be consistent but to secure to all others those rights and privileges for which we are contending ourselves," the convention declared its refusal to do anything "to keep three millions of our brethren and sisters in bondage" and called upon other labor groups "to speak out in thunder tones" along the same lines.

But the detestation of bondage common among northern working people induced very few of them to commit time and energy to abolishing that institution. Most were preoccupied with their own immediate economic and political goals. Few believed those goals related in any practical way to the abolition of chattel slavery. The racism that pervaded the nation reinforced such parochialism and undermined sympathy for the slaves as fellow human beings. So too did fears that emancipated bondsmen would flee the South, surge into the North, and there compete with free white workers (especially the economically more vulnerable unskilled) for jobs. Some northern workers who were averse to slavery nonetheless regarded abolitionists as fanatics bent on destroying their own favored political party (whether Democratic or Whig) as well as the federal Union (and thereby the liberties for free white men that the Union represented). Others noted that many abolitionist leaders came from the ranks or spoke in defense of large-scale employers of wage labor. The growing hostility toward such employers discussed earlier—a hostility that often embraced the whole range of economic, political, cultural, and religious values that employers seemed to treasure—helped steer many wage earners away from organized antislavery.

In the early 1830s, few abolitionists did much to challenge these perceptions or soften these antagonisms. True, a handful judged not only chattel slavery but also free-labor capitalism to be in conflict with human rights and justice. "Heartless, soul-destroying competition," wrote William I. Bowditch in 1852, undermined the "sublime doctrine of Christianity—the brotherhood of the human family." More commonly, however, abolitionists proudly subscribed to Adam Smith's free-market doctrines and placed their hopes for justice in the automatic functioning of the free-labor system. Efforts by northern wage earners to improve their conditions by collective action failed to win their sympathy. The first issue of Garrison's *Liberator*, in fact, attacked the New

England Association of Farmers, Mechanics, and Other Work-ingmen, specifically decrying attempts "to inflame the minds of our working class against the more opulent, and to persuade men that they are contemned and oppressed by a wealthy aristocracy." "Where is the evidence," Garrison asked a few weeks later, "that our wealthy citizens, as a body, are hostile to the interests of the laboring classes? It is not found in their commercial enterprises, which whiten the ocean with canvas, and give employment to the useful and numerous class of men; it is not found in their manu-facturing establishments, which multiply labor and cheapen the necessities of the poor."

Nor did economic inequality necessarily arouse abolitionist ire. Garrison believed that "a republican government . . . where the avenues to wealth, distinction, and supremacy are open to all . . . must, in the nature of things, be full of inequalities." "Pov-erty, wholesome poverty," wrote Wendell Phillips, "is no unmixed evil; it is the spur that often wins the race; it is the trial that calls out, like fire, all the deep great qualities of a man's nature." Theo-dore Parker concluded that "want is the only schoolmaster to teach" the lessons of "industry and thrift" to the shiftless. Lewis Tappan's abolitionist *Emancipator* conceded, with little evident concern, "that of the laborers for wages, a part will receive enough to accumulate, and a part only enough to subsist, on the simple principle that each receives what he earns."

Slave owners and their political allies, particularly in the Dem-ocratic party, appealed to northern workers alienated by this stance. Northern workers, declared John C. Calhoun and those who took their cues from him, lived harder lives than did south-ern slaves. If the latter had fewer formal rights, the former had less economic security. For that matter, Calhoun contended, "the manual laborers and operatives" of the free states *were* "essentially slaves," the only difference being that while "our slaves are hired for life and are well compensated,—yours are hired by the day and not cared for."

Some leaders of the northern labor movement found such rhetoric useful and regarded the Calhounites as allies in the fight against northern employers. Most who felt this way found a home in the northern Democratic party, accepting that party's equation of—and common enmity toward—abolitionism, disunionism, evangelical and Sabbatarian zeal, and contempt for the interests and wishes of white working people.

A prime example was George Henry Evans, the Welsh-born printer who became antebellum America's leading land reformer. Earlier in his career, Evans had championed the cause of anti-slavery. "We are now convinced," he wrote in 1831, that "EQUAL RIGHTS can never be enjoyed, even by those who are free, in a nation which contains slaveites enough to hold in bondage two millions of human beings." In that year, Evans's *Daily Sentinel* was the only newspaper in New York to defend Nat Turner's insurrection in Virginia. "They were deluded," Evans declared of the rebels, "but their cause was *just.*" Three years later, Evans vehemently denounced those—including wage earners—who had joined in antiabolition violence in New York City.

During the following decade, however, Evans executed a complete about-face. By the 1840s he was directly *counterposing* support for the interests of *northern* free workers to participation in abolitionist campaigns. "Wage slavery," he had decided, was "even more destructive of life, health and happiness than chattel slavery." Indeed, he added, "the efforts of those who are endeavoring to substitute wages for chattel slavery are greatly misdirected, and if they cannot be convinced of their error, they should, if possible, be prevented from making more converts to their erroneous doctrine."

There is, however, a particular irony in Evans's personal evolution. Even as he repudiated his early antislavery impulses, Deep South planters were embarking on a course of action that would eventually convince great numbers of other northern wage earners that their interests were directly menaced by the "Slave Power." And the defense of the "peculiar institution" would shortly pit slavery's most aggressive champions precisely against those northern farmers and wage earners most interested in the status of western lands.

— 7 —

"A Firebell in the Night": The Struggle Escalates

The debates over the Missouri Compromise and their aftermath rocked the planter elite. At the level of constitutional theory, complained North Carolina senator Nathaniel Macon, the 1820 compromise "acknowledge[d] the right of Congress to interfere" with slavery in the territories generally. On a practical level, warned South Carolina senator William Smith, it guaranteed territory for enough future free states to break the South's grip on the Senate. Thomas Jefferson, now in his late seventies, told a northern friend that the whole affair foreshadowed the complete dissolution of the United States. "This momentous question, like a firebell in the night, awakened me and filled me with terror. I considered it at once the [death] knell of the Union." As a result of the eventual compromise, he acknowledged, the matter was "hushed indeed, for the moment. But this is a reprieve only, not a final sentence." During the debates, political lines had been drawn on a regional basis; that geopolitical division, Jefferson believed, would now "never be obliterated." On the contrary, he predicted, "every new irritation will mark it deeper and deeper."

The Missouri controversy furnished still another cause for alarm. The wide-ranging congressional debate had given a dangerous public forum to subversive ideas. "The Missouri question," warned South Carolina governor John Geddes in 1820, "has given rise to the expression of opinions and doctrines respecting this specie of property, which tend not only to diminish its value, but also threaten our safety." Free black residents of the capital had filled the House galleries during the debates and listened intently to antislavery speeches. Who knew how far those words might travel? Such fears multiplied when it developed that prior to Denmark Vesey's 1822 insurrectionary bid, Vesey had used an antislavery speech by New York senator Rufus King to encourage his own comrades. "The events of the summer of 1822," declared the low-country Carolina planter and propagandist Robert J. Turnbull a few years later, "will long be remembered as amongst the choicest fruits of the agitation of that question in Congress." Because of the open debate it occasioned over the rights and wrongs of bondage, he explained, "our slaves thought there was a charter of liberties granted them by Congress."

Fears for the future of bound labor grew with the approach of abolition in the West Indies (with which the Carolinas had strong historic ties), the spread of immediatist abolitionism in the North, and the disturbingly acrimonious public debates over slavery in Virginia. In response, proslavery figures rushed to bolster the defense of the peculiar institution. That effort, as we have seen, was partly ideological. It was also eminently and aggressively practical. One of its most dramatic episodes occurred in 1832, when John C. Calhoun and other Carolinians tried to lead southern slave owners in a frontal challenge to the power of the federal government.

The Carolinians' immediate grievances were tariffs on imported manufactures that Congress enacted in 1828 and 1832. Before the sharpening of sectional differences, southern nationalists like Calhoun had supported protectionism in the interests of building up national strength. By the early 1830s, the same men were rejecting high tariffs as arbitrary taxes levied by northern industry upon southern agriculture. In November 1832, prominent South Carolina planters met in special convention and resolved that henceforth the tariffs "shall not be lawful . . . within the limits of this state," and added that any military attempt to enforce such federal power would be considered "inconsistent with the longer continuance of South Carolina in the Union."

Behind this stance lay sentiments stronger and calculations deeper than those connected simply with imports and exports. "Great as is this evil," explained Robert J. Turnbull, "it is perhaps the least of the evils which attend an abandonment of one iota of the principle in controversy. Our dispute involves questions of the most fearful import to the institutions and tranquility of South Carolina. I fear to name them. The bare thought of these is enough to rouse us to resistance were there no other motive." As Calhoun explained, the tariff was

> but . . . the occasion, rather than the real cause of the present unhappy state of things. The truth can no longer be disguised, that the peculiar domestick institutions of the Southern States, and the consequent direction which that and her soil and climate have given to her industry, has placed them in regard to taxation and appropriation in opposite relation to the majority of the Union.

This circumstance, Calhoun held, left the South with only three alternatives: (1) assert the "protective power in the reserved rights of the states"—that is, "nullify" the federal tariffs; (2) "submit to have their domestick institutions exhausted"; or (3) "in the end be forced to rebel." By opting for nullification, South Carolina would serve notice that it would permit Washington to impose *no* measures harmful to planter interests.

That South Carolina should take the initiative in this campaign—as it did in the drive to strengthen the ideological defense of slavery—was hardly coincidental. Throughout the antebellum era, the planters of that state proved the most sensitive to all threats against slavery's stability. Some of the largest plantations in the South were to be found there. Preoccupied with what one referred to as the "dense slave population at our own firesides," South Carolina planters harbored some of the region's deepest fears of slave uprisings. News of the Turner insurrection in Virginia had terrified Charleston, and the state legislature had hastily dispatched a special cavalry unit to protect that city from Turner's sympathizers and potential allies.

But South Carolina's particular sensitivity also led it to misjudge the actual relationship of forces in 1832. It exaggerated the antislavery intentions of northern politicians as well as Northerners' control over the federal government. That miscalculation led to a second one: the Carolinians' belief that other Southerners would rally around the nullification cause. This became clear when President Andrew Jackson reacted to South Carolina's challenge by reinforcing the federal fort in Charleston harbor and obtaining a "force bill" from Congress that authorized the use of military power to carry out federal law. Carolina's plea for support elsewhere in the South fell on deaf ears. Few southern leaders considered nullification the proper means with which to advance southern interests. That sharp critic of the 1820 Missouri Compromise, North Carolina's Nathaniel Macon, flatly rejected nullification as unconstitutional. Many who rejected nullification did assert a state's *right* to secede should it choose to do so. But few white Southerners believed that the menace then emanating from Washington as yet merited such drastic action.

After a period of tense confrontation, armed conflict was averted. Congress (prodded by both Jackson and Henry Clay) agreed to reduce tariffs over the next nine years; South Carolina repealed its nullification ordinance in 1833. But the failure of most of the South to mobilize in behalf of nullification did not return national politics to the status quo ante. Too much had transpired during the previous decade and a half to permit that.

The practical defense of slavery now advanced along two parallel roads. First, attempts to carry slavery into new lands increased. The collapse of nullification made it more urgent to strengthen the proslavery party in Washington, D.C. The acquisition of new slave states would serve that end by increasing the southern population and congressional (especially Senate) representation. In a resolution presented to the Senate in December

1837, Calhoun outlined the proper uses of federal power. "This Government," it read, "is bound so to exercise its powers as to give, as far as may be practicable, increased stability and security to the domestic institutions of the States that compose the Union," adding that "the intermeddling of any State or States, or their citizens, to abolish slavery in this District, or any of the Territories, on the ground, or under the pretext, that it is immoral or sinful; or the passage of any act or measure of Congress, with that view, would be a direct and dangerous attack on the institutions of all the slaveholding States." Here was the mirror opposite of abolitionist doctrine; it might fairly be called "the nationalization of slavery." And it rested on an assumption shared with the abolitionists: the survival of the South's slave-labor system required the active collaboration of the federal government.

In the meantime, restrictions on the conduct of both slaves and free blacks in the South would be augmented, and all advocates of emancipation silenced—especially in the South, but also throughout the country. The perceived need for such repression followed from a particular evaluation of the domestic peril. According to this analysis, southern security was endangered chiefly by the conduct of southern free blacks; skilled, urban, educated, and generally worldly slaves; and northern agitators, both black and white. The uncontrolled activities of all these groups threatened to stir up the enslaved population as a whole and to divide, demoralize, and thereby disarm the white majority.

The menace posed by free blacks and relatively privileged individual slaves seemed amply documented in the record of slave rebellions. Gabriel Prosser was a blacksmith. Nat Turner was literate and unusually mobile. Denmark Vesey was a free black artisan who had traveled extensively as a seaman (to the West Indies, among other places), was multilingual, literate, well read, and well informed. Many of Vesey's chief collaborators were craftsmen and house servants.

Even before Vesey, slave owners had feared that free blacks undermined the institution of slavery. They were known to assist slaves in flight from their owners. Free black districts in southern cities gave fugitives nearby sanctuaries where they might circulate with relative ease without attracting unwanted attention. Schools and churches serving free blacks regularly attracted slaves as well, infecting the latter with dangerous ideas, both temporal and spiritual. Indeed, as more than one critic of colonization had noted, planters feared that the very status of "free black" gave slaves a dangerous goal to which they could aspire.

In the aftermath of the Vesey sensation, therefore, masters in one state after another redoubled their efforts to drive free blacks from their midst. Short of that, they aimed to reduce free blacks to an unprecedentedly oppressed and powerless condition. South Carolina legislated against individual manumission and barred other free blacks from entering the state. Its new Free Colored Seamen's Act required that all free black sailors employed on ships in a harbor be incarcerated in the local jail until the vessel weighed anchor.

The Turner rebellion inaugurated another rash of repressive laws, aimed at free blacks and slaves alike. The same Virginia legislature that deemed positive steps toward gradual emancipation "inexpedient" rushed to enact a more severe slave code, outlawed the buying of food from slaves, and allocated thousands of dollars to finance colonization of the state's existing free black population. Throughout the South, new laws aimed to make it more difficult than ever for a slave to learn to read. "To be able to read and write is certainly not necessary to the performance of those duties which are required of slaves," declared the Charleston City Council in 1826, "and on the contrary is incompatible with the public safety." Literacy would enable bondsmen "to carry on illicit traffic, to communicate privately among themselves, and to evade those regulations that are intended to prevent confederation among them." When told that slaves needed to read the Bible, Virginia's Whitemarsh Seabrook replied that anyone who wished slaves to read the whole Bible belonged in a "room in the Lunatic Asylum." "Millions of those now in heaven," agreed the *Farmers' Register* in 1836, "never owned a bible." These anti-literacy campaigns were effective; by 1860, only about 5 percent of all slaves had managed to learn to read.

Slavery's advocates acknowledged that such measures departed from the paternalist ideal. "We have been compelled to curtail some privileges," wrote James Henry Hammond, and "we have been debarred from granting new ones. . . . [W]e have in some measure to abandon our efforts to attach them to us, and control them through their affection and pride. We have to rely more and more on the power of fear." But none of this, Hammond argued, reflected either innate planter cruelty or intrinsic flaws in the society. Strong measures were necessary to retain control over the enslaved population, who were being agitated by those bent on "loosening all ties between master and slave." To reassert those ties, Hammond explained, "we must, in all our intercourse with them, assert and maintain strict mastery, and impress upon them that they are slaves. . . . We are determined to continue [being] masters, and to do so we have to draw the rein tighter and tighter day by day to be assured that we hold them in complete check."

Hammond and others blamed "the abolitionist agitation" for stirring up southern slaves. It followed that, to secure the institution of bondage, repression must target not only blacks but dangerous whites as well. Rebels like Prosser, Vesey, and Turner, after all, had been encouraged by open debate and divisions in white society. (That Turner knew about and valued differences among whites concerning slavery was apparent in his intention to spare the lives of any Frenchmen, Quakers, or Methodists he encountered "on account . . . of their being friendly to liberty.")

Beginning in the 1820s, therefore, and with an intensity that escalated through the Civil War, planters declared war upon all open criticism of the peculiar institution. In the aftermath of the Missouri debates, South Carolina's governor urged legislation that would "oppose at the threshold, everything likely in its consequences to disturb our domestic tranquility." Georgia offered a $5,000 reward for bringing William Lloyd Garrison to answer for his actions before a court in the state. Southern officials suppressed antislavery books, newspapers, lectures, and sermons and strove generally to deny critics of bondage access to any public forum.

Enforcement was obtained through either official or extralegal action. In July 1835, a Charleston crowd broke into the local post office, seized stacks of antislavery literature, and publicly set them ablaze. State officials endorsed the deed; so did Andrew Jackson's Postmaster General, Amos Kendall, who was also a slaveholder. As if to demonstrate to South Carolina that Washington, D.C., was indeed in safe hands, Jackson asked Congress for laws to prohibit "under severe penalties, the circulation in the Southern States, through the mail, of incendiary publications intended to instigate the slaves to insurrection." In the summer of 1835, leading Boston businessmen gathered to promise "our countrymen of the South" full support in the defense of slavery and to register "regret and indignation at the conduct of the abolitionists." In Cincinnati, Utica, and New York City, groups of Northerners showed themselves ready to help put down antislavery subversives. Crowds led by prominent merchants and professionals and filled out with white wage earners abused abolitionists and threatened them with violence. In Alton, Illinois, in 1837, a crowd destroyed the printing press of abolitionist Elijah Lovejoy and then shot and killed him when he tried to resist.

The ban on antislavery speech extended to the nation's capital. As abolitionist petitions streamed into the House of Representatives, southern members insisted that their northern colleagues join in refusing them consideration. Representative Henry Wise of Virginia warned in February 1835 that "slavery is interwoven with our very political existence, is guaranteed by our Constitution . . . and they cannot attack the system of slavery without attacking the institutions of our country, our safety, and our welfare." On the contrary, the need to reconcile the interests of the various states demanded that slavery's "consequences must be borne by our Northern brethren" too. Indeed, suggested Virginia senator William C. Rives, "for the people of the non-slaveholding States to discuss the question of slavery, at all, is to attack the foundations of the union itself."

In May 1836, the House bowed to such pressure and instituted a regular "gag rule," according to which "all petitions, memorials, resolutions, propositions, or papers relating in any way or to any extent whatever to the subject of slavery" shall be tabled and "no further action shall be taken thereon." The vote on this rule found northern Whigs generally opposed, confronting a majority composed of southern Whigs and Democrats of both sections. From 1840 to 1844, an even more exclusionary rule prevailed; under its provisions, the House declined even to take note of antislavery petitions.

Repression, however, failed to bury antislavery opinion. On the contrary, escalating attacks against free expression of antislavery opinion convinced ever more Northerners that the peculiar institution was not simply repulsive and immoral in the abstract but a tangible and immediate threat to their own liberties. It was partly for this reason that (as Daniel Webster noted to a friend early in 1838) "the anti Slavery feeling is growing stronger & stronger every day." The abolitionist crusade, Henry Clay warned a year later, "should no longer be regarded as an imaginary danger."

Mounting popular hostility to slavery and resentment at proslavery repression, in turn, exerted increasing pressure on northern politicians, Whigs and Democrats alike. This became clear in early 1842, when former President John Quincy Adams, now a Massachusetts congressman, precipitated a confrontation over the gag rule. In January, Adams introduced a number of petitions related to slavery but not technically excluded by the rule; he then used them as a pretext to expound at length upon the evils of bondage. This violation of the spirit, if not the letter, of the gag rule finally led Henry Wise to move to censure Adams. The protracted debate that followed ended in a vote to table (and thereby kill) Wise's motion; the voting followed sectional lines, defying considerations of party unity.

Some six weeks later, Joshua Giddings, congressional representative of Ohio's Western Reserve, rose in the House to defend a group of slaves who had mutinied aboard the U.S. ship *Creole*, killing one seaman in the process. That speech provoked another censure motion, and this one carried the House by a vote of 125–69. (Democrats of both sections now joined southern Whigs to form the majority.) Thus rebuked, Giddings immediately re-signed his House seat and returned to Ohio to campaign for re-election against a Democratic challenger. The Western Reserve responded with a massive show of support. On election day, the district gave Giddings an incredible 95 percent of its votes. A rue-ful Henry Wise termed Giddings's return to Congress that May "the greatest triumph ever achieved by a member of the House."

This explosion of popular resentment signaled the beginning of the end of the gag rule. In 1844, the House voted to rescind it by a vote of 108–80, and more than three-quarters of northern Democratic congressmen now supported repeal. The same kind of public pressure would soon compel them to prove their hos-tility to planter dictates in a more direct (and more momen-tous) way.

In the meantime, northern residents were expressing revulsion against slavery in another form. In an 1842 ruling, the Supreme Court held that the national government alone had jurisdiction where escaped slaves were concerned. The legislatures of several northern states used that decision to forbid their own elected offi-cials from aiding those pursuing fugitives.

The genesis of the "personal liberty law" eventually passed in Massachusetts reveals the role played by an aroused population. In Boston in 1842, public pressure forced the release from jail of an accused fugitive, George Latimer. Fearing that Latimer would then flee the area, his putative owner (James B. Grey of Norfolk, Virginia) consented to sell Latimer to an antislavery minister. The clergyman, in turn, then set Latimer free. In the aftermath, 65,000 citizens signed a petition urging the state government's noncooperation with all slave hunters. Within months, such a personal liberty bill passed both houses of the state legislature with overwhelming majorities and was quickly signed into law. Similar measures were enacted in Vermont and Ohio that year and by Connecticut in 1844. In 1847, the Pennsylvania legislature re-ceived more petitions opposing cooperation with fugitive hunting than it had on any issue during the previous decade. That led to the quick drafting and passage of a law similar to the Bay State's.

The Pennsylvania bill won endorsement from both Democrats and Whigs. John Greenleaf Whittier gave voice to the spirit animating these developments in his poem "Massachusetts to Virginia":

> We wage no war, we lift no arm, we fling no torch within
> The fire-damps of the quaking mine beneath your soil of sin;
> We leave ye with your bondmen, to wrestle, while ye can,
> With the strong upward tendencies and godlike soul of man!
>
> But for us and for our children, the vow which we have given
> For freedom and humanity is registered in heaven;
> No slave-hunt in our borders,—no pirate on our strand!
> No fetters in the Bay State,—no slave upon our land!

The passage of these laws was an important signal: popular support for even the original constitutional compromises was eroding. Southern spokesmen said as much. The enactment of personal liberty laws, asserted Virginia's state legislators, was a "disgusting and revolting exhibition of faithless and unconstitutional legislation," an attempt to foist "palpable frauds upon the South, calculated to excite at once her indignation and her contempt." John C. Calhoun called these state laws "one of the most fatal blows ever received by the South and the Union." Henry Clay reported them to be "most irritating and inflammatory to those who live in Slave states." A Pennsylvania newspaper laconically replied, "Anti-slavery public sentiment will make anti-slavery law."

By the late 1830s, then, conflicts touching on the stability and future of slave labor were taking on the form of a self-perpetuating and escalating spiral. At the heart of things lay planter fears about the volatility of chattel slavery. Bound laborers could be controlled and worked profitably only if they were kept intimidated, uneducated, isolated from dangerous influences, and convinced that resistance was hopeless. That, in turn, required confronting them with overwhelming force and a white majority united in support of black servitude.

Exactly here, however, lay the difficulty. Over time, planters found themselves faced with a growing sector of the nation's white population animated by economic interests, cultural dispositions, and political values increasingly antithetical to slave labor. The southern elite responded to this palpable danger by moving to tighten its political grip—over slaves, free blacks, dissenting southern whites, "outside agitators," and the federal government. This aggressive conduct, however, served precisely to deepen the slave owners' political isolation in the country—by challenging the liberties of northern free whites, opposing their practical interests, and affronting their sensibilities. Their actions, thus, stimulated public support for attacks on planter power. Even northern politicians inclined to conciliate the South grew fearful for their careers and bent before rising antislavery winds. Thwarted, southern leaders responded with still firmer (and more offensive) measures.

The consequent sharpening of the underlying conflict could be traced in the history of American Protestantism. In 1837 the Presbyterian Church underwent a major split because of conflicts between its "Old School" and "New School" affiliates. The issues formally in contention did not concern chattel slavery. But southern congregations sided with the Old School primarily in reaction to the spread of antislavery sentiment among northern New School adherents. In 1850, the New School's Presbyterian General Assembly made this underlying issue clearer by formally denying that God sanctioned human bondage. By that time, the country's two largest Protestant denominations had also split over the same general issue. In 1844–45, northern Methodists and Baptists tried to outlaw slaveholding among church leaders. Both denominations split, with the South's partisans organizing themselves, respectively, in the Methodist Episcopal Church, South, and the Southern Baptist Convention.

What did it all mean? Theodore Weld—with Birney and the Tappan brothers, a leader of the evangelical wing of abolitionism—thought he knew. "Nothing short of miracles," he wrote in 1842, "constant miracles, and such as the world has never seen can keep at bay the two great antagonistic forces . . . They must drive against each other, till *one* of them goes to the bottom. *Events*, the master of men, have for years been silently but without a moment's pause, settling the basis of two great parties, the nucleus of one slavery, of the other, freedom."

This popular polarization revealed itself with special clarity in—and received a powerful stimulus from—the struggle over the annexation of Texas and the subsequent war with Mexico. Americans, chiefly from the trans-Allegheny South and Missouri, had begun systematically to colonize the Mexican province of Coahuila-Texas in the 1820s. At first the Mexican government had viewed this influx as a way to develop a sparsely populated region. Although Mexico formally outlawed slavery in 1829, American colonists received special permission to keep "permanent indentured servants," about a thousand of whom lived in Texas in 1830.

Eventually, however, growing conflicts with the Texans—and concern about the United States' increasingly vocal wish to absorb Texas—compelled a radical reevaluation among Mexican leaders. In 1830, new legislation outlawed further immigration from the United States. Mounting tensions between the Mexican government and the colonists finally yielded war in the fall of 1835. By the following spring Texas was an independent slaveholding republic, and its leaders promptly requested admission into the United States.

In the United States, however, the population of the free states was palpably hostile to absorbing so vast a slaveholding region, and the strength and extent of that opposition for some time discouraged annexationists, President Andrew Jackson among them. Jackson's Vice President and successor, New York Democrat Martin Van Buren, had always shown himself sensitive to planter interests. He had opposed abolition in the District of Columbia, supported the congressional gag rule, and endorsed Jackson's proposed ban on abolitionist literature from the mails, all of which earned him the sobriquet "a northern man with southern principles." But growing northern antislavery sentiment now left him politically vulnerable. President Van Buren decided to come out against the annexation of Texas.

In his bid for reelection in 1840, Van Buren faced a Whig ticket headed by William Henry Harrison and John Tyler. A combination of factors (including a tendency to blame Democratic monetary policy for the panic of 1837 and the depression that began two years later) made Harrison President. Harrison's death from pneumonia after just one month in office raised the Virginian John Tyler to the presidency. It then quickly became apparent that Tyler's understanding of Whiggery was quite distinct from that of his congressional colleagues. Confrontations over a range of issues were capped by Tyler's decision to reopen negotiations with the Republic of Texas.

The North was no readier to annex Texas than it had been in the mid-1830s. The Massachusetts legislature warned that statehood for Texas would imperil the nation's peace and prosperity and instructed its congressional delegation "to spare no exertions" in opposing it. John C. Calhoun (Tyler's new Secretary of State) was defiant. His 1844 correspondence with British ambassador John Packenham (which was leaked to the press) aggressively and repeatedly identified annexation as crucial to the defense of slavery and a priority for slavery's champions. With a storm of northern public protest at its back, the Senate failed in June to muster the two-thirds support required to ratify Tyler's proposed treaty of annexation.

In the presidential contest of 1844, the Whigs nominated Henry Clay. That Kentucky planter, with his Jeffersonian ambivalence about slavery, waffled on the Texas issue. Southern Democrats, by now determined to bring the Lone Star Republic into the Union and thereby bolster their own political power, blocked Van Buren's bid for renomination. Instead, the Democratic convention picked Tennessee slaveholder James K. Polk as its standard bearer. Afterward, South Carolina's Francis Pickens crowed, "We have triumphed. Polk is nearer to *us* than any public man who was named. He is a large Slave holder & plants cotton—free trade—Texas—States rights out & out." Polk's platform shrewdly paired a call for annexing Texas with an issue close to the heart of many emigrant-minded families in the Midwest—the demand that the United States assume sole jurisdiction over the Oregon Territory (then still disputed with Britain) all the way up to the border of Russian-owned Alaska.

Polk rolled to victory in popular balloting notable on a number of counts. The Democrat obtained 50 percent of the popular vote but 15 out of 26 states and 62 percent of the votes cast in the electoral college. The Whigs suffered a particularly severe setback in the lower South. In 1840, Georgia, Mississippi, and Louisiana had all lined up behind Harrison; four years later, the contest between the ardently expansionist Polk and the vacillating Clay propelled them into the Democratic camp alongside South Carolina and Alabama. Polk's triumph opened the door to annexation, which was secured not through a treaty but a simple congressional resolution passed by majority vote in each house in February 1845. (That resolution also left open the possibility—particularly attractive to the vote-hungry South—that the vast land mass of Texas might eventually be divided into five states.)

The annexation of Texas badly strained U.S.-Mexican relations. But full-scale war occurred because Polk was determined to wrest still more land from that country. Mexico regarded the Nueces River as Texas's southern border. Texas and Washington, however, asserted that the true border was farther south, at the Rio Grande, an assertion which removed additional thousands of square miles from Mexico's domain. To press this claim, Polk dispatched troops under General Zachary Taylor southward and, in January 1846, ordered them to cross the Nueces. When, as expected, fighting ensued, Polk won a congressional declaration of war.

With the exchange of bullets, war fever swept across much of the United States. But none were so enthusiastic as the South's planter leadership. The Charleston *Courier* crowed that "every battle fought in Mexico and every dollar spent there, but insures the acquisition of territory which must widen the field of Southern enterprise and power in the future. And the final result will be to readjust the power of the confederacy, so as to give us control over the operation of government in all time to come."

By September 1847, U.S. troops were in Mexico City. In March 1848, the Treaty of Guadalupe Hidalgo transferred the provinces of California and New Mexico to the United States and fixed the international border at the Rio Grande. Almost 1.2 million square miles of land—half Mexico's national domain—and nearly 80,000 people were transferred to the United States; in exchange, Washington paid Mexico the sum of $15 million.

This military victory (and geographical windfall) bore a considerable political price, however. A growing tendency to see the conflict as a slaveholders' adventure stimulated antiwar sentiment in the free states, first of all and most forcefully in New England. When Polk failed to make good on his campaign promise to fight for all of Oregon—settling instead with Britain on more moderate terms—a great many farmers of the upper Midwest felt betrayed as well.

The Whig party opposed Polk's Mexico policy. Vermont Whig Solomon Foot warned, "You are rushing headlong and blindfold upon appalling dangers, before which the stout heart shrinks, and brave men turn pale. You are rekindling the slumbering fires of a volcano [that] . . . will consume all the plain." "If I were a Mexican," swore Ohio senator Thomas Corwin, a mainstream Whig leader, "I would tell you, 'Have you not room in your own country to bury your dead men? If you come into mine, we will greet you with bloody hands, and welcome you with hospitable graves.' " When told that the United States had to prosecute the war to obtain the territories it required, Corwin responded, "I have never yet heard a thief, arraigned for stealing a horse, plead that it was the best horse that he could find in the country."

Antiwar sentiment found still stronger voice in the House of Representatives, where northern voters enjoyed a representation in closer consonance with their numbers. The freshman Illinois Whig congressman Abraham Lincoln dismissed Polk's justification for war as "the sheerest deception" and compared it with "the half insane mumbling of a fever-dream." The Administration's advocates, Lincoln added, could only hope "to escape scrutiny by fixing the public gaze upon the exceeding brightness of military glory." In 1846, Whig members of the House of Representatives pushed through a resolution asserting that the war had been "unnecessarily and unconstitutionally begun by the President of the United States."

This Whig bark was actua'ly much worse than its bite. Party leadership lay in the hands of men determined to straddle internal differences on the war and slavery. They voted funds to sustain the fighting even as they criticized the initiation of the conflict and demanded that the final peace treaty include no additional annexations of Mexican territory. More consistently antiwar and antislavery Whigs lambasted this policy as unprincipled and cowardly. But the Whig stance did enable that party to reap the benefits of mounting northern hostility to the war and its expansionist purpose.

— 8 —

"Keep It Within Limits": Western Lands and Free Soil

From the 1840s onward, principled abolitionists made up only a part—and a declining proportion at that—of Northerners anxious about the future of slavery. A large northern majority remained uncommitted to nationwide abolition and expressed little if any active concern for African-Americans. Many Northerners (and especially Midwesterners) repeatedly endorsed legislation to restrict the rights of free blacks in their states. By 1840, only five free states—Maine, New Hampshire, Vermont, Massachusetts, and Rhode Island—allowed blacks to vote on an equal basis with whites.

Nevertheless, hostility to the institution of slavery steadily grew in the North during these years. Even more of an anathema was the prospect of slavery's expansion beyond its current borders. "It is one of the things about which there is an almost entire concurrence of opinion among reflecting men of every party and degree in the free states," believed the Whiggish Newark, New Jersey, *Daily Advertiser*. John C. Calhoun estimated in 1847 that two-thirds of the northern population actively opposed the spread of slavery. A typical expression of this outlook appeared a few years later in the pages of Cincinnati's *Daily Unionist*, a newspaper published by journeymen printers on strike against the city's major dailies. "We are no abolitionists in the popular sense of the term," it noted, "but we would belie our convictions of democracy if we did not oppose slavery's expansion over new lands."

Some old considerations were still at work here: additional slave states meant additional proslavery votes in both Congress and the electoral college and thus greater proslavery power over the national government. Principled abolitionists naturally opposed slavery in the new territories as well. But for many Northerners there were additional reasons for concern. Northern farmers wanted western lands for their own use as homesteads, and many urban working people shared the farmers' dream. Neither group wanted those lands preempted by slave plantations. Neither wished to dwell among slaves, compete with slave labor, or be governed locally by slave-owning politicians. Even many plebeians who expected to remain in the East wanted the West guaranteed as "free soil" for the future benefit of neighbors, children, grandchildren, and future immigrants.

This firm and widespread determination increased the pressure on both Whigs and Democrats to produce credible free-soil credentials.

The Van Buren wing of the northern Democratic party was in a particularly exposed position. The dominant southern wing of their party reviled and rebuffed Van Burenites in the 1840s for failing to defend the interests of the slave states with sufficient firmness and consistency. Simultaneously, however, an antislavery northern population blamed them for compromising the interests of the free North. Van Buren was worried in 1842 because "the Democrats in the State [his native New York] have suffered so often and so severely in their advocacy of Southern men, and Southern measures." A few years later, in February 1845, Congressman Preston King of New York warned that Democrats would "fall in every free state except Illinois" if they were "made responsible" for annexing a slaveholding region the size of Texas. Later still it was Van Buren's turn to fret that war with Mexico would expose Democrats to the "charge . . . that it is waged for the extension of slavery." Given northern hostility to such a conflict, he wrote, "the Democracy of the Free States would, I very much fear, be driven to the sad alternative of turning their backs upon their [Southern] friends, or of encountering political suicide with their eyes open."

These readings of the popular political temperature were perceptive. In 1846, antiwar forces did register important electoral gains. In March, a coalition of Whigs and breakaway Democrats led by John P. Hale won majorities in both houses of the New Hampshire legislature. Included in the first order of business were resolutions denouncing both the annexation of Texas and war with Mexico and endorsing "every just and well-directed effort for the suppression and extermination of that terrible scourge of our race, human slavery." Congressional elections later in the year brought a net Whig gain of 38 seats in the House of Representatives, almost two dozen of them from Pennsylvania, New York, and Ohio alone—the heart of Van Burenite country. Democrats lost 14 seats just in New York State, and Democratic governor Silas Wright, a Van Buren man, failed in his bid for reelection.

The message was not lost on the losers. "The Mexican war," Wright privately acknowledged, "is rapidly becoming unpopular with the people of this section of the Union," explaining that "the great and universal objection made to it is that its effect is to be . . . to extend slavery." "The abolitionists are gaining in New York," reported Democratic senator John M. Niles of Connecticut in 1846, "and recruiting from the Democrats. . . . There have been enough northern Democrats who have sacrificed themselves to southern interests and I do not wish to see any more." "Are we required," wondered Representative Jacob Brinkerhoff, an Ohio Democrat, ". . . eternally to combat the inborn sentiments and instincts of our own people for their [slaveholders'] benefit?" Even some more conservative Democrats, Polk loyalists, felt the heat. A leader of this faction, New York senator Daniel Dickinson, considered it prudent to declare his "respect with a feeling akin to reverence" for "the sentiment entertained by the great masses of those I represent upon the subject of slavery. I know how deeply its existence is deplored by the true philanthropist."

In the summer of 1846, the Van Burenites determined to stake out a public position that would improve their standing at home. Representative David Wilmot, a Van Burenite from Pennsylvania, introduced a rider to a House appropriations bill that would make it "an express and fundamental condition to the acquisition of any territory from the Republic of Mexico by the United States" that "neither slavery nor involuntary servitude shall ever exist in any part of said territory." It was crucial, believed Connecticut Democrat Gideon Welles, to "satisfy the northern people that we are not to extend the institution of slavery as a result of the war." "The adoption of the principle of the 'Wilmot proviso,'" believed Jacob Brinkerhoff, "is the only way to *save* the Democratic party of the free states." Otherwise "they are destined to defeat and doomed to a position in the minority, from . . . Iowa to . . . Maine."

Once again, debate and the vote that followed polarized along broadly sectional rather than partisan lines. Michigan's Lewis Cass and New Hampshire's Charles Atherton deplored the Proviso in private. But opposing it openly (as they confided to President Polk) would place them "in great peril with their constituents." In the event, only four northern Democrats stood with Polk against the Proviso. The House of Representatives passed the measure, and all but one northern state legislature added its formal support. The Senate refused its assent.

The Wilmot Proviso provoked Deep South planters as nothing else had in years. At the most general level, it stigmatized their peculiar institution as singularly undeserving of further expansion, an insult they were by no means prepared to accept passively. But foreclosing slavery's westward expansion posed more immediate dangers in declining control over the federal government and growing internal insecurity. It would reduce the land area in which poor but ambitious southern whites might carve out farms and enter the ranks of the slaveholders. That, in turn, could increase tensions within the existing slave states. The evident decline of slavery in the upper South magnified slave-owner fears of isolation, as did the continued expression in that region of antislavery opinions. "How long," wondered one of John C. Calhoun's correspondents, "will Maryland, Western Virginia, Kentucky, Eastern Tennessee, and even the western part of North Carolina feel it in their interest to retain slaves?"

Restricting the slaveholding domain also increased the danger of slave resistance and rebellion. Drawing "a line of political and social demarcation around the Slave States," the Charleston *Mercury* warned in 1847, would leave them flanked "on every side . . . with those who will continually excite our slaves to insubordination and revolt, which [agitation] it would be folly to suppose would forever be resisted." Proviso supporters like David Wilmot himself anticipated a similar, if less violent, outcome. "Slavery," Wilmot asserted, "has within itself the seeds of its own destruction. Keep it within limits, let it remain where it now is, and in time it will wear itself out."

Opponents of the Wilmot Proviso lined up behind one of three alternative legislative formulas. Some (most notably Polk himself) sought to extend the Missouri Compromise line (at 36 degrees 30 minutes latitude) westward through the Mexican cession to the Pacific. Others wanted more. Calhoun, applying his general nationalization-of-slavery doctrine, insisted that Congress and its agents (including territorial governments) must respect all the property rights of all American citizens wherever they traveled or settled in all lands held by the states in common. This constitutional interpretation would eviscerate not only the Wilmot Proviso but also the compromise of 1820 and, indeed, all federal attempts to limit the spread of slavery in the West, including the Northwest Ordinance.

Polk's Vice President, George Dallas, broached a third alternative; Michigan Democratic senator Lewis Cass (a particularly vocal and energetic exponent of territorial expansion in general) became its first vociferous champion. According to their "popular sovereignty" plan, Congress would make no a priori judgment about slavery in any territory but would leave that issue to local voters and legislators to decide. This formula promised to spare Congress repeated divisive disputes over slavery and thus help mute the debate nationally. But even here sectional division could not be entirely suppressed. Northern supporters of "popular sovereignty" generally assumed that territorial governments could vote to outlaw slavery. Most Southerners believed that slavery was automatically legal in all federal territories. The right to outlaw bondage by popular sovereignty, they held, arose only once a territory became a state with full rights of self-government. Supporters of both views for a time chose to leave this ambiguity undisturbed for the sake of party unity.

As the election of 1848 approached, then, slavery's future in the lands taken from Mexico remained undecided. Leaders of both major parties strove mightily to avoid taking the kind of clear and resolute position on the matter that might finally sever partisan ties.

Virtually from its birth, the Whig party had been divided between a strongly antislavery ("Conscience") faction and a more powerful conservative ("Cotton") bloc tied by commercial and political considerations to sectional compromise. (At one point, the Boston *Whig*, a Conscience mouthpiece, denounced Whigs linked commercially to textiles and the South—such as Abbott Lawrence and Nathan Appleton—for prostituting principles "for the sake of slaveholding gold" and "thinking more of sheep and cotton than of men.") In 1841, just one year after the Whigs waged their first coordinated national presidential campaign, their cohesion had been badly strained by the selection of Kentucky slaveholder John White as Speaker of the House. A common aversion to annexation and war with Mexico had later helped sustain Whig unity. But the Treaty of Guadalupe Hidalgo rendered the party's official "No Territory" stance moot. Compelled now to address the future of the expanded American West, most northern Whigs supported the Wilmot Proviso; Southerners opposed it. In late 1847, this renewed intraparty dissension nearly prevented the Whigs' House majority from electing its own candidate (Massachusetts's Robert Winthrop) as Speaker. "While I am not enough of an antislavery man for some of our Northern friends," Winthrop observed, "I am too much of a Wilmot Proviso man for some of our Southern friends."

To paper over these differences, the national Whig convention in 1848 nominated Zachary Taylor, a Mexican war hero and a major Louisiana planter—but a man who harbored the kind of moderate views about the slavery-expansion issue more commonly associated with the upper South, where he was born and raised. The Democrats once again rejected Martin Van Buren, this time in favor of Lewis Cass.

Cass's platform implied support for popular sovereignty. Some Deep South politicians committed to more aggressively proslavery policies and candidates bridled. But dissatisfaction at least as intense united those at the other end of the political spectrum. Van Burenites, incensed at their treatment by the Democratic leadership, joined with Liberty party leaders, Conscience Whigs, and others in 1848 to fashion a new political organization, the Free Soil party. From ten to twenty thousand delegates drawn from every free state in the Union gathered in Buffalo that August to attend the Free Soil convention.

The new party expanded on the Wilmot Proviso to craft its defining platform plank: "No more slave states and no more slave territory." Slavery, the party declared, was "a great moral, social, and political evil—a relic of barbarism which must necessarily be swept away in the progress of Christian civilization." Seeking to expand the free-soil appeal, the platform also endorsed another measure whose popularity had steadily been building: "the free grant [of land] to actual settlers" of the West. (Thus did the call for land reform wend its way from one side of the partisan and sectional spectrum to the other.) When Martin Van Buren expressed unqualified support for the Wilmot Proviso, he received the Free Soil nomination for the presidency. Although the new party called for salvaging the West "for the Caucasian race," free black leaders such as Samuel Ringold Ward, Henry Highland Garnet, Charles L. Remond, Henry Bibb, and Frederick Douglass nonetheless cheered the Free Soil party's emergence as a major blow against slavery.

Earlier attempts to translate popular antislavery into votes had yielded only modest results. The vast majority of Northerners opposed to bondage and its expansion had clung to one of the two major parties. Some did so out of faith in northern Whig or Democratic promises to defend antislavery interests. Even more important, however, was the fact that most Northerners for years considered other issues on which Whig and Democratic candidates usually clashed—tariffs, banking, internal improvements, and temperance—to be more immediate and compelling than slavery.

This helps explain why in 1840 James Birney received only some 7,000 votes running as the Liberty party's first presidential candidate. By one estimate, 90 percent of the 70,000 to 100,000 enfranchised members of abolitionist societies had cast their ballots for Birney's Whig and Democratic opponents. Many abolitionist-minded Whigs were particularly reluctant to abandon a presidential candidate of their own party (Harrison) reputedly open to antislavery influence. In 1841, Liberty candidates running for state office amassed a total vote three times the size of the 1840 total, and the Liberty vote grew by half again in 1842. By 1844 the Liberty total had reached 65,000, possibly costing Clay the electoral votes of both New York and Michigan and therewith the election. The progress thus measured since 1840 was significant, but in absolute and tangible terms the rewards remained small. Birney's 1844 vote still amounted to less than 2.5 percent of all ballots cast that year.

Measured against the Liberty party's experience, the first Free Soil results were impressive. In 1848, Van Buren received 290,000 votes, 10 percent of the national total and nearly one in every seven cast in the free states. That achievement denied an outright popular-vote majority to both Cass and Taylor (who won the presidency in the electoral college). Free Soil voters also sent a dozen antislavery men to the U.S. House of Representatives in 1848. And the election of eight Free Soilers to the Ohio legislature's lower house induced that state's Democratic legislators to offer a bloc to Free Soil leader Salmon P. Chase in early 1849. In return for backing Democrats seeking the posts of speaker and clerk, Free Soilers won repeal of Ohio's notorious "Black Laws" and sent Chase to the U.S. Senate.

Like the Liberty party, but on a larger scale, the Free Soil party demonstrated its strongest appeal in commercially developing rural and small-town areas of the North. Free Soil voting strength proved greatest in New York and Massachusetts; there, in fact, as in Vermont, Van Buren received more votes than did Lewis Cass. But the new party also demonstrated a notable strength among certain groups of northern industrial workers. Lynn shoemakers proved particularly receptive, and the party carried that city in 1848 in a three-cornered contest. In 1852, the Free Soil ticket received 10 percent more votes in the shoe towns of Massachusetts than it did statewide. In Lowell, Massachusetts, Free Soilers and Democrats combined forces in 1851 to elect a slate of state legislators pledged both to legally restricting the working day and to opposing slavery's extension. That same year, the new Sozialistischer Turnerbund (a large and growing organization dominated by German-born craft workers, small shopkeepers, and professionals then settling in the free states) announced that it "in general subscribes to the principles underlying the radical Free Soil Party and urges all members to support that party in every way possible."

Once again, however, the Free Soil vote understated the strength of antislavery sentiment in the North. Whig newspapers continued to insist that only their party "could rightfully claim the appellation of the Free Soil Party," and many cherished the hope that Zachary Taylor would block the further expansion of slavery. When addressing antislavery Democratic voters, meanwhile, Lewis Cass's backers frequently presented him as a Wilmot man.

Even so, the Free Soil vote of 1848 deprived both major parties of a popular majority. The Democrat, Cass, received only 42.5 percent, taking the electoral votes of Maine and New Hampshire in New England, virtually the entire Midwest, and retaining those of Virginia, Arkansas, Mississippi, Alabama, and South Carolina won in 1844, to which were now added those of Texas. The Whigs won 47.5 percent of the nation's popular votes, in the process picking up a number of states lost to Polk four years earlier—New York and Pennsylvania in the North, Georgia and

Louisiana in the South (as well as Florida, a state since 1845)—while retaining control in Kentucky, Tennessee, and North Carolina.

Once he was in office, Zachary Taylor's conduct gratified some antislavery supporters but embittered much of the South. To avoid yet another divisive congressional debate about territorial slavery, Taylor tried during 1849 to bring both California and New Mexico into the Union as (free) states. In a startling replay of the Harrison–Tyler succession, however, Taylor died suddenly in July 1850, putting his more conservative Vice President, Millard Fillmore of New York, in the White House.

In this setting, Congress decided the status of the Mexican cession in a different way. A series of five resolutions, adopted after a bruising and lengthy debate, made up what became known as the Compromise of 1850. These resolutions explicitly outlawed bondage nowhere in the West. California was simply accepted into the Union as a state (bearing an antislavery constitution of its own device). Neither did Congress directly address the issue of slavery as it organized New Mexico and Utah as territories (although territorial governments in both places later explicitly legalized slavery there). To placate antislavery sentiment, another law prohibited the slave trade (but not slavery itself) in the District of Columbia.

To mollify slave owners, finally, a new fugitive slave bill was adopted. Article IV of the federal constitution already authorized the recapture of fugitive slaves, and an act of February 1793 had specifically empowered an owner or an owner's agent "to seize or arrest such fugitive from labour," bring the latter before a state judge, justify the claim, and then return the fugitive "to the state or territory from which he or she fled." As noted, however, a growing number of northern state legislatures had sought during the 1840s to obstruct this legal procedure with personal liberty laws. The 1850 fugitive slave bill, in turn, was intended to foil that obstructionism. It empowered any marshal pursuing accused runaways in a free state to force free-state citizens to join his posse. It also established a body of special federal commissioners to preside in all such cases (in place of the less dependable local northern judges) and denied jury trials to the accused.

Frederick Douglass believed that the fugitive slave law was "designed to involve the North in complicity with slavery" and thereby "deaden its moral sentiment" against the peculiar institution. More immediately, it was intended to nullify the North's proliferating personal liberty laws and to destroy the so-called Underground Railroad, a network of black and white opponents of slavery that helped runaway slaves flee the South. Its most famous "conductor" was Harriet Tubman, who had escaped from slavery only in 1849. During the next decade, Tubman returned to the South fifteen times, repeatedly risking recapture and summary punishment, to liberate more than two hundred slaves. With (and without) such assistance, the number of successful escapes increased to about a thousand per year by the late antebellum years, especially from those slave states closest to the free North.

The impact of slave flight was far greater than these numbers might suggest. Some fugitives (like Frederick Douglass) became effective antislavery speakers and organizers, their testimonies belying proslavery propaganda and steadily undermining proslavery assumptions in the North. Closer to home, successful escapes by some slaves inspired and emboldened those who remained behind while they reminded masters that there were limits to what even slaves could tolerate. A remarkable field hands' song thus advised:

> Go way, Ole Man,
> Go way, Ole Man
> W'ere you been all day?
> If you treat me good
> I'll stay till Judgment Day,
> But if you treat me bad,
> I'll sho' to run away.

By further undermining the control of upper South masters over their human property, therefore, the threat of escape to the

North added to Deep South fears that the domain of slavery was shrinking. The new fugitive slave law, it was hoped, would reduce the number of future escapes and drive earlier escapees like Douglass, Tubman, Henry Bibb, and Samuel Ringold Ward into hiding. It registered some successes in that regard. Douglass judged that the "chief effect" of the law's passage "was to produce alarm and terror among the class subject to its operation, and this it did most effectually and distressingly." From his home in Rochester, New York, Douglass saw "fugitive slaves who had lived for many years safely and securely in western New York and elsewhere . . . suddenly alarmed and compelled to flee to Canada for safety as from an enemy's land—a doomed city—and take up a dismal march to a new abode, empty-handed, among strangers." Samuel Ringold Ward joined the exodus, "and thousands followed his example." Although Douglass had by this time paid his former master for his freedom, his friends nonetheless urged him to flee. Though he decided to remain, he did so "not without apprehension"—and not without squads of supporters guarding his house by night.

In New York, Boston, Philadelphia, Pittsburgh, Cincinnati, and other northern cities, leading politicians and business figures organized mass meetings in support of the 1850 congressional compromise. Leaders of both major parties congratulated themselves on having finally buried the dangerous slavery issue and thereby rescuing the Union from conflict and division. Millard Fillmore called it "a settlement in principle and substance—a final settlement of the dangerous and exciting subjects which they embraced." "Much . . . may be effected by a conciliatory temper and discreet measures," approved the prominent and wealthy Whig patron Philip Hone. "All praise to the defenders of the Union!" Lewis Cass now declared confidently, "I do not believe any party could now be built in relation to this question of slavery. I think the question is settled in the public mind." Martin Van Buren led his closest followers back into the Democratic party, thereby halving the Free Soil vote in 1852.

A closer look, however, shows national reconciliation to have been far more apparent than real. Passage of the five congressional resolutions in 1850 reflected little deliberate compromise among disputing forces. That is why, in fact, an earlier attempt to pass a single "omnibus" bill through Congress had come to naught; no single, stable, identifiable majority there would support all the five measures it contained. Representatives of the upper North and the lower South showed the least interest in compromise. Breaking the omnibus bill into five separate resolutions was the only way to pass them—on the basis of distinct, constantly shifting majorities.

Nor did the success of these parliamentary maneuvers guarantee sectional peace. Much of the North found the new fugitive slave law unpalatable, and many northern congressmen (Daniel Webster prominent among them) who backed the bill confronted indignant protests from their constituents. So long as slavery seemed geographically contained and remote, free-state residents could despise it without feeling much direct personal involvement in its workings; slavery could thus remain the peculiar institution of the South, not a problem or responsibility of the North. By sending slave hunters into the free states and requiring even antislavery citizens to aid them, however, the new law made such rationalizations impossible.

Here as elsewhere, therefore, the demand for stepped-up federal guarantees for slavery compelled Northerners to confront slavery as a national, not just a sectional, issue. The Baptists of New York objected to being involved "in a business against which their moral sense and their best sympathies revolt with instinctive and unutterable aversion." Ohio's legislature in 1851 declared the fugitive slave law "repugnant to the express provisions of the Constitution," especially the latter's due-process clause. In Boston, Syracuse, Christiana, Pennsylvania, Racine, Wisconsin, and elsewhere, free blacks and antislavery whites forcibly rescued fugitives from their pursuers, in some instances wounding and even killing the slave catchers. More ominous still to the South was the reaction of other Northerners. Local juries refused to convict the immense majority of those indicted for participating in these illegal rescues.

It was against this background that Harriet Beecher Stowe's novel about slavery, fugitive slaves, and slave hunters, *Uncle Tom's Cabin*, appeared. It was originally serialized in the abolitionist *National Era* from mid-1851 through the spring of 1852. Within another year, a bound edition sold 1.2 million copies, making it one of the best-selling novels of its time and surely the most effective piece of antislavery literature ever written. Far from anesthetizing northern antislavery feelings, the new fugitive slave law had helped to inflame them.

Dissatisfaction with Congress's actions also ran deep in the lower South. Political leaders there welcomed the fugitive slave law but were deeply chagrined by Congress's failure explicitly to guarantee slavery in the Utah and New Mexico territories. The admission of the free state of California, moreover, threatened the South's effective legislative veto in the U.S. Senate. James Henry Hammond and Senator Robert Barnwell Rhett of South Carolina urged secession; so did William Lowndes Yancey of Alabama. Governor John Quitman of Mississippi saw "no hope of an effectual remedy for existing and prospective evils but separation from the Northern States."

In the short term, the events of 1850 took their heaviest toll on the national Whig party. Zachary Taylor's conduct and northern Whig opposition to the fugitive slave bill angered southern Whigs and embarrassed them at home. In 1852, the party's national convention polarized along sectional lines; northern delegates backed the presidential candidacy of Winfield Scott (who had ties to free-soil Whigs gathered around New York's William Seward) while Southerners supported Millard Fillmore. Scott finally obtained the nomination, but the convention attempted to mute the intraparty division by adopting a platform that "acquiesced" in the congressional resolutions of 1850.

This latest attempt to satisfy both sides of an increasingly acrimonious dispute accomplished little. Scott's campaign managers, regarding the South as already lost, set out to broaden the Whigs' northern electoral base. Their strategy called for playing down support for the 1850 compromise and courting the big immigrant (including Catholic) electorate of northern towns and cities— precisely those, that is, whom conservative northern Whigs considered a degraded, depraved, and hopelessly Democratic rabble.

In the event, this effort only deepened the crisis of Whiggery. Conservative northern Whigs, including Webster and Fillmore, were incensed; so were southerners like Alexander Stephens and Robert Toombs (both of Georgia). On election day 1852, many such men and their supporters either abstained or cast protest votes, usually for Democratic candidate Franklin Pierce, whose platform lauded states' rights and the 1850 compromise. Only two of the nation's fifteen slave states (upper South Kentucky and Tennessee) gave their electoral votes to Scott, and in the Deep South the Whigs' popular vote plummeted from the 50 percent mark of 1848 to 37 percent in 1852. Many free-soil Whigs, however, were just as disgusted with their party's evasiveness. Franklin Pierce claimed victory with 51 percent of the popular vote.

The advancing disintegration of the national Whig party forced leaders of both its conservative and its free-soil wings to seek a general reorganization of national party politics—to redefine and restructure partisanship along new axes. The Fillmore faction (Webster died in the fall of 1852) dreamed of fusing with centrist Democrats in support of unconditional Unionism, sectional compromise, and maintenance of social order in both sections— and to the exclusion of all other issues. Conscience Whigs (such as Charles Sumner and Henry Wilson of Massachusetts) sought an alliance with other free-soil forces, especially Wilmot Democrats, that could stop and roll back "Slave Power" aggression. Wilson soon decided that "the time has come to dissolve the infamous union of the Whigs of the north and south. If the northern Whigs will now act they can unite with them 160,000 Free Soilers and tens of thousands of Democrats and carry with a rush every Free State."

The plans of both groups were frustrated by the continuing cohesion of the Democratic party. In the immediate afterglow of

Pierce's victory (and the Whig debacle), indeed, Democrats seemed invincible and unprecedentedly solid. "Never since Washington," wrote Massachusetts Cotton Whig Amos Lawrence in early 1853, "has an Administration commenced with the hearty [good] will of so large a portion of the country." This state of affairs was destined to last little more than a year.

In early January 1854, Democratic senator Stephen A. Douglas of Illinois introduced his Nebraska Bill in Congress. Short in stature but big in lung power and influence, the "Little Giant" designed his bill to facilitate the political organization, settlement, and economic development of the Nebraska Territory—a vast region obtained half a century earlier in the Louisiana Purchase but not yet politically organized. Concerning the legal status of slavery there, the bill took a leaf from the Compromise of 1850 and left local voters "perfectly free to regulate their domestic institutions in their own way, subject only to the Constitution of the United States."

This popular-sovereignty formula implicitly superseded the strict geographic limits placed on the northward and westward spread of slavery by the Missouri Compromise. It represented a concession to southern congressmen, who had killed a still earlier version of the bill they had deemed unsound for slavery. But the South's Senate leadership wanted still more. To assure the right of slave owners to enter all territories with their slaves (and finally to annul an agreement that had rankled for decades, and to establish what one writer called "an outpost" for Missouri slavery), southern senators now demanded an explicit revocation of the Missouri Compromise as it pertained to the Nebraska Territory. Douglas acquiesced, and on Monday morning, January 23, he introduced a new bill that satisfied all the South's requirements. It also divided the original territory into two parts, Nebraska in the north and Kansas in the south. Many Northerners presumed that this Kansas Territory, located due east of Missouri, was being carved out specifically for proslavery settlers.

In a Senate speech a week later, Salmon P. Chase warned

Douglas in blunt language of what this new legislation would provoke. "You may pass it here," he granted. "You may send it to the other House. It may become law. But its effect will be to satisfy all thinking men that no compromise[s] with slavery will endure, except so long as they serve the interests of slavery." The resulting conflict would surely redefine and realign party organization. "No great question so thoroughly possesses the public mind as this of slavery," Chase noted. "This discussion will hasten the inevitable reorganization of parties." "It will," he said (employing imagery reminiscent of Solomon Foot's prophecy about Texas/Mexico), "light up a fire in the country which may, perhaps, consume those who kindle it." Douglas scorned the Cassandras. "Gentlemen mistake the people of the North," he replied confidently, "if they think they can be led into any such crusade." "I accept your challenge," he continued; "raise your black flag, call up your forces; preach your war on the Constitution as you have threatened it here. We will be ready to meet all your allied forces."

In the event, it was Chase who proved the more accurate seer. Yes, the bill became law. The Senate passed it on March 3. After a prolonged and stormy debate, the House added its assent by a vote of 113–100 about seven weeks later. (Two-thirds of all northern congressmen opposed the bill, but northern Democrats supported Douglas by a narrow margin.) President Franklin Pierce, who had privately approved the bill in January and later made support for it "a test of Democratic orthodoxy," signed the measure into law on May 30.

But the bill's legislative history proved far less important than its impact on the people of the free states. "Arguments will avail nothing," anti-Nebraska congressman Edwin Morgan had concluded during the House debates. Only a popular mobilization could now hope to stop Buchanan & Co., by instilling in them the fear "that their constituents will be *after* them." Just such a mass movement of public protest now arose. By the time the House passed the bill more than three hundred large anti-Nebraska rallies had occurred.

People from all layers of northern society, holding a spectrum of free-soil views, joined this anti-Nebraska movement. Among them were some of the North's biggest merchants, bankers, and manufacturers. Long advocates of compromise and friendly relations with the slave owners, they now pleaded with southern leaders to reject the bill in order to avoid inflaming the already powerful antislavery sentiment in the North. Boston cotton manufacturer and Whig leader Amos Lawrence begged slave owners to "pause before they proceed further to disturb the peace which we hoped the Compromise of 1850 would have made perpetual." Business and political figures in the manufacturing center of Newark, New Jersey, regretted that the bill threatened to "open anew the whole controversy and conflict between the free and slave-holding states," a polarization "destructive of peace and harmony of the States, dangerous to the interests of the Republic, and causing serious apprehensions for the perpetuity of the Republic." As George Julian of Indiana noted scornfully, many such men "made the sacredness of the bargain of 1820 and the crime of its violation the sole basis of their hostility . . . [and] talked far more eloquently about the duty of keeping covenants, and the wickedness of reviving sectional agitation than [about] the evils of slavery."

At the other end of the political spectrum stood more strongly antislavery-minded forces, both native- and foreign-born. They denounced the Nebraska Bill not (or not only) for endangering national unity but because it "authorizes the further extension of slavery" despite the fact that "we have, do now, and shall continue to protest most emphatically against both white and black slavery." The great body of antiexpansion opinion lay somewhere between these poles. Four states (Connecticut, Rhode Island, Maine, and Michigan) expressed their people's anger against the Nebraska act by ratifying new personal liberty laws; Ohio and Wisconsin later followed suit.

All such protests, Douglas insisted, reflected only ignorance of his bill's true meaning. "The storm will soon spend its fury," he predicted, "and the people of the north will sustain the measure when they come to understand it." They would remember that

Congress had already abandoned the Missouri Compromise formula in admitting the Utah and New Mexico territories in 1850. They would realize, moreover, that popular sovereignty was more democratic (enshrining the principle of local self-government) than a strict geographic line drawn in Washington. In any case, Douglas explained to northern audiences, slavery was effectively excluded from Kansas by inhospitable climate and soil; popular sovereignty would therefore simply ratify the "free soil" verdict of nature. (He thus ignored the fact that slavery already existed in similarly situated and endowed Missouri.) Once the free states grasped the facts, Douglas was sure, the Kansas-Nebraska Act would become "as popular at the North as at the South."

A late-summer speaking tour suggested otherwise. A scheduled speech in New Jersey's capital, Trenton, had been carefully prepared by a group of Democratic party officials and officeholders; a band and procession greeted the Little Giant at the train depot. So, however, did a crowd filled with angry wage earners, organized by shoemaker Charles Skelton, a labor leader and congressman affiliated with Douglas's own party. The Trenton crowd jeered and shouted at the Little Giant until the train finally pulled out of the station to the accompaniment of "a parting salute of groans" (as a newspaper account recorded).

As Douglas arrived in boomtown Chicago on September 1, he had every reason to anticipate a warmer reception. A crowd of 8,000 came to hear him speak. Once again, party functionaries had prepared extensively for the visit, renting a hall in an Irish neighborhood considered safe and (according to Douglas's critics) hiring a group of men to cheer the speaker and discourage hecklers. But extensive precautions proved no more foolproof than they had in New Jersey. The Chicago crowd turned out to be hostile in its large majority. Douglas explained, he promised, he thundered—all in vain. As in Trenton, members of the audience punctuated his speech with hisses, groans, and shouts. Nothing the speaker did could silence them. In the wee hours of the next morning, a frustrated Douglas finally abandoned the effort and denounced his tormentors as he left the podium. "Abolitionists of

Chicago," he raged, according to legend, "it is now Sunday morning. I'll go to church, and you may go to hell." The rest of Douglas's tour brought him more of the same. "I could travel from Boston to Chicago," he would bitterly recall, "by the light of my own [burning] effigy."

The enactment of Douglas's bill in 1854 shifted national attention to Kansas itself. Forces in the free states organized to encourage and help finance settlers opposed to slavery. Proslavery forces centered in Missouri mounted an opposing campaign. Even homesteaders initially more concerned with farm making than politics soon became embroiled in the escalating struggle for control of the territorial government.

By the fall of 1855, the free-state forces enjoyed numerical superiority. Franklin Pierce, however, gave official recognition to a territorial government dominated by proslavery forces—a government, moreover, that decreed the laws of Missouri in force in Kansas as well. Public office and jury service were restricted to those with demonstrable proslavery opinions. Publicly to deny the right to hold slaves became punishable by five years' imprisonment. To assist fugitive slaves risked a ten-year sentence. The penalty for inciting slave rebellion was death.

By year's end Kansas contained two rival governments, one proslavery and one free-soil. On May 21, 1856, proslavery settlers bolstered by additional reinforcements from Missouri invaded the free-state settlement of Lawrence, destroyed its two newspapers, and demolished or looted nearby homes and businesses. This act dramatized a territory-wide conflict in which six free-state partisans had already lost their lives. Developments in Washington the next day further magnified the national impact of this news. On May 22, South Carolina representative Preston S. Brooks strode into the Senate to chastise Charles Sumner for delivering a stinging speech entitled "The Crime Against Kansas." Approaching the seated Sumner, Brooks raised his walking stick and proceeded to beat the Massachusetts senator into bloody unconsciousness. Unaware of that assault but smarting at the attack on nearby Lawrence, John Brown and a small company of antislavery partisans exacted a bloody revenge on May 23 near Pottawatomie Creek, summarily executing five proslavery settlers.

John Brown appears in most standard texts as a solitary, bizarre, even demented individual. And Brown was certainly an atypical man. He was, after all, a religious zealot. But if unusual, Brown was nevertheless very much the product of his time and place, and both his feelings and his actions—religious and political alike—reveal much about the world that produced him. He was born in 1800 (the year of Gabriel Prosser's conspiracy and of Nat Turner's birth) into a family of New England stock that was deeply attached to the country's revolutionary traditions and stirred by the great spiritual excitement of the age. As an adult, Brown made his living as a sheepherder, tanner, and merchant. But he set little store by commercial success for its own sake. "To get a little property together," he once wrote his son, ". . . is really a low mark to be firing at through life." Far more important were personal independence, equal rights, self-government, self-discipline, and self-respect—traditional values of northern small producers, values that Brown identified with authentic Christianity.

Of all society's ills, none enraged Brown in the way that chattel slavery did. Here, surely, was the "sum of all villainies." Brown was not simply a free-soiler but a longtime abolitionist. He found particularly offensive (as one of his associates recalled) "that class of persons whose opposition to slavery was founded on expediency," those who were "desirous that Kansas should be consecrated to free white labor only, not to freedom for all and above all." Like his father before him, John Brown aided fugitive slaves. In 1831, he and his neighbors cheered at the news of Nat Turner's insurrection. In the mid-1850s, five of John Brown's sons moved west to Kansas as free-soil homesteaders. He himself journeyed to Kansas when his sons called on him for aid. There Brown "soon alarmed and disgusted" many in the free-state camp "by asserting the manhood of the Negro race, and expressing his earnest, anti-slavery convictions with a force and vehemence" unusual there.

Recently, a historian of that period once again labeled Brown "a psychopathic ne'er-do-well," approving an earlier writer's dismissal of Brown as one of those who "care nothing for the final result but take advantage of the excitement to commit acts of rapine plunder and murder and then attribute it to one or other of the contending political parties." John Brown looked different to the former slave and abolitionist leader Frederick Douglass. To him, Brown was nothing less than "one of the . . . greatest heroes known to American fame." To Brown himself, the sanguinary action at Pottawatomie was simply the taking of an eye for an eye in a struggle pitting good against evil. Nor was Brown alone in that evaluation of the stakes involved and the means that they justified. By the end of 1856, the struggle for control of Kansas—a territorial civil war that anticipated the larger one yet to come—claimed the lives of some two hundred people.

— 9 —

"Anti Nebraska Feeling Is Too Deep":
Origins and Triumph
of Republicanism

As Salmon Chase had predicted, the Kansas-Nebraska Act and its aftermath sharply accelerated the reorganization of political life in the country. In the congressional and state elections of 1854 and 1855, electoral tickets representing makeshift anti-Nebraska coalitions demonstrated striking popularity. In the 1854 elections to the House of Representatives, more than 70 percent of all northern Democratic incumbents lost their seats. In 1855, every pro-Nebraska candidate who ran for the Senate from a free state went down to defeat. "The Anti Nebraska feeling is too deep," conceded Stephen A. Douglas's Illinois ally James Shields, "more than I thought it was." "To tell you an unwelcome truth," sighed another pro-Douglas Democrat, New York's William Marcy, "the Nebraska question has sadly shattered our party in all the free states."

Committed foes of slavery recognized the Kansas uproar as a turning point and worked to channel the protest forces into the creation of a new, more broad-based antislavery party. The final fruit of their labor, the Republican party, held its national organizing convention in Pittsburgh in February 1856. Four months later in Philadelphia, the new party announced the presidential candidacy of John C. Frémont, who had by then won a national reputation as a western explorer and statesman.

The Republican platform (drafted by a committee chaired by David Wilmot) focused on the issue of slavery and its extension. It denounced the repeal of the Missouri Compromise, the substance and results of the Administration's Kansas policy, and called for the admission of Kansas as a free state. Like the Free Soil party, the Republicans branded slavery "a relic of barbarism," reaffirming "that all men are endowed with the inalienable right to life, liberty, and the pursuit of happiness, and that the primary object and ulterior design of our Federal Government were [sic] to secure these rights to all persons under its exclusive jurisdiction." The party thus endorsed the denationalization-of-slavery premise, which held that the norm, under the Constitution, was freedom; federal power was obliged to acknowledge and defend freedom wherever its writ extended. Congress therefore had the "right and imperative duty . . . to prohibit [slavery] in the Territories." The platform went on, indeed, to deny the right "of Congress, of a Territorial Legislature, of any individual, or association of individuals, to give legal existence to Slavery in any Territory of the United States." These planks made up most of the platform. As a distinct afterthought, it also endorsed "appropriations by Congress for the improvement of rivers and harbors of a national character" and federal aid in the construction of "a railroad to the Pacific Ocean."

The road leading from Kansas-Nebraska in 1854 to Republicanism in 1856 was by no means a straight one. Political nativism constituted the most important detour. It took organizational form in the early 1850s in the American party, more commonly called the Know-Nothing party because membership was secret and members professed ignorance about it. Under the leadership of conservative New York City merchant James W. Barker, the party grew dramatically in 1854. By the beginning of 1855, it reportedly had more than a million members.

The Know-Nothings' voting base proved considerably broader and more heterogeneous than its membership. By the 1850s, people with widely divergent outlooks and major disagreements on a range of issues were ready to blame their various grievances on "alien" influences in American life. Devotees of temperance, Sabbatarianism, and evangelical reform generally—often with Whig backgrounds—despised "infidel and Sabbath-breaking Germans" and denounced the Roman Church for indulging the depravity of the laboring poor generally. Ardent democrats and religious rationalists (native- and foreign-born alike) opposed the same church as a citadel of authoritarian reaction. Northern employers disliked the readiness of too many immigrant workers to join trade unions and strikes. Many native-born workers (including trade unionists) blamed immigration for increasing job competition that enabled bosses to depress wages and working conditions.

A similar pattern emerged on the slavery issue. Antislavery militants blamed immigrant (especially Irish Catholic) voters for propping up a proslavery Democratic party. Defenders of slavery and champions of sectional compromise (including Louisiana Catholics) denounced European-born radicals (especially Germans) for their ignorance of "American institutions and methods" and their consequent disregard for the "rights of the South." More broadly still, planters and their southern allies increasingly resented immigrants, most of whom settled in free states and thereby increased free-state representation in Congress. Even objects of nativist wrath could embrace some parts of the nativist program. In Ohio, antislavery Germans flirted with antislavery nativists who made war on Catholic Democrats. In Boston, the Catholic *Pilot* endorsed a nativist-inspired extension of the naturalization period in order to disenfranchise German-born radicals. In Louisiana, Catholic Creole planters also supported the Know-Nothing party. For a historical moment, thus, the nativist banner could attract a broad range of voters who agreed with one another on very little else.

Nativism's programmatic ambiguity and its heterogeneous appeal helped bring it impressive short-term success at a politically fluid time. In 1854, a coalition of nativist and free-soil candidates swept the Massachusetts state election with almost two-thirds of the vote. Nativists garnered a quarter of the total vote in New York State and two-fifths in Pennsylvania (in the process winning the mayoralty of Philadelphia). The following year brought still more victories—in New England and the middle Atlantic region, in Kentucky, Texas, and elsewhere in the South as well. Some 120 members of the 34th Congress had received the support of the Know-Nothing party.

A party as heterogeneous as the Know-Nothings could remain united and survive only on one condition—that the issues that divided its supporters remained subordinated. Muting the slavery issue, moreover, was a major goal of the party's conservative hardcore leadership. Like conservative New York City merchant Daniel Barnard, they despised the Republicans, who stood only for "eternal hatred and eternal war against the South," and sought instead a new "conservative and national party." Such old (Fillmore) Whigs looked to the Know-Nothing organization (in the words of one of them) as "the only means for preserving a great Union party in opposition to abolition and sectional names." In 1854, accordingly, the Know-Nothings began formally to pledge their candidates for public office "to protect and uphold the Union of these States" and to

> discourage and discountenance any and every attempt, coming from any and every quarter, which you believe to be designed or calculated to destroy or subvert [the Union], or to weaken its bonds; and . . . use your influence, as far as it is in your power, in endeavoring to procure an amicable and equitable adjustment of all political discontents and differences, which may threaten its injury or overthrow. You do further promise and swear (or affirm) that you will not vote for any one to fill any office of honor, profit, or trust of a political character, whom you know or believe to be in favor of a dissolution of the Union of these States, or who is endeavoring to produce that result . . .

The subordination of all else to an amorphous nativist nationalism had proven to be a source of short-term victory. It also proved to be the party's fatal weakness. The fate of the Whig party had already suggested that by the middle 1850s it was no longer possible to straddle the slavery question. As that question, dramatized in Kansas, forced itself ever further to the forefront of the political stage, it destroyed the cohesion of the Know-Nothing party too. The editor of a Democratic newspaper in Pennsylvania accurately foresaw in 1855 that

> there are thousands in the new [Know-Nothing] party throughout the state with whom the anti-slavery sentiment is stronger than all other political purposes, and they will leave the ranks of the K.N.'s for the more congenial fellowship of the antislavery party, which is to be rendered more attractive under the ill-fitting name of *Republican*.

In June 1855, the Know-Nothing party's national council divided into a pro-Nebraska majority rooted in the South and a northern-based anti-Nebraska minority. The majority introduced a set of resolutions demanding enforcement of all existing laws upholding slavery (including the fugitive slave law), denying Congress's right to prohibit slavery in the territories or the District of Columbia, and forbidding discussion of slavery within the Know-Nothing party.

Like the Cotton Whigs before them, Know-Nothing leaders in the North harbored antislavery sentiments markedly less radical and less militant than did the founders of the Republican party. But developments among the northern electorate, coupled with the aggressive stance of the Know-Nothing party's proslavery element, forced their hand. To adopt the majority platform, the minority insisted, would doom Know-Nothingism in the free states. "The American party cannot stand an instant in New England," warned a New Hampshire member, "after its anti-slavery principles are gone." Accordingly, the minority presented what Massachusetts's Henry Wilson called "a moderate but positive antislavery position." It rejected the Kansas-Nebraska Act, sought the reestablishment of the Missouri Compromise line, and endorsed the admission of Kansas and Nebraska as free states. When the party's national council nonetheless approved the pro-Nebraska platform, most northern delegates stormed out of the meeting. An attempt at reunification in February 1856 ended the same way. An outcome feared by Amos Lawrence had been realized—that, through an internal conflict over slavery, "the American party from wh[om] we expected much good, will go to pieces."

The destruction of the national Know-Nothing party did not expunge anti-immigrant and anti-Catholic attitudes (in their various incarnations and meanings) from national politics. It did relegate them to a secondary, rather than a primary, role. The main line of partisan cleavage would now follow the division over the slavery issue.

The rump of the Know-Nothing party nominated Millard Fillmore as its candidate for President of the United States. Though his platform came down hard on the nativist issue, Fillmore's actual campaign laid far greater stress on "the perpetuation of the Federal Union" and "the unequalled recognition and maintenance of the reserved rights of the several states, and the cultivation of harmony and fraternal good-will between the citizens of the several states." The remnant of the Whig party subsequently nominated Fillmore too. The new faction of anti-Nebraska "North Americans" held a convention of its own in June 1856 and there placed the name of Republican presidential nominee John C. Frémont atop its own electoral ticket.

In selecting a presidential candidate in 1856, the Democratic National Convention passed over both Franklin Pierce, the incumbent, and Stephen A. Douglas, the single most powerful Democrat in the North; the calamitous state of affairs in Kansas, it was felt, had compromised the national standing of both of those men. Instead, James Buchanan of Pennsylvania (then ambassador to Great Britain) was chosen to head the ticket. Buchanan's platform pledged him to the Compromise of 1850, popular sovereignty, the Kansas-Nebraska act, antinativism, states' rights and a weak federal government, and opposition to both internal improvements and protective tariffs. The Democratic campaign elaborated on these themes, and the party's candidates presented themselves as guardians of national unity, popular rights, and regional and cultural diversity. By defending the course of compromise, only the Democrats would defend the nation against threats of "civil war and disunion." Popular sovereignty, moreover, was no mere legislative device but the embodiment of a basic principle—that of democratic self-government—and once again demonstrated the Democracy's basic "trust in the intelligence, the patriotism, and the discriminating justice of the American people."

Especially in the North, Democrats strove to depict the contest between themselves and their opponents as one between cultural tolerance and bigotry (against the South, against Catholics, against the foreign-born). Only the Democrats were ready to protect the rights of all white residents, native- and foreign-born alike, and regardless of religious faith. "Let this be made the issue in the Newspapers & in the Legislature & everywhere," Stephen A. Douglas had earlier advised. "That," Douglas assured another correspondent, "will bring the Germans and all other foreigners and Catholics to our side."

Just as it stressed its cultural toleration, the Democratic party presented itself as the true friend of the (white) producing classes. As in the age of Jackson, the party's 1856 platform declared, Democrats were "continuing to resist all monopolies and exclusive legislation for the benefit of the few at the expense of the many" (i.e., tariffs, appropriations for internal improvements). This remained a potent appeal. As a Connecticut politician later noted, there were "mechanics who think they show their independence by voting the ticket dubbed Democratic, to whom a Republican is an old Whig, and an old Whig an Aristocrat who would be glad to go back to the government of George 3rd." Nowhere did Democrats press these themes harder or more effectively than in New York City. In 1855, Democratic mayor Fernando Wood expressed support for the slogan of municipal relief or employment for the jobless; during the downturn of 1857, he translated words into deeds, supervising a substantial expansion of public works projects.

The electoral conflict of 1856 was fiercely fought, and voters rarely remained passive bystanders. A newspaper report from Philadelphia typically counted "ward meetings and mass meetings and committee meetings every day and every night"—indeed, it often seemed, "at every hour in the day and night." When the smoke cleared, James Buchanan and the Democratic party emerged victorious, having received 45 percent of the popular vote nationally and carried every southern state but Maryland and taken Illinois, Indiana, Pennsylvania, California, and New Jersey besides. Fillmore, candidate of conservative Know-Nothings and Whigs, received 22 percent of the popular vote. That support was disproportionately concentrated in the South. While only Maryland gave Fillmore its electoral votes (eight of them), the Know-Nothing–Whig candidate made a strong showing in Alabama, Arkansas, Florida, Kentucky, Louisiana, and Tennessee and carried every one of the South's major urban centers.

But it was northern support for John C. Frémont and his party that cast the longest shadow over the political landscape. Contrary to its opponents' hopes and predictions, the Republican party was evidently here to stay. Despite a brand-new, inexperienced, and often inept organization, Frémont received a full third of the nation's popular vote and 45 percent of all ballots cast in the free states. The Republican ticket took eleven out of sixteen free states. This was a spectacular increase over Van Buren's 1848 tally, indicating that slavery had become the most important question posed in national politics and, therefore, the decisive criterion in determining one's party loyalties. "They feel no differently now than they did at the time of the annexation of Texas," a contemporary observer believed; it had simply "required twelve years following of the south through the bogs before they could make up their minds to quit the [Democratic] fellowship."

Republicans found their firmest support among the same groups upon whom first the Liberty and then the Free Soil party had depended. Commercial farmers, modest entrepreneurs, and skilled workers of smaller urban centers responded to the Republican campaign most readily. Unskilled laborers, however, rarely followed suit. Neither—despite the prominence in Republican circles of western Pennsylvania ironmaster Thaddeus Stevens, Michigan merchant Zachariah Chandler, and former Massachusetts shoemakers Henry Wilson and John B. Alley—did most members of the North's economic elite. True, the Republicans ardently championed the values and economic expansion of the free-labor economy. But, as we have seen, the North's leading merchants had generally taken a more pragmatic attitude toward national politics. "In the old Whig times," observed a discouraged Republican organizer in Philadelphia, "we could go out into Market St. and easily get a few thousand dollars, but now all of our Merchants are trading with the West and South, we can't get a cent, with two or three exceptions." "Nearly all our monied men," he explained, "are for Buchanan or are wasting their powder on Fillmore."

For reasons touched upon in Chapter 2, occupational patterns in voting behavior tended to overlap with ethnic ones. Republicanism was strongest in small-town antislavery New England and sections of the upper Midwest settled by Yankee migrants—western New York State, northern and western Pennsylvania, eastern and northeastern Ohio, and northern Indiana, Illinois, and Iowa. English, Scots, and Welsh voters—who generally fared better than other immigrant groups in the northern economy—also tended to vote for Frémont. Scandinavians settled on small farms in the upper Midwest did so too.

Independent studies of two midwestern cities revealed a substantial number of Irish voting against Buchanan in 1856 (25 percent in Chicago, a majority in St. Louis); this bears further investigation. But the overwhelming majority of the nation's Irish electorate—consigned to unskilled labor, more skeptical of "free labor" propaganda, grateful for the services of urban Democratic machines, fearful both of Republican nativism and of job competition from emancipated slave laborers—stood by Buchanan and the Democrats.

German-American voters were much more divided. Like so many native-born counterparts, the wealthiest immigrants re-

sisted Republican appeals for fear of antagonizing southern planters and encourging social and political ferment generally. Catholic and more conservative Lutheran voters (who were evidently
more numerous in parts of the countryside and among the urban
unskilled) voted Democratic. Republicans most readily attracted
those Germans (especially numerous among freethinking and
Protestant small shopkeepers and craft workers) most deeply influenced by liberal and radical-democratic values and least suscep-
tible to the Democrats' economic and cultural blandishments.

The Republican leadership found little in the election returns
to surprise them. The social profile of their supporters reflected
the party's core principles and message. The Springfield *Republican* observed proudly:

> Those who work with their hands, who live and act independently,
> who hold the stakes of home and family, of farm and workshop, of
> education and freedom—these, as a mass, are enrolled in the re-
> publican ranks . . . They form the very heart of the nation, as op-
> posed to the two extremes of aristocracy and ignorance.

The political polarization revealed in the 1856 campaign and
balloting further stoked the fires of sectional conflict. Planters
were convinced that the furious public debates that raged during
the year had measurably increased the rebelliousness of their human property. Rumors of abortive slave revolts spread across
Texas, Tennessee, Missouri, Kentucky, Arkansas, Virginia, and
Maryland—perhaps because it was there, rather than in the core
of the cotton kingdom, that the system seemed least secure. On
the outskirts of Baltimore during the fall of 1856, a brawl erupted
pitting a large band of whites against another of free blacks. The
blacks carried the day and (according to a local free black newspaper) "gave three cheers for Frémont." A Nashville editor observed that "the recent Presidential canvass has had a deleterious
effect on the slave population. The negroes manifested an unusual interest in the result, and attended the political meetings of
the whites in large numbers. This is dangerous." A Memphis
newspaper recounted the case of the plantation mistress who "a

few days ago went into her kitchen and gave some directions to the negro cook, who replied with a sneer, 'When Frémont's elected, you'll have to sling them pots yourself.'"

This incident captured the larger peril. Republican campaign propaganda evidently stirred the boldest slaves. But so (noted the Memphis paper quoted above) did the alarmed speeches of southern Democrats. "We have seen crowds of negroes at the outskirts of political assemblages in this city, listening attentively" to Democratic speakers warning "that the prospects were very fair for the election of Frémont." All such words "inspire the hope among dissatisfied slaves that with an effort on their own part, they would be free in the event of the success of the most abused candidate." "If this eternal agitation of the slavery question does not cease, we may expect servile insurrections in dead earnest." Indeed, it seemed that not even the Republicans' defeat in 1856 could now assure safety. In Millwood, Virginia, free blacks and slaves accused of plotting a revolt two months after the election confessed that "they had heard white men and negroes talking [that] if Frémont was elected they would be free, and as they knew he was not [elected], they were prepared to fight for it."

The Republicans threatened slavery's stability, of course, because they had demonstrated such impressive strength in the North. That fact also undermined slaveholders' willingness to entrust their fate and the security of their property to the verdict of free-state voters. The planter elite's most consistent champions therefore demanded more and stronger built-in, institutional supports for slavery. Some insisted upon reopening the Atlantic slave trade. More demanded a definite federal slave code that once and for all committed the national government to enforcing and protecting slavery in all the territories. Embittered at the still-expanding northern population, southern politicians also began to sour on immigration as well as homestead legislation. A number of southern congressmen advocated imposing a range of new political restrictions upon the foreign-born. "The whole education of the foreigners and their prejudices when they come to this country," complained Mississippi senator Stephen Adams, "are against the institution of slavery." And a law handing western land over to independent small farmers, exclaimed the Charleston, South Carolina, *Mercury*, would be "the most dangerous abolition bill which has ever been directly passed by Congress" because it would attract to the West even larger numbers of presumably antislavery settlers from Europe and the northern free states.

One facet of the southern reaction revealed itself in a decision handed down in March 1857 by a Supreme Court majority composed of six Democrats, five of them Southerners. The occasion was a lawsuit involving the slave Dred Scott, who claimed that he had become legally free during the 1830s when his master took him out of the slave state of Missouri and into the free state of Illinois and the free territory of Wisconsin before returning southward. With Buchanan's behind-the-scenes encouragement, Chief Justice Roger B. Taney of Maryland (a Jackson appointee) rejected Scott's bid for freedom. Taney (who had been South Carolina's attorney general in the era of its Free Colored Seamen's Act) held that Scott had no rights in federal court because since the republic's foundation blacks had enjoyed "no rights which the white man was bound to respect." Taney then went on to endorse the view associated with John C. Calhoun—that any law restricting the free movement of property, including human property, throughout the territories was unconstitutional. Congress, in Taney's judgment, had thus never had the legal right to limit slavery's expansion, and the Missouri Compromise had been null and void on the day of its formulation.

Deep South Democrats were delighted. A constitutional doctrine previously championed only by a minority was now the law of the land. Most northern Democrats, however, were deeply chagrined. Following Stephen A. Douglas's lead, many had staked their reputations on the twin claims that (1) popular sovereignty was the only democratic way to decide the slavery issue and (2) this formula would, in fact, result in slavery's exclusion from the West. By now denying Congress (and its creatures, the territorial governments) the right to outlaw slavery, the Court was imposing a proslavery construction on Douglas's own doctrine.

Republicans, including party moderates, were infuriated and pointed in alarm to the direction in which the nation was moving.

The Dred Scott ruling seemed the clearest proof yet that champions of slavery meant to impose their views and their hated institution upon all parts and all residents of the United States. "Seventy years ago," noted a Pennsylvania newspaper in 1859, the country had outlawed the transatlantic slave trade and bondage itself in the Old Northwest, "and said to the Slave Trader, 'thus far you may go, but no farther.' This was the Jeffersonian Proviso." But what had transpired since then? the editor asked.

> Thirty years ago they rubbed out part of the line, and said to him, "You may go into the lands of the South, but not into the lands of the North." This was the Missouri Compromise. Five years ago they rubbed out the rest of the line, and said to him, "We leave it to the Settlers to decide whether you shall come in or not." This was the Nebraska Bill. Now they turn humbly to him, hat in hand, and say, "Go where you please; the land is all yours, the National flag shall protect you, and the National Troops shoot down whoever resists you." This is the Dred Scott decision.

How long would it be, asked Abraham Lincoln, before the Court took the next logical step and ruled explicitly that "the Constitution of the United States does not permit a *state* to exclude slavery from its limits?" How far off was the day when "we shall lie down pleasantly dreaming that the people of Missouri are on the verge of making their State free; and we shall awake to the reality, instead, that the Supreme Court has made Illinois a slave State"?

Meanwhile, the struggle over the future of Kansas continued. Early in 1858, President Buchanan called on Congress to admit Kansas as a slave state with a constitution (drafted by the proslavery territorial government at Lecompton) that was never approved by Kansas voters and obviously opposed by a majority of them. Buchanan's policy struck another blow at Douglas's northern political constituency. When the Administration tried to force northern Democrats into line behind "Lecompton," Stephen A. Douglas led the intraparty protest and resistance.

Douglas faced reelection in 1858. Illinois Whigs nominated former congressman Abraham Lincoln to oppose him. For weeks the two men stumped the state, attacking one another's position on the leading questions of the day—Kansas, Lecompton, and Dred Scott. These were the famous Lincoln-Douglas debates. Douglas took an aggressive approach, equating Republicanism with abolitionism and racial equality and invoking the specter of national disunity. Republicans, he told sympathetic downstate audiences, were bent on legislating racial equality and would impose terms on the South that must surely provoke disunion. No, Lincoln replied, he did not believe in and would not endorse full equality, much less social mingling, between white and black. That, he said, is not the substance of the debate. The "real issue" between Douglas and himself—and between the Democratic and Republican parties more generally—was

the sentiment on the part of one class that looks upon the institution of slavery *as a wrong* and of another class that does *not* look upon it as a wrong. The sentiment that contemplates the institution of slavery in this country as a wrong is the sentiment of the Republican party. It is the sentiment around which all their actions—all their arguments—circle, from which all their propositions radiate. They look upon it as being a moral, social and political wrong.

Senator Douglas repeatedly insisted that he did "not care" whether the exercise of popular sovereignty resulted in slavery's exclusion or consecration in the territories, Lincoln argued, because Douglas "looks to no end of the institution of slavery." The Republicans, on the other hand, were determined to take slavery and "place it . . . in the course of its ultimate extinction."

Douglas, in turn, denied that his party or his doctrines championed the spread of slavery. Those anxious to keep the territories free, he insisted, had no need for the draconian federal measures that Lincoln and the Republicans demanded. Popular sovereignty, fairly administered, would effectively exclude slavery from the West. Nor did the Dred Scott decision (which Douglas claimed to accept) remove that power, since if the people of a Territory want slavery, they will encourage it by passing affirmatory laws, and the necessary police regulations, patrol laws, and slave code; if they do not want it they will withhold that legislation, and by withholding it, slavery is dead as if it were prohibited by a constitutional prohibition, especially if, in addition, their legislation is unfriendly, as it would be if they were opposed to it.

Enunciated repeatedly, this position attracted most attention when presented before an audience in Freeport, Illinois; thereafter it was known as Douglas's "Freeport Doctrine."

These debates cast into sharp relief Douglas's differences with the Republican party as well as with explicitly proslavery Democrats. The Little Giant retained his Senate seat in 1858. But the whole affair deepened Douglas's isolation from the southern wing of his own party. Planters and their advocates now turned on the Little Giant with even greater fury than they had against another erstwhile northern ally, Martin Van Buren. Pro-Douglas and pro-Buchanan Democrats openly warred on one another for the next two years; an unacknowledged but very real split had in fact taken place. A leading organ of the party's northern wing now concluded that "upon no single issue is there adequate agreement for a common basis of action" among Democrats. "There is no such entity as a Democratic party."

Douglas's struggle to placate northern voters in 1857–58 hastened southern Democratic flight from the doctrine of popular sovereignty. That formula, declared Mississippi senator Jefferson Davis, had proved "a siren's song . . . a thing shadowy and fleeting, changing its color as often as the chameleon." Similar sentiments were heard even from previously moderate representatives of the upper South. Virginia's James Mason had supported the Kansas-Nebraska Act in 1854; he, like Davis, now considered himself betrayed. "You promised us bread," he accused Douglas, "and you have given us a stone; you promised us a fish, and you have given us a serpent; we thought you had given us a substantial right; and you have given us the most evanescent shadow and delusion."

For a growing number of the Deep South's leaders, Calhoun's demand for the "nationalization of slavery" now became a condition of continued national unity. In February 1859, for example, Mississippi senator Albert Gallatin Brown demanded guarantees over and above "the mere naked Constitution"—"*adequate* protection, *sufficient* protection . . . suited to the nature and description of property to be protected." This, he indicated, would constitute the South's platform in 1860. If the electorate rejected it, then "the Constitution is a failure . . . the Union a despotism . . . [and] I am prepared to retire from the concern."

Frémont, "Bleeding Kansas," Dred Scott, Lecompton—here was the background against which John Brown and about twenty associates, black and white, slave and free, launched their October 1859 raid on the federal arsenal in Harpers Ferry, Virginia. They evidently planned to seize the arms stored there, liberate nearby slaves, and then withdraw into the Allegheny Mountains and from there encourage, assist, and defend additional escapes and insurrections. Within twenty-four hours, however, U.S. marines under the command of Colonel Robert E. Lee and Lieutenant J. E. B. Stuart had surrounded the insurgents, raked them with rifle fire, and finally captured most of the survivors. Brown himself, severely wounded, was swiftly tried, convicted, sentenced to death, and hanged by the state of Virginia. Six captured associates shared his fate.

Though unsuccessful, the Harpers Ferry raid rocked the nation to its foundations. Northern Democrats and southern whites generally cited it as the inevitable result of Republican antislavery rhetoric. Some deduced the need for still firmer proslavery safeguards. Others, laying the groundwork for secession, called Brown's raid a warning of what a future within the Union held in store. Northern conservatives and some moderates responded by categorically repudiating Brown and all his works. Twenty thousand New York City merchants rushed in a single week to sign a call for a public meeting designed to reassure the South of their good intentions. At similar meetings in the past, conciliators had coupled appeals for national calm and compromise with intimations of personal distaste for slavery. Now, however, even these asides disappeared, replaced by declarations that slavery was in fact "just, wise, and beneficent," "ordained by nature," and "a necessity of both races."

But many antislavery radicals and even some moderate Republicans rejected Brown's means while honoring his antislavery principles and commitment. Church bells throughout the North pealed in mourning when Brown was hanged. The leading organ of German-American labor called Brown and his comrades "martyrs for freedom." In Cincinnati, '48er labor leader and journalist August Willich told an audience of black and German listeners "to whet their sabers and nerve their arms for the day of retribution, when Slavery and Democracy [the Democrats] would be crushed in a common grave." (An unsympathetic reporter was shocked to observe that Willich's words "received the rapturous applause of the motley gathering.") Frederick Douglass called the Brown raid a "desperate but sublimely disinterested effort to emancipate the slaves of Maryland and Virginia from their cruel taskmasters," and in its aftermath wrote:

> Men who live by robbing their fellow-men of their labor and liberty . . . have by the single act of slaveholding voluntarily placed themselves beyond the laws of justice and honor, and have become only fitted for companionship with thieves and pirates—the common enemies of God and of all mankind. While it shall be considered right to protect one's self against thieves, burglars, robbers, and assassins, and to slay a wild beast in the act of devouring his human prey, it can never be wrong for the imbruted and whip-scarred slaves, or their friends, to hunt, harass, and even strike down the traffickers in human flesh.

Awaiting execution, Brown received an eloquent letter from a black woman living in Indiana. "In the name of the young girl sold from the warm clasp of a mother's arms to the clutches of a libertine or a profligate," she wrote, "in the name of the slave mother, her heart rocked to and fro by the agony of her mournful separations, I thank you, that you have been brave enough to reach out your hands to the crushed and blighted of my race."

> You have rocked the bloody Bastille; and I hope that from your sad fate great good may arise to the cause of freedom . . . God writes national judgments upon national sins; and what may be slumbering in the storehouse of divine justice we do not know. We may earnestly hope that your fate will not be a vain lesson, that it will intensify our hatred of Slavery and love of freedom, and that your martyr grave will be a sacred altar upon which men will record their vows of undying hatred to that system which tramples on man and bids defiance to God.

The Democratic party held its national convention just six months after the Harpers Ferry raid—in April 1860, in Charleston, South Carolina. There southern delegates demanded a promise of federal protection of slavery in all the territories and a de facto veto in the selection of the party's presidential candidate (in order to block Stephen A. Douglas's anticipated nomination). When northern delegates rejected that ultimatum, Southerners bolted.

Both Democratic factions subsequently reconvened elsewhere—the northern-based majority in Baltimore, the southern-based minority in Richmond. The Baltimore convention reaffirmed the core of the national party's 1856 (Cincinnati) platform, to which were added pledges to enforce the fugitive slave law, respect the Dred Scott decision, and seek "the acquisition of the Island of Cuba." Stephen A. Douglas received the presidential nomination. (Senator Benjamin Fitzpatrick of Alabama first accepted and later rejected the vice presidential nomination, which ultimately went to Herschel V. Johnson of Georgia.) The Richmond convention adopted the platform presented by the Charleston minority and fielded a national electoral ticket headed by Kentucky's John C. Breckinridge (Buchanan's Vice President) and Oregon's Joseph Lane. The Democrats had finally succumbed to the same fate that had successively befallen the major evangelical Protestant denominations, the Whigs, and then the Know-Nothings.

Stephen A. Douglas refused to accept defeat, struggling in 1860 to challenge Breckinridge for the loyalty of the South and Lincoln for that of the North. "We must make war boldly against the Northern abolitionists and the Southern Disunionists, and give no quarter to either," he wrote a close ally that June. "We should treat the Bell & Everett men friendly and cultivate good relations with them, for they are Union men."

Douglas's last remark referred to the new Constitutional Union party, created in 1860 from conservative Whig and Know-Nothing fragments. Claiming that party platforms "have had the effect to mislead and deceive the people, and at the same time to widen the political divisions of the country," this new party declined to adopt one. Here was implicit acknowledgment that virtually any program of substance and clarity had become incompatible with national harmony and unity. The Constitutional Unionists contented themselves with a promise "to recognize no political principle other than the Constitution of the Country, the Union of the States, and the Enforcement of the Laws." Of course, that declaration ignored the fact that by 1860 the very nature and meaning of the Constitution, the Union, and the laws had themselves become highly controversial. On such shaky premises did John Bell of Tennessee and Edward Everett of Massachusetts, respectively, attempt to conduct presidential and vice presidential campaigns.

Stephen A. Douglas predicted that Breckinridge would win two states at most (the Deep South states of South Carolina and Mississippi). Bell and Everett, he thought, would take six border and upper South states (Kentucky, Tennessee, Delaware, Maryland, Virginia, and North Carolina). "We [northern Democrats]," Douglas wrote, "shall probably carry Missouri, Arkansas, Louisiana, Texas, Alabama & Georgia in the South, and hope to get enough more in the free States to be elected by the people."

Internal struggle also beset the Republicans as they prepared for their 1860 national convention. In the eyes of the party's more conservative elements, the elections of 1856 had demonstrated the urgency of winning the confidence (and votes) of middle-of-the-road Democratic, Whig, and Know-Nothing voters—especially in the populous states of Illinois, Indiana, Pennsylvania, and New Jersey, all of which (along with California) had been lost to Buchanan. This goal seemed to dictate, among other things, proving the party's nativist credentials. (Massachusetts Republicans helped to do so by pushing through an amendment to their state's constitution that barred immigrants from voting for an additional two years following the five-year federal naturalization period.) At the party's 1860 national convention, conservatives sought to give the presidential nomination to a figure identified with Know-Nothingism, such as Nathaniel P. Banks of Massachusetts or Edward Bates of Missouri.

Conservatives also argued that increasing the Republican vote necessitated a softening of the party's stand on slavery—specifically by welcoming genuine supporters of "popular sovereignty" who resented southern attempts to legalize slavery throughout the territories by fiat. The falling-out between Douglas and Buchanan Democrats, such men believed, offered a heaven-sent opportunity to redraw party boundaries to the Administration's disadvantage. When Buchanan in 1858 opposed Douglas's reelection to the Senate from Illinois, some leading East Coast Republicans called on their midwestern counterparts to throw their support behind the Little Giant. The debacle at Harpers Ferry the next year made it all the more necessary, argued Republican conservatives, to distance the national party from abolitionist "fanaticism."

Other Republicans rejected this conciliatory course, insisting instead that the key to the party's previous success and future gains lay in adherence to a clear and firm position against slavery and its expansion. They wished to retain the strong antislavery language of the 1856 Philadelphia platform and add a promise to repeal the fugitive slave law. They rejected nativist legislation out of a distinct combination of principle and pragmatism. Proscription based on birth and creed, they held, ran directly counter to the Republicans' basic philosophy. And antislavery immigrant (especially German) voters must be convincingly assured of the Republican party's welcome and friendship.

These struggles reached a climax at the 1860 Republican national convention in Chicago. Attempts to dilute the party's anti-slavery stand failed. An implicit condemnation of Harpers Ferry placed in the platform was worded broadly enough to apply also to Missouri "border ruffians" in Kansas. The 1856 endorsement of the Declaration of Independence and its egalitarian doctrines was pointedly repeated; the Dred Scott decision was firmly rejected, as was the Lecompton constitution. The 1860 platform again declared slavery unconstitutional throughout the territories and demanded that Kansas be admitted to the Union as a free state. Concerning the foreign-born, the Republicans supplemented their 1856 equivocations with a flat commitment to oppose "any change in our naturalization laws or any state legislation by which the rights of citizens hitherto accorded to immigrants from foreign lands shall be abridged or impaired." To its original, spare economic program, the party now added an endorsement of tariffs that would protect "the industrial interests of the whole country." It also appealed to land-hungry farmers and workers, native- and foreign-born alike, by demanding passage of the homestead bill then bogged down in the Senate.

The final decision confronting the delegates was the candidate. Salmon P. Chase, abolitionist and former Liberty party leader, was passed over as too radical to win over undecided voters. Both Bates and Banks were rejected as too prone to compromise on the essential issue of free soil and too offensive to foreign-born voters. New York's William Seward suffered from a too radical reputation and a too conservative record. Seward was also anathema to nativists, with whom he had repeatedly clashed in the New York Whig party. Seemingly by default, then, the convention finally settled on Abraham Lincoln; Hannibal Hamlin, an ex-Democrat from Maine, completed the ticket.

In fact, Lincoln proved a strong representative of the party's principles and well suited to address its potential constituency. A middle-of-the-road former Whig, Lincoln was neither radical nor conservative on the slavery issue; fittingly, he was neither one of the party's founders nor one of its Johnny-come-latelies. He was known to oppose nativism. "How can any one who abhors the oppression of negroes, be in favor of degrading classes of white people," he had asked years earlier. In Illinois, Lincoln had earned a modest but definite national reputation as a battler for free soil against the Republicans' chief rival for northern voters— Stephen A. Douglas. Of humble, southern, smallholder origins (his family had migrated out of Kentucky and through Indiana before settling in Illinois), Lincoln responded to a request for biographical detail in 1860 by quipping, "It can all be condensed into a simple sentence . . . 'The short and simple annals of the poor.'"

A good deal of Lincoln's attraction lay precisely here—in the perception that (like Andrew Jackson) this "Great Commoner" had raised himself up out of poverty by his own disciplined efforts, passed through the widest range of jobs under the longest list of employers, and eventually transformed himself into a prosperous and respectable man—an attorney, a state legislator, a congressman, and now a presidential candidate. Lincoln was a zealous and effective apostle of the right of personal advancement. "There is no *permanent* class of hired laborers among us," Lincoln said of northern society during the campaign. "Twenty-five years ago, I was a hired laborer. The hired laborer of yesterday labors on his own account today, and will hire others to labor for him tomorrow. Advancement—improvement in condition—is the order of things in a society of equals." Such opportunity, he insisted, would remain so long as the free-labor system was permitted to grow unimpeded—unimpeded, for example, by the economic obstacle of slave labor in the West and slave-owner domination of the government in Washington. The economic policies that he had supported since his earliest days in Illinois politics—and which were now enshrined in the 1860 Republican platform— were those he deemed most conducive to free-labor development and individual opportunity.

Lincoln delivered some of his most powerful remarks on these themes during a major labor conflict that gripped the city of Lynn, Massachusetts, the unchallenged national center of shoe

manufacturing. Declining wages, repeated layoffs, and the dis-
ruptions caused by the sewing machine's introduction sparked,
early in 1860, the largest strike the country had yet seen. More
than 20,000 men and women—more than a third of all shoe
workers in the state—participated. The strikers identified their
cause with the defense of individual dignity and independence,
calling on other shoe workers to "sink not to the state of the slave."
Women shoe workers paraded through the streets of Lynn on
March 7 carrying a banner that warned, "American ladies will not
be slaves!"

One day prior to that demonstration, Abraham Lincoln—not
yet a declared candidate for the Republican nomination—found
himself on a speaking tour nearby, in New Haven, Connecticut.
Southern planters and their advocates and allies were already citing the strikers' grievances as proof that "manufacturers all over
the world keep their laborers as near the starvation point as circumstances and the efficient operation of their factories will allow," while slave owners maintained their chattels in "comfort
and good treatment."

These issues were animatedly discussed and debated among the
striking shoe workers too. A reporter for the New York *Tribune*
overheard one such exchange. "What is the use," asked one shoe
worker, "of our making such a fuss about the slaves of the South?
I tell you we are almost as oppressed as they are. In fact, in one
sense we are worse oppressed, for they don't work so many hours
in the week as we do; and they get a living: while most of us
couldn't live, with our families, if we couldn't get trusted for the
necessaries of life [by the grocer], which we never expect to be
able to pay for at this rate." To which a second responded, "We
are worse treated than the slaves of the South, in every sense, so
far as I can see." A third striker, however, demurred. "You know,
gentlemen, we are not a quarter as bad off as the slaves of the
South, though we are, by our —— [sic: the editor has obviously
deleted an expletive] foolishness, ten times as bad off as we ought
to be. They can't vote, nor complain, and we can. And then just
think of it; the slaves can't hold mass meetings, nor 'strike,' and
we haven't lost that privilege yet, thank the Lord." According to

the *Tribune* reporter, this observation evoked loud cheers from a circle of listeners. "That's so," agreed the speaker who had begun the exchange, "but what'll those privileges amount to if they come to nothing?"

In his New Haven speech, Abraham Lincoln addressed precisely this point by contrasting the rights and opportunities of free workers with the enforced immobility of the slaves. "At the outset," he began, "I am glad to see that a system prevails in New England under which laborers can strike when they want to, where they are not obliged to work under all circumstances, and are not tied down and obliged to labor whether you pay them or not!" These words provided a springboard into Lincoln's by now familiar discussion of individual opportunity. And part and parcel of this right, he continued, was the right to move westward onto free soil:

> I desire [he said] that if you get too thick here, and find it hard to better your condition on this soil, [that] you may have a chance to strike and go somewhere else, where you may not be degraded, nor have your family corrupted by forced rivalry with negro slaves.

Lincoln's listeners that day responded to his words with prolonged applause. More instructive were subsequent developments in Lynn. Within a few weeks the shoe strike centered there was defeated. The economic and political power of the shoe bosses was simply too great for the strikers. The level of bitterness between employer and employee palpably increased, revealing itself, for example, in elections that fall for local public office. The shoe workers refused to vote for any candidate nominated by the city's Republican organization, which was very much controlled by the shoe bosses. They voted, instead, for the independent Working Men's party of Lynn.

But Abraham Lincoln's larger message—that whatever their grievances, northern workers' hopes and aspirations required defending the liberties they had already won against the threat of the "slave power"—was evidently taken to heart. The shoe workers of

Lynn gave decisive majorities to Republican candidates running for state office and to the slate of Republican electors committed to Abraham Lincoln.

Americans everywhere—North and South, men and women, slave and free—followed and took an active part in the four-way campaign of 1860. Issues, platforms, speeches, and candidates were reviewed and debated in corn fields and cotton fields, workshops and markets, family gatherings, churches, picnics, races, sewing circles, schoolhouses, slave quarters, taverns and beer gardens. It was plain to everyone that the outcome would determine the course of the nation's history for years to come. In much of the country, voter participation matched or exceeded previous records.

The final returns represented a stunning verdict, not only on the contending parties and candidates but, even more fundamentally, on further attempts to suppress differences over slavery in the interests of national compromise and unity. Stephen A. Douglas and his party received 29 percent of the popular vote nationally. In the North, a majority of voters supported Douglas only in New Jersey; of the slave states, only Missouri gave Douglas a popular plurality and all its electoral votes. The Constitutional Unionists claimed only 13 percent of the popular vote nationally (compared with Fillmore's 22 percent in 1856). Though they attracted most of the South's small urban vote, and displayed considerable strength throughout the upper South, Bell and Everett won popular majorities in only three (Kentucky, Tennessee, and Virginia) of the six states that Douglas thought would support them.

Together, then, the parties committed to compromise above all else received but 42 percent of all ballots cast nationwide, most of them concentrated in the lower North and upper South. Even this may overstate conciliationist sentiment, since a good many northern voters apparently stood by Douglas only because of his much-publicized opposition to the Lecompton constitution and other aspects of Buchanan's proslavery policy. More than one of

Douglas's southern campaigners, meanwhile, did his best to garner support among proslavery fire-eaters.

What is certain is that a big majority of voters in 1860—58 percent—rejected calls to further compromise and rallied instead to the most directly counterposed political standards and to the language of confrontation. Breckinridge's southern Democrats swept the slave-state countryside, even in Delaware and Maryland. In the process they rolled up 18 percent of all ballots cast nationally. The free states went heavily to Breckinridge's most consistent opponent, giving Lincoln 54 percent of all their ballots (equal to 40 percent of the popular vote nationally). Without making any important concessions to party conservatives and nativists, the party captured four of the five states lost to the Democrats in 1856. The Republican share of the vote jumped between 1856 and 1860 from 19 to 32 percent in California, from 40 to 51 percent in both Illinois and Indiana, and from 32 to 56 percent in Pennsylvania. Even in New Jersey, whose electoral votes Lincoln split with Douglas, the Republican total increased impressively, from 28 to 48 percent. In New York, Pennsylvania, and Rhode Island, anti-Republican fusion tickets failed to deprive Lincoln of his popular or electoral majorities.

As finally processed through the electoral college, Lincoln's popular-vote plurality became an outright majority. In just its second effort, the Republican party had elected a President of the United States.

It was a fateful victory. In its aftermath, more and more Southerners who had willingly—enthusiastically—backed Douglas or Bell in order to preserve the Union moved toward proslavery fire-eaters pressing the course of secession. Mobile, Alabama, editor John Forsyth, a Douglas supporter in 1860, now wrote the Little Giant that "with your defeat, the cause of the Union was lost." Forsyth preferred a war to being "stripped of 25 hundred millions of slave property & to have turned loose among us 4,000,000 of freed blacks." Similar messages reached Douglas's desk from North Carolina, Tennessee, Georgia, Louisiana, and elsewhere. "No compromise on earth," concluded one correspondent, "can ever unite the cotton states with the old Union."

— 10 —

"The Inexorable Logic of Events": Secession, War, and Emancipation

On December 20, 1860, little more than a month following Lincoln's election, a special convention elected by South Carolina voters resolved unanimously to take that state out of the federal Union. In the early weeks of 1861, six other lower South states—Mississippi, Florida, Alabama, Georgia, Louisiana, and Texas—followed that lead. In February, their representatives met in Montgomery, Alabama, to form a new southern federation, constitute themselves as a temporary Confederate Congress, adopt a provisional constitution, and elect a President. They chose Jefferson Davis of Mississippi, a planter, former U.S. congressman and senator, and Secretary of War under Franklin Pierce.

Eight slave states held back but warned that they would remain in the federal Union only if their more southerly neighbors were allowed to withdraw. In January, Robert M. T. Hunter of Virginia presented the U.S. Senate with additional conditions in the name of the upper South. These included a radical revision of the federal constitution to permanently ensure equal northern and southern control over both the presidency and the Supreme Court. When Republican leaders refused to eviscerate the Constitution or to permit others to dismember the Union, Virginia, North Carolina, Arkansas, and Tennessee joined the Confederacy.

The political crisis that finally precipitated Lincoln's election, secession, and then war had been many years in the making. By 1860, most northern voters had decided that only an explicitly antislavery party could protect their interests. That decision, in turn, convinced southern leaders that their position within the Union was untenable. Encouraged and assisted by a Republican federal government, they concluded, treacherous southern whites (in the upper South, the hill country, and towns and cities) would join with southern blacks, free and slave, to subvert the peculiar institution and the whole civilization that it supported. To avoid that outcome, leading planters gambled. They gambled that withdrawal from the old Union would secure their way of life once and for all. When secession yielded war, southern leaders gambled that they could gain on the battlefield a victory that had eluded them at the ballot box.

Instead, the Civil War hastened the destruction of the antebellum South. Some thirty years earlier, David Walker had written that while slave rebellions might not bring about "the destruction of the oppressors . . . yet the Lord our God will bring other destructions upon them—for not infrequently will he cause them to rise up against one another, to be split and divided, and to oppress each other, and sometimes to open hostilities with sword in hand." In fact, the Civil War combined both alternatives. Secession and the South's resort to arms "split and divided" the country as nothing else could. The war itself created the necessity (from the standpoint of the North) and the opportunity (from the standpoint of African-Americans) for blacks to act decisively and in great numbers in their own behalf. That same war, meanwhile, imposed unequal and mounting burdens on the majority of southern whites who owned no slaves. Many ultimately concluded that the cost of a last-ditch defense of slavery had far exceeded the benefits of unconditional white solidarity.

The coming of the Civil War would later be explained in a variety of ways. Some blamed human frailties; denying that there were sufficient real grounds for such a conflict, they stressed paranoia, impulsiveness, miscalculation, overreaction, venality, and demagogic rhetoric. "One extreme naturally begets another,"

James Buchanan sighed in 1866. "It would be difficult to determine which of the opposing parties was guilty of the greatest ex-
cess." On the side of antislavery forces, he wrote, "every epithet
was employed calculated to arouse the indignation of the Southern people. . . . Among the latter there sprung up a party as fa-
natical in advocating slavery as were the abolitionists of the North
in denouncing it." Before long matters were out of control: "Fanaticism never stops to reason."

Others attributed secession and war to a clash of regional cultures and ambitions. Twenty years after the fact, Jefferson Davis
flatly asserted that "African servitude was in no wise the cause of
the conflict, but only an incident." The actual cause, he wrote in
1881, was to be found in "sectional rivalry and political ambition," which "would have manifested itself just as certainly if slavery had existed in all the States, or if there had not been a negro
in America." Still other observers traced the war to a clash between two schools of constitutional interpretation. Looking back
on the Civil War, Alexander Stephens called it "a strife between
the principles of Federation, on one side, and Centralism, or
Consolidation, on the other. Slavery, so called, was but the question on which these antagonistic principles, which had been in
conflict from the beginning on diverse other questions, were finally brought into actual and active collision with each other on
the field of battle."

In 1860–61, however, leading planters explained secession
very differently, employing arguments that placed slavery, its justification, and its practical defense at the heart of the matter. In
1860, South Carolina's "Declaration of Causes" did defend secession on legal-constitutional grounds: Because "fourteen of the
States have deliberately refused for years past to fulfill their constitutional obligations . . . South Carolina is released from her
obligation." Precisely how, though, had the northern states broken the covenant? They had "assumed the right of deciding upon
the rights of property established in fifteen of the States and recognized by the Constitution; they have denounced as sinful the
institution of Slavery; they have permitted the open establishment
among them of societies, whose avowed object is to disturb the

peace and eloin [carry off] the property of the citizens of other States. They have encouraged and assisted thousands of our slaves to leave their homes; and those who remain have been incited by emissaries, books, and pictures, to servile insurrection."

In February 1861, Alexander Stephens became Vice President of the new Confederacy. In March, he stressed the relationship between slavery and secession with particular frankness. It had taken the formation of the Confederacy, Stephens explained, finally to "put at rest forever all the agitating questions [concerning] . . . the proper status of the negro in our form of civilization." Indeed, Stephens added, warming to his discussion of "our new government,"

> its foundations are laid, its cornerstone rests, upon the great truth that the negro is not equal to the white man, that slavery—subordination to the superior race—is his natural and normal condition. This our new government is the first in the history of the world based upon this great physical, philosophical, and moral truth.

The Deep South planters who spearheaded secession believed that Lincoln's victory challenged "the proper status of the negro in our form of civilization." On the surface, their fears may seem exaggerated. They certainly did to Stephen A. Douglas, who urged his own evaluation on the South in late 1860. Democrats still controlled both Congress and the Supreme Court, he pointed out, leaving Lincoln "tied hand and foot, powerless for good or evil." How could there, then, be "sufficient cause for destroying the best government of which the history of the world gives an example?"

The new President was also at pains to reassure the slave owners. "Do the people of the South really entertain fears that a Republican administration would, *directly* or *indirectly*, interfere with their slaves, or with them, about their slaves?" Lincoln asked in a letter to Alexander Stephens on December 22, 1860. "If they do, I wish to assure you, as once a friend, and still, I hope, not an enemy, that there is no cause for such fears. The South would be in no more danger in this respect, than it was in the days of Washington." Had Lincoln, in fact, not built up a record over the years of carefully observing the constitutional limits imposed on antislavery action? In his very first statement of principled opposition to slavery—voiced in the Illinois legislature in the 1830s—had he not simultaneously denounced abolitionism in equally strong terms? In the first months of 1861, Lincoln approved a constitutional amendment proposed by Ohio's Thomas Corwin that would explicitly bar Congress from ever interfering with slavery within the states. Both the House and the Senate gave it their requisite two-thirds approval.

Other Northerners also made last-ditch efforts to conciliate the planters. Prominent in this endeavor were key sections of the economic elite who feared alienating the slave owners more than they disliked slavery—especially merchants, bankers, and manufacturers who had strong connections with the South. Led or initiated by such businessmen, large compromise meetings occurred in New York, Boston, Philadelphia, and in hundreds of other locales. A contemporary reported that pro-compromise leaders were generally "men who are well to do worldly speaking . . . usually found in warm parlors . . . for good feeding . . . sleek and comfortable. I notice that they pay great attention to the prices of stock." Boston merchant John Murray Forbes reported that " 'club men' who live by wine, cards, tobacco and billiards . . . gravitate very strongly to secesh sympathies." Firmer Unionist principles, he added, could be found only among "the hard-handed people of the country." The conciliationist impulse crossed ethnic lines. The era's most powerful German-born Democrat was financier August Belmont, whom Stephen A. Douglas had made chairman of the northern Democratic party in 1860. Following Lincoln's election, Belmont orchestrated much of the upper-class clamor for concessions to forestall secession.

In the most elaborate compromise scheme put forward in the early months of 1861, Senator John J. Crittenden of Kentucky proposed a series of constitutional amendments that would outlaw slavery above the 36°30′ line while recognizing and protecting it in all territories "now held, or hereafter acquired" to the south. (This had been the sine qua non of Breckinridge's candidacy in 1860.) Other amendments that Crittenden proposed would have prohibited Congress from abolishing slavery in the District of Columbia or interfering with the internal slave trade, and provided compensation for any master prevented from recovering escaped slaves in the North. All these amendments were to be unrepealable, permanently in force, once ratified.

Though Crittenden's proposals contradicted popular sovereignty, Stephen A. Douglas vigorously endorsed them, echoing the single note sounded in the Bell-Everett campaign of 1860. "Better that all party platforms be scattered to the winds," Douglas declared on the floor of the U.S. Senate; "better that all political organizations be broken up; better that every public man and politician in America be consigned to political martyrdom than that the Union be destroyed and the country plunged into civil war." And Lincoln's own Secretary of State, New York's William Seward, joined the conciliationist chorus. "Away with all parties, all platforms, all previous committals," he said in offering a toast at a January 24 dinner party given by Douglas, "and whatever else will stand in the way of restoration of the American Union."

Other Republicans resisted. Horace Greeley's New York *Tribune* cautioned Congress that "the cotton loving merchants and manufacturers in our cities," who were always ready to "eat a little dirt for the sake of slavery," didn't represent the sentiment of the people. Listen instead, Greeley advised, to "the men who fill the workshops and till the farms, and work the quarries of the mines . . . In this large class there is *no* timidity and hesitation."

Greeley exaggerated. Many working people joined with industrialists and merchants in supporting the calls for compromise. On February 22, for example, a group of trade unionists from eight states met in Philadelphia to denounce both the secessionist "disorganizing traitors" and antislavery "congressional extremists." They then endorsed the Crittenden formula as the alternative to civil war and the destruction of "the best form of government ever instituted by man."

But other northern working people drew different conclusions from the country's democratic traditions. In the early months of 1861, rank-and-file Republicans filled newspaper columns and congressional mailboxes with letters and petitions demanding firm adherence to their party's free-soil principles. "Artful politicians—rich merchants and speculators, whose god is money, will counsel peace, regardless of principle," said a representative letter. "See that you yield not to their solicitations." When Illinois Republican congressman William Kellogg delivered a pro-compromise speech in early February, a convention of his constituents repudiated him. The compromise efforts of Ohio senator Thomas Corwin provoked a similar reaction. When Pennsylvania's Republican senator Simon Cameron declared his friendliness toward compromise, an editor of the Pittsburgh *Gazette* wrote him personally about the reaction in that industrial city:

> I find upon my return home, that the public mind is so inflamed against Compromise and so bitter against all efforts at concession, that my colleagues thought it most prudent to enter their dissent [against your statement] in today's paper . . . Those who are familiar only with the public sentiment at . . . Philadelphia, New York, and Washington can have no idea of the fierceness of the sentiment here in opposition to anything that looks like Compromise. It amounts almost to a fury.

One Massachusetts textile magnate confessed to Senator Crittenden in January that "if the Government should call for enlistments of State militia, the applicants would be more numerous than could be received, and there would be as many Democrats and Union men as Republicans."

Nor could August Belmont speak for all German immigrants. Many German-American workers and urban small proprietors actively opposed compromise. A large crowd gathered in the Philadelphia German Workers' Hall in response to a call from the city's German Republican Club in late November. It resolved "against any dilution of the Chicago platform, to surrender not even an iota of principle for the sake of compromise but rather to fight harder than ever for freedom, progress, and improving the condition of the working classes." In Chicago, German Republican organizations led by a carpenter, a shoemaker, a sashmaker, and a laborer voiced their contempt for the "several Chicago meat packers and grain merchants" who, because "they probably are not able to buy as much pork and flour as they were wont," were "doing everything they possibly can during the current week to support the compromisers in the Senate and House of Representatives." By early spring, the strength and dimensions of popular anti-compromise sentiment were clear. Republican congressmen who continued to endorse conciliation, admitted the pro-compromise New York *Herald*, "would be swept from the face of the earth."

This anti-compromise ground swell strengthened the hand of Abraham Lincoln, who balked at abandoning the core of the Republican platform, a platform that defined the party and on which it had just waged and won the 1860 campaign. A compromise on such essential issues now, Lincoln warned, would mean that "all our labor is lost and sooner or later must be done over again." "We have just carried an election on principles fairly stated to the people. Now we are told in advance, the government shall be broken up, unless we surrender to those we have beaten. . . . If we surrender, it is the end of us. They will repeat the experiment upon us *ad libitum*. A year will not pass, till we shall have to take Cuba as a condition upon which they will stay in the Union." The Crittenden package failed to win Senate approval on March 4, 1861.

The collapse of this latest effort at compromise revealed yet again the depth of the chasm that now separated North and South. Reassurances from Douglas and Lincoln were useless. A North Carolinian explained to a Massachusetts friend that "it is not Lincoln" the individual that the South feared so much as "the *fundamental idea* that underlies the whole movement of his nomination and canvass [campaign], & his election. It is the declaration of unceasing war against slavery as an institution."

This "idea"—that slavery was wrong, should be contained, and then eventually ended—had demonstrably taken hold of a huge portion of the northern population. That did indeed alarm slave-holders. Nor were Republican promises not to touch slavery where it already existed very comforting. Who could guarantee that Republicans would not tomorrow (or four years hence) call for still bolder antislavery measures? Waiting seemed only to risk a showdown at a later point when the relationship of forces would be even less favorable to the planters.

From the planters' standpoint, in any case, the Republican platform of 1860 was already bad enough. The Lincoln Administration was pledged to halt slavery's expansion. Lincoln made the point in his letter to Stephens. "You think slavery is *right* and ought to be extended; while we think it is *wrong* and ought to be restricted. That I suppose is the rub." It was, indeed. Southern planters believed that their peculiar institution needed to *grow* in order to survive. "Expansion seems to be the law and destiny and necessity of our institutions," noted a delegate to Alabama's secession convention. "To remain healthful and prosperous within . . . it seems essential that we should grow without." For men like this, Lincoln's election marked the beginning of the end of slavery. Again: secession seemed the only alternative.

Other fears were also at work. What impact, planters had to ask, would a Republican national government have on the slave population? The rise of the Republican party had quickly attracted the attention of southern blacks. The New Orleans *Picayune* had already reported with evident alarm the growth of "impudence" among the city's free black residents. When white residents of Richmond commanded a free black to stand aside and let them pass, the man "challenged them to a fight and said he had as good a right to be on the sidewalk as any of them." John Brown's 1859 raid on Harpers Ferry had created the most intense terror of slave insurrection ever known in the South. When Baltimore police in 1859 broke into the caulkers' ball (an annual free black festivity), they found the hall hung with banners bearing John Brown's likeness and a bust of Brown inscribed, "The martyr—God bless him."

Lincoln's election, many whites feared, would fan the flames of rebellion throughout the South. Inevitably, some sparks would land in the slave quarters, igniting open revolt. "Cohorts of Federal office-holders, Abolitionists, may be sent into [our] midst," warned a southern senator in early 1861, together with "postmasters . . . controlling the mails and loading them down with incendiary documents." "Now that the black radical Republicans have the power," exclaimed a South Carolinian more bluntly, "I suppose they will [John] Brown us all."

A related factor in the drive toward secession was planter doubt about the long-term loyalty of nonslaveholding southern whites. Since the seventeenth century, the South had intermittently witnessed sharp conflict between major planters and their poorer up-country neighbors. "I mistrust our own people more than I fear all of the efforts of the Abolitionists," a politician in Charleston, South Carolina, confessed in 1859. A Republican White House would certainly seek to exploit these southern differences in order to build its own antislavery party in the region. "The new dynasty will be sleeplessly engaged in building up a party in our midst," warned a southern newspaper after Lincoln's election.

Nor did this seem idle speculation. Weren't there already southern-born men (and women) ready to push forward with such work? Individual Republican leaders (like the Blair family in Maryland and Missouri) and writers (like Cassius Clay in Kentucky and Hinton Helper of the Carolina hill country) had already begun courting "the nonslaveholding whites of the South." Helper's book *The Impending Crisis of the South* had reportedly made an impression upon some southern-born residents of the lower Midwest. Its immediate impact in the South seemed minor, but perhaps this was because slave-state governments had successfully limited its circulation there. What would happen when the federal mails came under Republican control? Was it not foolish, once again, to wait until the situation had become even more perilous?

At first glance these fears, too, may seem to have been overblown. Many slaveless southern whites participated in and endorsed the slavery-based economy. "I have no slaves to lose," one

J. Henly Smith of Georgia wrote just weeks after Lincoln's election, "but I neither want to live nor leave my posterity to live in any country where African slavery does not exist." No matter how much some other small farmers may have disagreed with Smith, moreover, most fiercely opposed freedom for the black population. They blamed the blacks for their own condition, regarded them as inherently lazy and criminal, as inferiors incapable of really moral, upright, "independent" existence. Emancipation, these whites feared, would expose the South to social, economic, and physical perils even greater than those posed by slavery itself.

Still, many champions of slavery remained unconvinced of nonslaveholder loyalty. "I think I understand the advantages of slavery to a poor man," J. Henly Smith wrote to Alexander Stephens, but he added, "I am certain that the poor men of the South do not." If the matter were freely left up to them, therefore, "it is ended. They will fail to solve the problem correctly." Let men like Clay, Helper, and the Blairs speak freely long enough, warned another writer, and "they will have an Abolition party in the South, of Southern men." When that happened, "the contest for slavery will no longer be one between the North and the South. It will be in the South between people of the South."

Fears that Republicans would find support within the white South were stoked by the presence in southern towns and cities of free white wage workers, many of them immigrants from landlord-ridden Europe who felt little sympathy for planters and little stake in bound labor. Similarly unsettling was the fact that, in both the 1860 presidential election and state votes on secession, southern districts in which slavery was sparse or declining leaned toward compromise—or, at least, toward equivocation. The sooner all these people could be separated from northern Republicans by an international border, the more soundly would slaveholders sleep.

Four years later, in his second inaugural address, Abraham Lincoln presented a concise and accurate account of the origins of secession and war. In 1861, he recalled, "one eighth of the whole population were colored slaves," a fact which for the South represented "a peculiar and powerful interest. All knew that this interest was, somehow, the cause of the war." "To strengthen, perpetuate, and extend this interest" was the object of secession, while "to restrict the territorial enlargement of it" was the program of the new Administration.

Neither side, Lincoln acknowledged, had eagerly sought military conflict. On the contrary, "all dreaded it—all sought to avert it. . . . Both parties deprecated war." But when the interests of the two parties proved irreconcilable within a united country, "one of them would *make* war rather than let the nation survive; and the other would *accept* war rather than let it perish. And the war came."

Northerners greeted secession as a deadly assault upon their own rights, welfare, and security. Secession leaders sought to nullify, not a single law, but the results of an entire presidential election. Far worse, they intended to shatter a nation that was liberty's last, best hope. That could not be tolerated. "For the first time since the adoption of the Federal Constitution," Stephen A. Douglas declared in late April 1861, "a wide-spread conspiracy exists to destroy the best government the sun of heaven ever shed its rays upon" and to haul down a flag that was the "emblem of peace and union and of constitutional liberty." Unreconciled to the Republican platform, Douglas and those who followed him would nevertheless "protect this government and that flag from every assailant, be he who he may." "Give me a country first," he affirmed, "that my children may live in peace; then we will have a theater for our party organizations to operate upon."

Douglas was by no means alone in these sentiments. Lincoln's call to arms after the fall of Fort Sumter elicited a spirited reply. In Lowell, Massachusetts, a "Mechanics' Phalanx," captained by a carpenter, won a $100 prize for being the first army unit ready for camp. William Sylvis, a leader of the 1860 conference of trade unionists that endorsed the Crittenden compromise, now raised a volunteer unit made up of other iron molders. Alonzo Draper, a leader of the 1860 Lynn shoe strike, became a brigadier general in the Union Army. The minute book of a Philadelphia labor organization noted simply, "It having been resolved to enlist with

Uncle Sam for this war, this Union stands adjourned until the Union is safe or we are whipped." Members and former members of the German *Turnverein* supplied the Union with between 7,000 and 8,000 troops and entire units in Ohio, Illinois, New York, and Pennsylvania. Irish residents of Boston enlisted in the 9th Massachusetts Regiment, and Irish-born New Yorkers raised two units, the Irish Brigade and the 69th Regiment.

To be sure, the outbreak of war also led most southern whites to rally 'round the Confederacy. Those who benefitcd most—and most directly—from bound labor had managed to mobilize in their own behalf those who benefited less or not at all. There was a caveat, however. The unity of the white South would have to pass the test of war. And that would prove a severe test indeed.

As a military power, the Confederacy enjoyed a number of distinct advantages. The old South's cavalier tradition, for example, had encouraged proficiency in horsemanship and marksmanship. It also presented Jefferson Davis with most of the country's most talented cavalry and infantry officers. But the Confederate war effort also suffered from the debilitating economic and political ills revealed during the antebellum era. The South proved no match for the Union either in sheer numbers (of citizens, workers, or troops) or in industrial power (and therefore in uniforms, boots, rifles, ammunition, artillery, wagons, or warships).

A conflict that many had expected to be brief and glorious therefore grew bloody, costly, and eventually hopeless. As the war dragged on, southern whites with the smallest stake in slavery found themselves bearing the greatest burdens to keep the peculiar institution secure; the fabric of Confederate unity began to fray and unravel.

In May 1861, local forces helped federal troops to detach the yeoman up-country counties of western Virginia from the Confederacy. An attempt was made to duplicate that achievement in hilly eastern Tennessee, but it failed for lack of sufficient Union support. By the spring of 1862, spreading disaffection within the Confederacy expressed itself in the bitter slogan: "A rich man's war and a poor man's fight." The British consul at Charleston reported to London in 1863 that "labouring men are frequently discharged from their employment and subjected to contumely [insult] for not taking up arms. They are frequently arrested and sent to gaol." By 1864, underground peace societies based in eastern Tennessee as well as northern Alabama, Georgia, and North Carolina were aiding Confederate deserters and supplying intelligence to Union forces. A group of captured Union soldiers imprisoned in Charleston managed to escape in 1864—with the help not only of blacks but also of local Irish and Germans, some of them deserters from and others still active in the Confederate Army. "As a general rule," the escaped prisoners wrote in their report, "the foreign born population (Chiefly Germans) are loyal [to the Union]."

The disintegration of popular support for the Confederacy accelerated sharply with the fall of Atlanta in the autumn of 1864. Jefferson Davis found army morale and cohesion in Georgia all but gone: "two thirds of our [army] men are absent—some sick, some wounded, but most of them absent without leave." The Confederate governor of North Carolina, Zebulon Vance, commented bitterly on the dearth of guerrilla interference with Sherman's destructive march in early 1865: "With a base line of communication of 500 miles in Sherman's rear, through our own country, not a bridge has been burnt, a cart thrown from its track, nor a man shot by our people whose country has been desolated! They seem everywhere to submit." "It shows," he added, "what I have always believed, that the great *popular heart* is not now and never has been in this war!" Another southern observer, "mingling freely with the common people," reported "with much regret that among that class generally there is a strong Union feeling," or at least a belief "that the people could not fare any worse under Lincoln than [they] are faring under Jeff [Davis]."

Even more dramatically, meanwhile, a war begun by the South to perpetuate slavery was serving instead to accelerate that system's destruction. Neither Lincoln nor Davis foresaw that outcome. "Neither party expected for the war, the magnitude, or the duration which it has already attained," Lincoln later recalled. "Neither anticipated that the *cause* of the conflict might cease with, or even before, the conflict itself should cease." At first, indeed, Lincoln himself had steadfastly rejected "radical and extreme measures" against slavery in hopes of limiting the war's bitterness, devastation, and duration.

Frederick Douglass's vision proved clearer. "Any attempt," he warned in May 1861, "to separate the freedom of the slave from the victory of the Government . . . any attempt to secure peace to the whites while leaving the blacks in chains . . . will be labor lost. The American people and the Government at Washington may refuse to recognize it for a time; but the 'inexorable logic of events' will force it upon them in the end; that the war now being waged in this land is a war for and against slavery; and that it can never be effectually put down till one or the other of these vital forces is completely destroyed."

The insistent and courageous initiative of southern slaves compelled the Union's military and civilian leaders to confront the implicit "logic of events" as an immediate, unavoidable reality. In March 1861, a month before the fall of Sumter, eight slaves escaped from their masters and presented themselves before Fort Pickens, a federal installation in Florida. The fort's commander found the fugitives "entertaining the idea" that Union forces there "were placed here to protect them and grant them freedom." At the end of May, three fugitives in tidewater Virginia sought sanctuary from the federal commander of Fort Monroe, General Benjamin Butler of Massachusetts.

Standing orders dictated the return of such people to their masters. To Butler, this seemed absurd. Rebels boasted that loyal slaves would powerfully bolster their war effort. Now the slaves were withdrawing their labor from the enemy and offering it to the Union. Must rebel masters really "be allowed to use this property against the United States," Butler asked, "and we not be allowed its use in the aid of the United States?" Surely not, he concluded. Instead, Butler declared the three slaves "contraband of war" and put them to work in his quartermaster department; Lincoln endorsed the decision.

Through such initially modest, incremental, and pragmatic steps—prodded at every turn by free blacks and slaves—did

Union policy eventually evolve into one of determined emancipation. In the middle of 1862, Lincoln issued his preliminary Emancipation Proclamation, which went into effect on January 1, 1863. The President was the first to admit the nature of that process. "I claim not to have controlled events," he told a group of Kentuckians in the spring of 1862, "but confess plainly that events have controlled me."

Washington's attitude toward blacks serving in uniform changed in the same way. Mounting casualties and African-American pressure combined to transform Union policy—from adamantly excluding blacks to accepting them as military laborers to welcoming their participation in combat. By war's end, nearly 200,000 African-Americans had donned Union blue, 80 percent of them recruited in the slave states. Perhaps the most telling testimony to their effectiveness came from Major General Patrick Cleburne, a division commander in the Confederacy's Army of Tennessee. In a confidential memo of January 1864, Cleburne acknowledged that "slavery . . . has now become, in a military point of view, one of our chief sources of weakness" and "a source of great strength to the enemy." Slaves who remained under the formal control of the South in fact functioned as "an omnipresent spy system" for the Union. Confederate troops had seen ex-slaves in Union uniforms "face and fight bravely against their former masters." "My present position in reference to the rebellion," Abraham Lincoln told critics in September 1864, was "the only position upon which any Executive can or could save the Union":

> Any different policy in regard to the colored man deprives us of his help, and this is more than we can bear. We can not spare the hundred and forty or fifty thousand now serving us as soldiers, seamen, and laborers. This is not a question of sentiment or taste, but of physical force which may be measured and estimated as horsepower and steam-power are measured and estimated. Keep it and you can save the Union. Throw it away, and the Union goes with it.

The adoption of an antislavery war policy and the recruitment of black soldiers transformed Union forces into an army of emancipation. The significance of black troops freeing black slaves was lost on no one, whether friend or foe. Some episodes captured this symbolism with special vividness. Passing through plantation districts, thus, some black units questioned local slaves to identify the cruelest overseer in the vicinity; if they could find the man, they would "tie him backward on a horse and force him to accompany them" as they marched. In August 1864, a raiding party recruited from the 2nd South Carolina Volunteers liberated slaves along South Carolina's Combahee River. The Volunteers were almost all former slaves, and the raiding party's commanding officer that day was Colonel James Montgomery, who had fought alongside John Brown in the Kansas wars. The raiding party's scout was Harriet Tubman.

Early the next year, in February 1865, black Union troops strode into Charleston, South Carolina, singing that John Brown's "truth goes marching on." Among the slaves who flocked to their side was an old woman who, throwing aside her crutch, cried out because the day of Jubilee had arrived. Seven months later, black workers in the same city laid the cornerstone for an African Methodist Episcopal church. The AME had flourished in that city from 1817 until 1822, when it was banished for alleged involvement in the Denmark Vesey slave insurrection plot. Now, after forty-three years, Charleston residents watched as a new sanctuary was erected, built entirely by black labor. The architect was Robert Vesey, Denmark Vesey's son.

In early April 1865, the approach of Union troops forced the Confederate government to evacuate Richmond. As he fled, Jefferson Davis swore defiantly that "again and again we will return, until the baffled and exhausted enemy shall abandon in despair his endless and impossible task of making slaves of a people resolved to be free."

The irony in Davis's words was certainly unconscious; his vow was completely empty. Within a week, Lee had surrendered; within another month, Davis was captured and imprisoned. But the Union's capture of Richmond served to make Davis's point, albeit in an unexpected way. The first bluecoats to enter the former Confederate capital included black cavalrymen and infantrymen. Many *were* former slaves; their presence showed their "resolve to be free." A white resident noted bitterly how black cavalrymen, their swords held high in victory, exchanged "savage cheers" with black residents who were "exulting" in liberation. Later, a crowd of black soldiers and townsfolk headed toward Lumpkin's Jail, where a group of slaves awaited their scheduled sale at auction. Catching sight of the crowd through the barred windows, the prisoners began to sing:

> Slavery chain done broke at last!
> Broke at last! Broke at last!
> Slavery chain done broke at last!
> Gonna praise God till I die!

The black soldiers and civilians promptly opened wide the prison doors, freeing its inmates. Surely, a black minister subsequently concluded, that day in Richmond was God's "finishing touch, as though He would speak audible words of approval to the nation."

Revolutions are dramatic. Their dramatic power reflects the clash within them of the familiar and the strange, between the old and the new. Individuals and types well known to us from past association suddenly interact in startling, inverted ways—ways that seem nearly surreal when judged by the standards of that past. In 1781, defeated British troops marching out of Yorktown, Virginia, invoked this sense of unreality when their band struck up a tune called "The World Turned Upside Down." Fourscore years later, both black and white Southerners experienced a similar feeling of inversion as lines of triumphant black soldiers moved northward toward Richmond. "The change seems almost miraculous," one black sergeant said. "The very people who, three years ago, crouched at their masters' feet, on the accursed soil of Virginia, now march in a victorious column of freedmen, over the same land." Local whites found it considerably more bizarre and wondered aloud (according to AME minister and army chaplain Henry M. Turner) "whether they are actually in another world, or whether this one is turned wrong side out."

BIBLIOGRAPHICAL ESSAY

This book covers a broad range of topics over a long period of time. The relevant monographic literature is vast, and a complete bibliographic guide through it would require at least a volume of its own. In what follows, therefore, I have limited myself to listing the books and articles of which I have made the most use. In another space-saving decision, I have rarely mentioned a work more than once, even when I have drawn upon it to explicate a variety of aspects of antebellum history. I apologize in advance for whatever unintended slights these guidelines may entail. Of course, a book like this one requires making use of the findings of authors with whose overarching interpretations I disagree. I have noted some of those disagreements below.

Introduction: Freedom, Slavery, and the Legacy of the American Revolution

The Introduction's brief treatment of the slavery issue in the revolutionary era leans heavily upon David Brion Davis, *The Problem of Slavery in the Age of Revolution, 1770–1823* (Ithaca, 1975); Benjamin Quarles, *The Negro in the American Revolution* (1961; reprint, New York, 1973); the essays contained in Ira Berlin and Ronald Hoffman, eds., *Slavery and Freedom in the Age of the American Revolution* (Charlottesville, 1983); Edward Countryman, *The American Revolution* (New York, 1985); and *Notes of the Debates in the Federal Convention of 1787 Reported by James Madison*, ed. Adrienne Koch (1966; reprint, New York, 1969). The discussion of Jefferson and slavery also draws upon Dumas Malone, *Jefferson and His Time*, 6 vols. (Boston, 1948–77). Additional quotations from Jefferson's writings come from his *Notes on the State of Virginia*, ed. William Peden (1787; reprint, New York, 1972), and *The Writings of Thomas Jefferson*, ed. Paul Leicester Ford, 10 vols. (New York, 1892–99). See also John Chester Miller, *The Wolf by the Ears: Thomas Jefferson and Slavery* (New York, 1977). The letter sent by Postmaster General Gideon Granger to Senator James Jackson was published in Walter Lowrie, ed., *American State Papers: Documents, Legislative and Executive of the Congress of the United States, Part VII: Post Office* (Washington, D.C., 1834). On the Haitian revolution, the classic analysis remains C. L. R. James's *The Black Jacobins: Toussaint L'Ouverture and the San Domingo Revolution* (rev. ed., New York, 1963). The revolution's external impact is examined in Alfred N. Hunt, *Haiti's Influence on Antebellum America: Slumbering Volcano in the Caribbean* (Baton Rouge, 1988). W. E. B. Du Bois noted the role that fear of slave revolts played in banning the slave trade in *The Suppression of the African Slave Trade to the United States of America, 1638–1870* (1896; reprint, Baton Rouge, 1969). John Taylor warned of the dangers posed by free blacks to slave society in *Arator: Being a Series of Agricultural Essays, Practical and Political: In Sixty-four Numbers*, ed. M. E. Bradford (1818; reprint, Indianapolis, 1977).

Other subjects raised and works used in the Introduction are discussed elsewhere in this essay.

1. *"Our Laborers Are Our Property"*: *The Southern Slave Economy*

For an intelligent and useful guide to the general subject of slavery in historiography, see Peter J. Parish, *Slavery: History and*

Historians (New York, 1989). Peter Kolchin, *Unfree Labor: American Slavery and Russian Serfdom* (Cambridge, Mass., 1987), examines the subject in an unusual comparative perspective.

Kenneth M. Stampp emphasized thirty-five years ago that "slavery was above all a labor system" in *The Peculiar Institution: Slavery in the Antebellum South* (New York, 1956). That observation provides the point of departure for this chapter (and for much of the rest of this book, for that matter). The system's colonial origins can be traced in Edmund S. Morgan, *American Slavery, American Freedom: The Ordeal of Colonial Virginia* (New York, 1975); T. H. Breen, "A Changing Labor Force and Race Relations in Virginia, 1660–1710," *Journal of Social History*, 7 (1973): 3–25 (conveniently reprinted, along with a host of other valuable essays, in Breen, ed., *The Shaping of Southern Society: The Colonial Experience* [New York, 1976]); Thad W. Tate and David L. Ammerman, eds., *The Chesapeake in the Seventeenth Century: Essays on Anglo-American Society and Politics* (New York, 1979); Peter Wood, *Black Majority: Negroes in Colonial South Carolina from 1670 through the Stono Rebellion* (New York, 1974); Ira Berlin, "Time, Space, and the Evolution of Afro-American Society on British Mainland North America," *American Historical Review*, 85 (1980): 44–78. The place of slavery in colonial law is treated in A. Leon Higginbotham, Jr., *In the Matter of Color: Race and the American Legal Process: The Colonial Period* (New York, 1978). Mark Tushnet picks up the account in *The American Law of Slavery, 1810–1860: Considerations of Humanity and Interest* (Princeton, 1981). Stampp's *The Peculiar Institution* remains unsurpassed in its treatment of the nineteenth-century master's fundamental economic purpose and many of his techniques. Of tremendous value in illuminating a series of slave-owner concerns is James O. Breeden, ed., *Advice among Masters: The Ideal in Slave Management in the Old South* (Westport, Conn., 1980). Also very useful is the collection edited by Paul F. Passkoff and Daniel J. Wilson, *The Cause of the South: Selections from De Bow's Review, 1846–1867* (Baton Rouge, 1982). Additional insight on this subject is found in Drew Gilpin Faust's masterful biography, *James Henry Hammond and the Old South: A Design for Mastery* (Baton Rouge, 1982). I have drawn upon that work for other purposes as well.

In their *Time on the Cross: The Economics of American Negro Slavery* (Boston, 1974), Robert William Fogel and Stanley L. Engerman set out to challenge what they considered to be an unexamined orthodoxy on the economics of American slavery. Stampp's book was their principal target. While noting that in the South "the relationship between its ruling and its servile class was marked by patriarchal features which were strongly reminiscent of medieval life," Fogel and Engerman nonetheless conclude that "shrewd capitalistic businessmen . . . ran the slave plantations" and "developed a highly capitalistic form of agriculture" (129, 232). Under their hands, slavery came strongly to resemble (a rather idealized version of) free-labor capitalism, even in the relationship between master and slave. They argued, for example, that "in slave, as in free society, positive incentives in the form of material awards, were a powerful instrument of economic and social control"; indeed, that "pecuniary awards were as integral a part of slavery as punishment" (241–42). They also asserted that such incentives helped raise the productivity of the average slave's labor well above the level that prevailed in northern society. *Time on the Cross* called forth stinging ripostes, including Paul A. David, Herbert G. Gutman, Richard Sutch, Peter Temin, and Gavin Wright, *Reckoning with Slavery: A Critical Study in the Quantitative History of American Negro Slavery* (New York, 1976); Herbert G. Gutman, *Slavery and the Numbers Game: A Critique of "Time on the Cross"* (Urbana, 1975). Fogel's subsequent *Without Consent or Contract: The Rise and Fall of American Slavery* (New York, 1989) modifies some of the initial assertions without altering his basic argument. (But see also Engerman's criticisms of Edward Pessen's stress on similarities between antebellum North and South in the *American Historical Review*, 85 [1980]: 1158–59.)

This debate has helped clarify a range of empirical and interpretive issues. In *The Political Economy of the Cotton South: Households, Markets, and Wealth in the Nineteenth Century*

(New York, 1978), Gavin Wright provides a wealth of important statistical data about the structure of the cotton kingdom and (inter alia) explains the high returns to slave labor in the cotton fields by noting the growth of international demand for that crop and its geographically limited supply.

Eugene D. Genovese first presented his own evaluation of the plantation system in *The Political Economy of Slavery: Studies in the Economy and Society of the Slave South* (New York, 1965). This has been supplemented and modified in subsequent books, including *The World the Slaveholders Made: Two Essays in Interpretation* (New York, 1969); *Roll, Jordan, Roll: The World the Slaves Made* (New York, 1974); and (with Elizabeth Fox Genovese) *Fruits of Merchant Capital: Slavery and Bourgeois Property in the Rise and Expansion of Capitalism* (New York, 1983). These bold and often brilliant works note the origins of New World slavery in the development of world capitalism but place overriding emphasis (in accounting for its actual functioning and ideological development) on its pre-capitalist aspects. *Fruits of Merchant Capital* thus depicts the antebellum southern elite as "a decisively, if hybrid, nonbourgeois ruling class" (144) and "the southern slave system as fundamentally noncapitalist" (148). James Oakes has produced two thoughtful books on antebellum southern society. In the first (*The Ruling Race: A History of American Slaveholders* [New York, 1982]), he registered agreement "with those who stress the capitalist nature of the slave system in the Old South" (xi). Laurence Shore advanced a similar thesis on the terrain of planter ideology in *Southern Capitalists: The Ideological Leadership of an Elite, 1832–1885* (Chapel Hill, 1986). But in *Slavery and Freedom: An Interpretation of the Old South* (New York, 1990), Oakes judged the view that "modern slavery was capitalist in every way that matters" to be not "wholly adequate," since it "underestimates the distinctive economic consequences of slave labor" (55). In *Half Slave and Half Free*, I have suggested that both the practical and ideological dimensions of the South's slave-labor system reflected its genuinely hybrid character.

A number of excellent documentary collections shed light on a variety of aspects of slavery. I have consulted John W. Blassingame, ed., *Slave Testimony: Two Centuries of Letters, Speeches, Interviews, and Autobiographies* (Baton Rouge, 1977); George P. Rawick, ed., *The American Slave: A Composite Autobiography*, 19 vols. (Westport, Conn., 1972), a compilation of interviews recorded by the Federal Writers' Project of the WPA and Fisk University, most of them organized by state; James Mellon, ed., *Bullwhip Days: The Slaves Remember—An Oral History* (New York, 1988); Milton Meltzer, ed., *A History of the American Negro*. Vol. 1: *1619 to 1865* (New York, 1965); Robert S. Starobin, *Blacks in Bondage: Letters of American Slaves* (1974; reprint, New York, 1988); Willie Lee Rose, ed., *A Documentary History of Slavery in North America* (New York, 1976); Gilbert Osofsky, ed., *Puttin' On Ole Massa: The Slave Narratives of Henry Bibb, William Wells Brown, and Solomon Northup* (New York, 1969); Philip S. Foner and Ronald L. Lewis, eds., *The Black Worker: A Documentary History*. Vol. 1: *The Black Worker to 1869* (Philadelphia, 1978); and Douglass C. North and Robert Paul Thomas, eds., *The Growth of the American Economy to 1860* (Columbia, S.C., 1968). Frederick Douglass's magnificent autobiography, *The Life and Times of Frederick Douglass* (1892; reprint, New York, 1969), is indispensable. Contemporary testimony from another quarter on these and other matters can be found in Frederick Law Olmsted's reports: *Journey through the Seaboard Slave States* (New York, 1856); *Journey through Texas* (New York, 1857); and *Journey in the Back Country* (New York, 1860).

My depiction of the evolving economy, social structure, and distribution of wealth (in this chapter as in the next) makes use of the following works: Alice Hanson Jones, *Wealth of a Nation to Be: The American Colonies on the Eve of the Revolution* (New York, 1980); John J. McCusker and Russell R. Menard, *The Economy of British America, 1607–1789* (Chapel Hill, 1985); Gary B. Nash, "Social Development," and James A. Henretta, "Wealth and Social Structure," both in *Colonial British America: Essays in the New History of the Early Modern Era*, ed. Jack P. Greene and J. R. Pole (Baltimore, 1984); Jackson Turner Main,

The Social Structure of Revolutionary America (Princeton, 1965); Edward Pessen, *Riches, Class and Power before the Civil War* (Lexington, Mass., 1973); James A. Henretta and Gregory H. Nobles, *Evolution and Revolution: American Society, 1600–1820* (Lexington, Mass., 1987); Louis M. Hacker, *The Triumph of American Capitalism: The Development of Forces in American History to the Beginning of the Twentieth Century* (1940; reprint, New York, 1965); Curtis P. Nettels, *The Emergence of a National Economy, 1775–1815* (New York, 1962); Lance Davis et al., *American Economic Growth: An Economist's History of the United States* (New York, 1972); Paul W. Gates, *The Farmer's Age: Agriculture, 1815–1860* (New York, 1960); *The Economic Growth of the United States, 1790–1860* (New York, 1961); Stuart Bruchey, *The Roots of American Economic Growth, 1607–1861: An Essay on Social Causation* (New York, 1968). Relevant statistical series are also provided in Bureau of the Census, *Historical Statistics of the United States: Colonial Times to 1970*, 2 vols. (Washington, D.C., 1975); Richard A. Easterlin, "Interregional Differences in Per Capita Income, Population, and Total Income, 1840–1950," and Robert E. Gallman, "Commodity Output, 1839–1899," both in William N. Parker, ed., *Trends in the American Economy in the Nineteenth Century* (Princeton, 1960); Lee Soltow, *Men and Wealth in the United States, 1850–1870* (New Haven, 1975); Stanley Lebergott, "The Pattern of Employment Since 1800," in Seymour Harris, ed., *American Economic History* (New York, 1961): 281–310; idem, *Manpower in Economic Growth* (New York, 1964); and idem, *Labor Force and Employment, 1800–1960* (New York, 1966). Thomas Weiss proposes some adjustments to Lebergott's data in his "Revised Estimates of the United States Workforce, 1800–1860," in Stanley L. Engerman and Robert E. Gallman, eds., *Long-Term Factors in American Economic Growth* (Chicago, 1986).

Ulrich B. Phillips, *American Negro Slavery: A Survey of the Supply, Employment and Control of Negro Labor as Determined by the Plantation Regime* (1918; reprint, Baton Rouge, 1966), is an apology for the system that nonetheless contains a wealth of information about plantation labor. Still immensely useful, too, is Lewis Cecil Gray, *History of Agriculture in the Southern United States to 1860*, 2 vols. (1932; reprint, Gloucester, Mass., 1958). See also Roger L. Ransom's thoughtful *Conflict and Compromise: The Political Economy of Slavery, Emancipation, and the American Civil War* (New York, 1989). Sam Bowers Hilliard, *Atlas of Antebellum Southern Agriculture* (Baton Rouge, 1984) provides an arresting depiction of the geographic and economic growth of the Old South. Barbara Jeanne Fields's fine study of the decay of the peculiar institution in the northerly reaches of the upper South, *Slavery and Freedom on the Middle Ground: Maryland During the Nineteenth Century* (New Haven, 1985), is rich in both evidence and analysis. Willie Lee Rose, *Slavery and Freedom* (New York, 1981), brings great erudition and subtlety to the study of a number of facets of antebellum southern life. The workings of the "task" and incentive systems are discussed in Philip D. Morgan, "The Ownership of Property by Slaves in the Mid-Nineteenth-Century Low Country," *Journal of Southern History*, 49 (1983): 399–420; and idem, "The Task System and the World of Lowcountry Blacks, 1700–1880," *William and Mary Quarterly*, 39 (1982): 563–99.

Historians have long known that the slave-labor system yielded profits. Too often, however, that issue has become confused with another one—the broader effects of this labor system upon overall regional economic development. Slavery's impact upon and compatibility with urbanization and industrialization are examined in Fred Bateman and Thomas Weiss, *A Deplorable Scarcity: The Failure of Industrialization in the Slave Economy* (Chapel Hill, 1981); Richard C. Wade, *Slavery in the Cities: The South, 1820–1860* (London, 1964); Robert S. Starobin, *Industrial Slavery in the Old South* (London, 1970). Ira Berlin and Herbert G. Gutman analyzed the ethnic stratification of the South's urban labor force in "Natives and Immigrants, Free Men and Slaves: Urban Workingmen in the Antebellum American South," *American Historical Review*, 88 (1983): 1175–1200. Berlin's *Slaves without Masters: The Free Negro in the Antebellum South* (New York,

1974) remains the sole comprehensive work on its subject. More: examining the situation of the southern black population's free minority within the context of the slave system as a whole, it is one of the most insightful studies of the antebellum South published in the last few decades. Leonard P. Curry, *The Free Black in Urban America, 1800–1850: The Shadow of a Dream* (Chicago, 1981), slices the material in a different way, surveying conditions of urban free blacks throughout the United States. The book contains much important data, but the attempt to describe patterns applicable to both North and South raises as many questions as it answers. My own discussion of free blacks also utilizes data derived from antebellum population censuses.

A growing literature deals with the place of the small-scale farmer in the southern economy. Notable recent contributions to this subfield include Eugene D. Genovese, "Yeoman Farmers in a Slaveholders' Democracy," in *Fruits of Merchant Capital*, already cited; Paul D. Escott, "Yeoman Independence and the Market: Social Status and Economic Development in Antebellum North Carolina," *North Carolina Historical Review*, 61 (1989): 275–300; James D. Foust, "The Yeoman Farmer and Westward Expansion of U.S. Cotton Production," Ph.D. dissertation, University of North Carolina at Chapel Hill, 1968; Steven Hahn, *The Roots of Southern Populism: Yeoman Farmers and the Transformation of the Georgia Upcountry, 1850–1890* (New York, 1983); J. William Harris, *Plain Folk and Gentry in a Slave Society: White Liberty and Black Slavery in Augusta's Hinterlands* (Middletown, Conn., 1985); Lacy K. Ford, *The Origins of Southern Radicalism: The South Carolina Upcountry, 1800–1860* (New York, 1988); John C. Inscoe, *Mountain Masters, Slavery, and the Sectional Crisis in Western North Carolina* (Knoxville, Tenn., 1989); John M. Allman II, "Yeomen Regions in the Antebellum Deep South: Settlement and Economy in Northern Alabama, 1815–1860," Ph.D. dissertation, University of Maryland, 1979. James C. Bonner's "Profile of a Late Antebellum Community" (*American Historical Review*, 49 [1944]: 663–80) was a pioneer work that retains its value. It is reprinted, together with a number of other fine studies, in Elinor Miller and Eugene D. Genovese, eds., *Plantation, Town, and Country* (Urbana, 1974).

2. *"Each Person Works for Himself":*
The Ideal and Reality of Free Labor

Chapter 2 opens with excerpts from J. Hector St. John de Crèvecoeur's *Letters from an American Farmer* (1782; reprint, New York, 1957), which are followed by the observations of Alexis de Tocqueville in his *Democracy in America*, 2 vols. (1835–40; reprint, New York, 1945). Similar themes are developed in Marvin Fisher, *Workshops in the Wilderness: The European Response to American Industrialization, 1830–1860* (New York, 1967). My discussion of Daniel Webster's relationship to the northern mercantile and manufacturing elite is based upon Richard N. Current, *Daniel Webster and the Rise of National Conservatism* (Boston, 1955), and Irving H. Bartlett, *Daniel Webster* (New York, 1978). Webster's speech celebrating economic development in 1847 is reprinted in Michael Brewster Folsom and Steven D. Lubar, eds., *The Philosophy of Manufactures: Early Debates over Industrialization in the United States* (Cambridge, Mass., 1982). Thomas P. Cope's views are found in *Philadelphia Merchant: The Diary of Thomas P. Cope, 1800–1851*, ed. Eliza Cope Harrison (South Bend, 1978); Philip Hone is quoted from *The Diary of Philip Hone, 1828–1851*, ed. Allan Nevins (New York, 1927).

This chapter's discussion of economic development, social stratification, and wealth distribution in the free states is based on many of the titles cited in the bibliography for Chapter 1. In addition, George Rogers Taylor, *The Transportation Revolution, 1790 to 1860* (New York, 1951), remains an immensely valuable synthesis that should be supplemented by Diane Lindstrom's *Economic Development in the Philadelphia Region, 1810–1850* (New York, 1978). Additional information on the antebellum northern elite comes from Frederic Cople Jaher's encyclopedic *The Urban Establishment: Upper Strata in Boston, New York, Charleston,*

Chicago, and Los Angeles (Urbana, 1982) and Douglas T. Miller, *Jacksonian Aristocracy: Class and Democracy in New York, 1830–1860* (New York, 1967). Also instructive is Irvin O. Wyllie, *The Self-Made Man in America: The Myth of Rags to Riches* (New York, 1954).

The study of northern agriculture has produced a number of classics, including Percy W. Bidwell and John I. Falconer, *History of Agriculture in the Northern United States, 1620–1860* (New York, 1941); Paul W. Gates, *The Farmer's Age* (cited earlier); and Clarence Danhof, *Change in Agriculture: The Northern United States, 1820–1870* (Cambridge, Mass., 1969). Growing interest in rural life is evidenced in Steven Hahn and Jonathan Prude, eds., *The Countryside in the Age of Capitalist Transformation: Essays in the Social History of Rural America* (Chapel Hill, 1985). Agrarian tenantry is treated in Sung Bok Kim, *Landlord and Tenant in Colonial New York: Manorial Society, 1664–1775* (Chapel Hill, 1978), and Edward Countryman, *A People in Revolution: The American Revolution and Political Society in New York, 1760–1790* (Baltimore, 1981).

The revival of interest in agricultural history has spawned a fascinating debate about the extent to which market production dominated rural life at various points in time. Michael Merrill kicked it off with his "Cash Is Good to Eat: Self-Sufficiency and Exchange in the Rural Economy of the United States," *Radical History Review*, 15 (1977): 42–71. Other contributions include Robert Mutch, "Yeoman and Merchant in Pre-Industrial America: Eighteenth-Century Massachusetts as a Case Study," *Societas*, 7 (1977): 279–302; Carole Shammas, "How Self-Sufficient Was Early America?" *Journal of Interdisciplinary History*, 13 (1982), 247–72; Robert A. Gross, "Culture and Cultivation: Agriculture and Society in Thoreau's Concord," *Journal of American History*, 69 (1982): 42–61; Joyce Appleby, "Commercial Farming and the 'Agrarian Myth' in the Early Republic," *Journal of American History*, 68 (1982): 833–49; Winifred Rothenberg, "The Market and Massachusetts Farmers, 1750–1855," *Journal of Economic History*, 41 (1981): 283–314; and James T. Lemon, "Agriculture and Society in Early America," *Agricultural History Review*, 35 (1987): 76–94.

Most satisfactory are James A. Henretta, "Families and Farms: *Mentalité* in Pre-Industrial America," *William and Mary Quarterly*, 35 (1978): 3–32; Joan M. Jensen, "Cloth, Butter and Boarders: Women's Household Production for the Market," *Reviews in Radical Political Economy*, 12:2 (1980): 14–24; and especially Christopher Clark, "Household Economy, Market Exchange and the Rise of Capitalism in the Connecticut Valley, 1800–1860," *Journal of Social History*, 13 (1979): 169–89; and idem, *The Roots of Rural Capitalism: Western Massachusetts, 1780–1860* (Ithaca, 1990). These works clarify important differences in rural life and outlook that correspond to different degrees of market dependence. They also lay bare the pressures and mechanisms through which semisubsistence farming evolved into fully fledged commercial agriculture. To illustrate one aspect of earlier rural life, I have quoted a passage from John Bradbury, *Travels in the Interior of America, 1809–1811*, vol. 5 of *Early Western Travels, 1748–1846*, ed. Reuben Gold Thwaites (Cleveland, 1904).

The history of manufacturing has attracted more attention than agriculture. In addition to the general economic histories cited above, consult Harold F. Williamson, ed., *The Growth of the American Economy* (New York, 1944). Victor S. Clark, *A History of Manufactures in the United States.* Vol. 1: 1607–1860 (1929; reprint, New York, 1949) is a classic that retains considerable value. See also Peter Temin, *The Jacksonian Economy* (New York, 1969); Thomas C. Cochran, *Frontiers of Change: Early Industrialism in America* (New York, 1981); and David A. Hounshell, *From the American System to Mass Production, 1800–1932: The Development of Manufacturing Technology in the United States* (Baltimore, 1984).

The evolution of work, working conditions, and the work force in the pre-Civil War North has been examined from many angles. An older work of continuing utility is Norman Ware, *The Industrial Worker, 1840–1860: The Reaction of American Industrial Society to the Advance of the Industrial Revolution* (1924; reprint,

Chicago, 1964). A provocative overview of industrial evolution and sequential changes in the industrial and managerial organization is David M. Gordon, Richard Edwards, and Michael Reich, *Segmented Work, Divided Workers: The Historical Transformation of Labor in the United States* (Cambridge, Eng., 1982). See also Amy Bridges, "Becoming American: The Working Classes in the United States before the Civil War," in *Working-Class Formation: Nineteenth-Century Patterns in Western Europe and the United States*, eds. Ira Katznelson and Aristide R. Zolberg (Princeton, 1986); and the articles by Sean Wilentz, Michael Reich, Leon Fink, and Mari Jo Buhle in *Perspectives on American Labor History: The Problems of Synthesis*, eds. J. Carroll Moody and Alice Kessler-Harris (De Kalb, Ill., 1989).

The urban work force of the revolutionary era is analyzed in Gary B. Nash, *The Urban Crucible: Social Change, Political Consciousness, and the Origins of the American Revolution* (Cambridge, Mass., 1979). The subject of indentured servitude in the North is investigated in Abbott Emerson Smith, *Colonists in Bondage: White Servitude and Convict Labor in America, 1607–1776* (1947; reprint, New York, 1971); David W. Galenson, *White Servitude in Colonial America: An Economic Analysis* (Cambridge, Eng., 1981); Farley Grubb, "The Incidence of Servitude in Trans-Atlantic Migration, 1771–1804," *Explorations in Economic History*, 22 (1985): 316–39; and Sharon V. Salinger, *"To Serve Well and Faithfully": Labor and Indentured Servants in Pennsylvania, 1682–1800* (Cambridge, Eng., 1987). The urban work force of the early national period is considered in Allan Pred, "Manufacturing in the Mercantile City, 1800–1840," *Annals of the Society of American Geographers*, 56 (1966): 307–25; and David Montgomery, "The Working Class of the Pre-Industrial City," *Labor History*, 9 (1968): 3–22.

The rise of factory production has been chronicled in Hannah Josephson, *The Golden Threads: New England's Mill Girls and Magnates* (New York, 1949); Anthony F. C. Wallace, *Rockdale: The Growth of an American Village in the Early Industrial Revo-*

lution (New York, 1978); Jonathan Prude, *The Coming of Industrial Order: Town and Factory Life in Rural Massachusetts, 1810–1860* (Cambridge, Mass., 1983); Philip Scranton, *Proprietary Capitalism: The Textile Manufacture at Philadelphia, 1800–1885* (New York, 1983); Barbara Tucker, *Samuel Slater and the Origins of the American Textile Industry, 1790–1860* (Ithaca, 1984); Cynthia J. Shelton, *The Mills of Manayunk: Industrialization and Social Conflict in the Philadelphia Region* (Baltimore, 1986). The most rounded study remains Thomas Dublin's *Women and Work: The Transformation of Work and Community in Lowell, Massachusetts, 1826–1860* (New York, 1979). This book is as rich in evidence and understanding as it is careful and modest in style. Dublin has also edited a most illuminating set of letters, *Farm to Factory: Women's Letters, 1830–60* (New York, 1981), the introduction to which contains a fine, concise analysis of the early evolution of the rural New England economy. Another excellent and more extended treatment of the relationship between agricultural change and early factory development is Mary Alice Feldblum's (unfortunately) unpublished Ph.D. dissertation, "The Formation of the First Factory Labor Force in the New England Cotton Textile Industry, 1800–1848" (New School for Social Research, 1977), whose rich literary documentation I have quoted liberally.

The transformation of craft production has attracted an even larger number of students. The most important works on this subject include Alan Dawley, *Class and Community: The Industrial Revolution in Lynn* (Cambridge, Mass., 1976); Paul G. Faler, *Mechanics and Manufacturers in the Early Industrial Revolution: Lynn, Massachusetts, 1780–1860* (Albany, 1981); Howard Rock, *Artisans of the New Republic: The Tradesmen of New York City in the Age of Jefferson* (New York, 1979); Susan E. Hirsch, *Roots of the American Working Class: The Industrialization of the Crafts in Newark, 1800–1860* (Philadelphia, 1978); Bruce Laurie, *Working People of Philadelphia, 1800–1850* (Philadelphia, 1980); Sean Wilentz, *Chants Democratic: New York City and the Rise of the American Working Class* (New York, 1984); and Steven

J. Ross, *Workers on the Edge: Work, Leisure, and Politics in In-dustrializing Cincinnati, 1788–1890* (New York, 1985). Mary Blewett, *Men, Women, and Work: Class, Gender, and Protest in the New England Shoe Industry, 1780–1910* (Urbana, 1988), stresses the gendered division of labor within that industry and its impact. Other studies that focus upon women and wage work include Alice Kessler-Harris, *Out to Work: A History of Wage-Earning Women in the United States* (New York, 1982); Fay E. Dudden, *Serving Women: Household Service in Nineteenth-Century America* (Middletown, Conn., 1983); and Christine Stansell, *City of Women: Sex and Class in New York, 1789–1860* (New York, 1986).

Unskilled labor still awaits thorough treatment. Pieces of the puzzle can be found in works nominally focused upon other subjects. One example is Stephan Thernstrom, *Poverty & Progress: Social Mobility in a Nineteenth-Century City* (Cambridge, Mass., 1964).

We need far more information about the origins and daily life of free blacks in the North. (The end of northern slavery is examined in Arthur Zilversmit, *The First Emancipation: The Abolition of Slavery in the North* [Chicago, 1967], but only in its ideological dimensions.) Leon F. Litwack, *North of Slavery: The Negro in the Free States, 1790–1860* (Chicago, 1961), remains the only general work, whose findings may be supplemented by those of Leonard P. Curry (already cited); James Oliver Horton and Lois E. Horton, *Black Bostonians: Family Life and Community Struggle in the Antebellum North* (New York, 1979); and Gary B. Nash, *Forging Freedom: The Formation of Philadelphia's Black Community, 1720–1840* (Cambridge, Mass., 1988). In my discussion of free black life in the North (and on a range of other subjects), I have quoted from Frederick Douglass's autobiography as well as from *The Life and Writings of Frederick Douglass*, ed. Philip S. Foner, 5 vols. (New York, 1950–75). I have also used data on northern free blacks published in the population census.

Studies that illuminate the economic experience of antebellum immigrants include Marcus Lee Hansen, *The Atlantic Migra-*

tion, 1607–1860 (1940; reprint, New York, 1961); Maldwyn Allen Jones, *American Immigration* (Chicago, 1960); E. P. Hutchinson, *Immigrants and Their Children* (New York, 1956); Theodore Hershberg et al., "Occupation and Ethnicity in Five Nineteenth-Century American Cities: A Collaborative Inquiry," *Historical Methods Newsletter*, 7 (1974): 174–216; Nora Faires, "Occupational Patterns of German-Americans in Nineteenth-Century Cities," in Hartmut Keil and John B. Jentz, eds., *German Workers in Industrial Chicago, 1850–1910: A Comparative Perspective* (De Kalb, Ill., 1983); Herbert G. Gutman, "Work Culture and Society in Industrializing America," in his collection by the same name (New York, 1976); the contributions to *Immigrants in Industrial America*, ed. Richard L. Ehrlich (Charlottesville, 1977); Roland W. Berthoff, *British Immigrants in Industrial America, 1790–1950* (1953; reprint, New York, 1968); Charlotte Erickson, *Invisible Immigrants: The Adaptation of English and Scottish Immigrants in Nineteenth-Century America* (1972; reprint, Ithaca, 1990); Robert Ernst, *Immigrant Life in New York City: 1825–1863* (New York, 1949); Oscar Handlin, *Boston's Immigrants, 1790–1880: A Study in Acculturation* (rev. ed., Cambridge, Mass., 1959); Kathleen N. Conzen, *Immigrant Milwaukee, 1836–1860: Accommodation and Community in a Frontier City* (Cambridge, Mass., 1976); Allen F. Davis and Mark H. Haller, eds., *The Peoples of Philadelphia: A History of Ethnic Groups and Lower-Class Life, 1790–1840* (Philadelphia, 1973); Lynn H. Lees and John Modell, "The Irish Countryman Urbanized: A Comparative Perspective on the Famine Migration," *Journal of Urban History*, 3 (1977): 391–408; Oliver MacDonagh, "The Irish Famine Emigration to the United States," *Perspectives in American History*, 10 (1976): 357–446; Kerby A. Miller, *Emigrants and Exiles: Ireland and the Irish Exodus to North America* (New York, 1985); a number of the articles in Keil and Jentz, *German Workers in Industrial Chicago* (already cited); Stanley Nadel, *Little Germany: Ethnicity, Religion, and Class in New York City, 1845–80* (Urbana, 1990); Bruce Levine, *In the Spirit of 1848: German Immigrants, Labor Conflict, and the Coming of Civil War* (Urbana, 1992); Hasia R. Diner, *Erin's Daughters in America: Irish Immi-*

grant *Women in the Nineteenth Century* (Baltimore, 1983); Theodore C. Blegen, *Norwegian Migration to America: 1825– 1860* (1931; reprint, New York, 1969). I have also made use of Edith Abbott, ed., *Historical Aspects of the Immigration Problem: Select Documents* (Chicago, 1926).

The impact of economic crisis on early industrial society is depicted in Reginald C. McGrane, *The Panic of 1837* (Chicago, 1924), and Samuel Rezneck, "The Social History of an American Depression," *American Historical Review*, 40 (1935): 662–87. The relationship between changes in wealth and location is discussed in Stanley L. Engerman, "Up or Out: Social and Geographic Mobility in the United States," *Journal of Interdisciplinary History*, 5 (1975): 469–89.

3. "A Complete Revolution in Social Life": Cultural Change in the Antebellum North

The changing status of middle-class women of the antebellum North has been explored in an imposing body of scholarship. Some of the most influential works have been Cott, *The Bonds of Womanhood* (already cited); Kathryn Kish Sklar, *Catharine Beecher: A Study in American Domesticity* (New York, 1976); Linda K. Kerber, *Women of the Republic: Intellect and Ideology in Revolutionary America* (Chapel Hill, 1980); Mary Beth Norton, *Liberty's Daughters: The Revolutionary Experience of American Women, 1750–1800* (Boston, 1980); Julie A. Matthaei, *An Economic History of Women in America: Women's Work, the Sexual Division of Labor, and the Development of Capitalism* (New York, 1982); Susan Strasser, *Never Done: A History of American Housework* (New York, 1982). Mary Beth Norton, "The Evolution of White Women's Experience in Early America," *American Historical Review*, 89 (1984): 593–619, provides a summary of recent literature. Benjamin Franklin's comments about his wife's contribution to their printing business are taken from *Benjamin Franklin: The Autobiography and Other Writings*, ed. L. Jesse Lemisch (New York, 1961).

The following works illuminate links between evolving gender roles and other changes in the antebellum North's social, cultural, and political life: Ellen Carol DuBois, *Feminism and Suffrage: The Emergence of an Independent Women's Movement in America, 1848–1869* (Ithaca, 1978); Blanche Glassman Hersh, *The Slavery of Sex: Feminist Abolitionists in America* (Urbana, 1978); Barbara Berg, *The Remembered Gate: Origins of American Feminism—The Woman and the City* (New York, 1978); Barbara Leslie Epstein, *The Politics of Domesticity: Women, Evangelism, and Temperance in Nineteenth Century America* (Middletown, Conn., 1981); Mary Ryan, *Cradle of the Middle Class: The Family in Oneida County, New York, 1790–1865* (Cambridge, Mass., 1981); Elisabeth Griffith, *In Her Own Right: The Life of Elizabeth Cady Stanton* (New York, 1984); Nancy A. Hewitt, *Women's Activism and Social Change: Rochester, New York, 1822–1872* (Ithaca, 1984); and Carroll Smith-Rosenberg, *Disorderly Conduct: Visions of Gender in Victorian America* (New York, 1985). Considerable detail about and a general feeling for the spirit of antebellum reform movements are found in Alice Felt Tyler, *Freedom's Ferment: Phases of American Social History from the Colonial Period to the Outbreak of the Civil War* (1944; reprint, New York, 1962), and Ronald G. Walters, *American Reformers, 1815–1860* (New York, 1978).

The distinction between the standards of the northern middle class and various strata of working-class women was pointed out a generation ago in Gerda Lerner, "The Lady and the Mill Girl: Changes in the Status of Women in the Age of Jackson, 1800–1840," *Midcontinent American Studies Journal*, 10 (1969): 5–14. Her point has been amplified in studies of female (and especially Irish-born) wage earners cited earlier. See also Carol Groneman, "Working-Class Immigrant Women in Mid-Nineteenth-Century New York: The Irish Woman's Experience," *Journal of Urban History*, 4 (1978): 255–73, and other articles by the same author; and Amy Gilman Srebnick, "True Womanhood and Hard Times: Women and Early New York Industrialization, 1840–1860," Ph.D. dissertation, State University of New York at Stony Brook, 1979.

Information about popular leisure activities in the North can be found in Foster Rhea Dulles, *A History of Recreation: America Learns to Play* (rev. ed., New York, 1965), and Melvin L. Adelman, *A Sporting Time: New York City and the Rise of Modern Athletics, 1820–70* (Urbana, 1986). Frederic Cople Jaher's *The Urban Establishment* (already cited) has some interesting things to say about upper-class leisure. The chasm between the northern middle class's concept of propriety and common forms of male working-class entertainment is discussed in many recent studies on the antebellum working class. See also Susan G. Davis, *Parades and Power: Street Theatre in Nineteenth-Century Philadelphia* (Philadelphia, 1986); David Grimsted, *Melodrama Unveiled: American Theater and Culture, 1800–1850* (Chicago, 1968); Peter George Buckley, "To the Opera House: Culture and Society in New York City, 1820–1860," Ph.D. dissertation, City University of New York, 1984; Elliott J. Gorn, "Good-Bye Boys, I Die a True American: Homicide, Nativism, and Working-Class Culture in Antebellum New York City," *Journal of American History*, 74 (1987): 388–410; and idem, *The Manly Art: Bare-Knuckle Prize Fighting in America* (Ithaca, 1986); Ian R. Tyrell, *Sobering Up: From Temperance to Prohibition in Antebellum America, 1800–1860* (Greenwood, 1979); W. J. Rorabaugh, *The Alcoholic Republic: An American Tradition* (New York, 1979); Jed Dannenbaum, *Drink and Disorder: Temperance Reform in Cincinnati from the Washingtonian Revival to the WCTU* (Urbana, 1984); and Richard B. Stott, *Workers in the Metropolis: Class, Ethnicity, and Youth in Antebellum New York City* (Ithaca, 1990).

An inclusive survey of religion in the antebellum era is found in Sidney Ahlstrom's *A Religious History of the American People* (New Haven, 1972). The nature and growth of evangelical Protestantism in the North and of the "benevolent empire" are treated in William McLoughlin, *Revivals, Awakenings, and Reform* (Chicago, 1978); Timothy Smith, *Revivalism & Social Reform: American Protestantism on the Eve of the Civil War* (1957; reprint, Baltimore, 1980); Clifford S. Griffin, *Their Brothers' Keep-*

ers: *Moral Stewardship in the United States, 1800–1865* (New Brunswick, 1960); Allan Stanley Horlick, *Country Boys and Merchant Princes: The Social Control of Young Men in New York* (Lewisburg, Pa., 1975); Richard Carwardine, *Trans-Atlantic Revivalism: Popular Evangelicalism in Britain and America, 1790–1865* (Greenwood, 1978); Paul Boyer, *Urban Masses and Moral Order in America, 1820–1920* (Cambridge, Mass., 1978); and Paul Johnson, *A Shopkeeper's Millennium: Society and Revivals in Rochester, New York, 1815–1837* (New York, 1978). Jama Lazerow's "A Good Time Coming: Religion and the Emergence of Labor Activism in Antebellum New England" (Ph.D. dissertation, Brandeis University, 1982) taps a vein of working-class evangelicalism that has attracted the attention of other students of labor history. The subject cries out for reconsideration. For an introduction to the relationship between abolitionism and antebellum Protestantism, see John R. McKivigan, *The War Against Proslavery Religion, 1830–1865* (Ithaca, 1984). See also Jean R. Soderlund, *Quakers & Slavery: A Divided Spirit* (Princeton, 1985).

Antebellum American Catholicism has received considerably less attention than Protestantism. On the politics of the clerical hierarchy, I have relied chiefly upon H. Daniel-Rops, *The Church in an Age of Revolution, 1789–1870* (New York, 1965); Joseph N. Moody, ed., *Church and Society: Catholic Social and Political Thought and Movements, 1789–1950* (New York, 1953); and Kenneth Scott Latourette, *The Nineteenth Century in Europe: Background and the Roman Catholic Phase* (vol. 1 of *A History of Christianity in the Nineteenth and Twentieth Centuries*) (New York, 1958). On the nature of popular Irish Catholicism, see Emmet Larkin, "The Devotional Revolution in Ireland, 1850–75," *American Historical Review,* 77 (1972): 625–52; David W. Miller, "Irish Catholicism and the Great Famine," *Journal of Social History,* 9 (1975): 81–98; and Jay P. Dolan, *The Immigrant Church: New York's German and Irish Catholics, 1815–1865* (Baltimore, 1975).

Antebellum free thought demands a new look. We now rely

upon Albert Post, *Popular Freethought in America, 1825–1850* (New York, 1943), for the only overview and supplement it with information presented in a number of monographs on labor history already cited.

4. *"The Anointed Lords of Creation":*
Culture and Society in the Antebellum South

In depicting family and gender patterns in the planter class, I have referred to Anne Firor Scott, *The Southern Lady: From Pedestal to Politics, 1830–1930* (Chicago, 1970); Catherine Clinton, *The Plantation Mistress: Woman's World in the Old South* (New York, 1982); and Elizabeth Fox Genovese, *Within the Plantation Household: Black and White Women of the Old South* (Chapel Hill, 1988). See also Suzanne Lebsock, *The Free Women of St. Petersburg: Status and Culture in a Southern Town, 1784–1860* (New York, 1984). The hopelessness of challenging the alliance of slavery and patriarchy from within the Big House is suggested in Gerda Lerner, *The Grimké Sisters from South Carolina: Pioneers for Woman's Rights and Abolition* (New York, 1967). The relationship between evangelical Protestantism and the southern social order has been treated in Richard R. Beeman and Rhys Isaac, "Cultural Conflict and Social Change in the Revolutionary South: Lunenburg County, Virginia," *Journal of Southern History*, 66 (1980): 525–50; Rhys Isaac, *The Transformation of Virginia, 1740–1790* (Chapel Hill, 1982); Dickson D. Bruce, Jr., "Religion, Society and Culture in the Old South: A Comparative View," *American Quarterly*, 26 (1974): 399–416; Donald Matthews, *Religion in the Old South* (Chicago, 1977); Anne C. Loveland, *Southern Evangelicals and the Social Order, 1800–1860* (Baton Rouge, 1980); John H. Boles, ed., *Masters and Slaves in the House of the Lord: Race and Religion in the American South, 1740–1870* (Lexington, Ky., 1988), especially the articles by Alan Gallay and Blake Touchstone; Mitchell Snay, "American Thought and Southern Distinctiveness: The Southern Clergy and the Sanctification of Slavery," *Civil War History*, 35 (1989):

311–28. Family and cultural patterns in the antebellum South's up-country require much more study than they have thus far received. Suggestive observations can be found in William L. Barney, "Patterns of Crisis: Alabama White Families and Social Change, 1850–70," *Sociology & Social Research*, 63 (1979): 524–43; and Elliot Gorn, " 'Gouge and Bite, Pull Hair and Scratch': The Social Significance of Fighting in the Southern Backcountry," *American Historical Review*, 90 (1985): 18–43.

The study of family, religion, and cultural life among slaves has yielded rich returns over the past twenty years. My discussion makes heavy use of Herbert G. Gutman, *The Black Family in Slavery and Freedom, 1750–1925* (New York, 1976); Eugene Genovese's *Roll, Jordan, Roll* (already cited); Charles Joyner, *Down by the Riverside: A South Carolina Slave Community* (Urbana, 1984); Lawrence W. Levine, *Black Culture and Black Consciousness: Afro-American Folk Thought from Slavery to Freedom* (New York, 1977); George P. Rawick, *From Sundown to Sunup: The Making of the Black Community* (Westport, Conn.: Greenwood, 1972); Albert J. Raboteau, *Slave Religion: The "Invisible Institution" in the Antebellum South* (New York, 1978); Leslie Howard Owens, *This Species of Property: Slave Life and Culture in the Old South* (New York, 1976); Thomas L. Weber, *Deep Like the Rivers: Education in the Slave Quarter Community, 1831–1865* (New York, 1978); Sterling Stuckey, *Slave Culture: Nationalist Theory and the Foundations of Black America* (New York, 1987); John T. O'Brien, "Factory, Church, and Community: Blacks in Antebellum Richmond," *Journal of Southern History*, 44 (1978): 509–36; Jacqueline Jones, *Labor of Love, Labor of Sorrow: Black Women, Work, and the Family from Slavery to the Present* (New York, 1985); John Blassingame, *The Slave Community* (2nd ed., New York, 1979); and C. Eric Lincoln and Lawrence H. Mamiya, *The Black Church in the African American Experience* (Durham, 1990). Data on family breakups resulting from sale and migration can also be found in Michael Tadman, *Speculators and Slaves: Masters, Traders, and Slaves in the Old South* (Madison, 1989), and Robert William Fogel, *Without Consent or Contract* (already cited).

Insight into social values and leisure activities in the antebellum white South can be found in W. J. Cash, *The Mind of the South* (New York, 1941); William R. Taylor, *Cavalier and Yankee: The Old South and American National Character* (New York, 1961); Clement Eaton, *The Growth of Southern Civilization, 1790–1860* (New York, 1961); David Bertelson, *The Lazy South* (New York, 1967); Bertram Wyatt-Brown, *Southern Honor: Ethics and Behavior in the Old South* (New York, 1982); idem, *Yankee Saints and Southern Sinners* (Baton Rouge, 1985); Dale A. Somers, *The Rise of Sports in New Orleans, 1850–1900* (Baton Rouge, 1972); Steven M. Stowe, *Intimacy and Power in the Old South: Ritual in the Lives of the Planters* (Baltimore, 1987); William Ransom Hogan, "Amusements in the Republic of Texas," *Journal of Southern History*, 3 (1937): 397–421; and Guion Griffis Johnson, *Ante-Bellum North Carolina* (Chapel Hill, 1937); and Raimondo Luragi, *The Rise and Fall of the Plantation South* (New York, 1978).

5. *"Called by the Same Name":*
The Many Meanings of Liberty

The United States as the site of humanity's spiritual and political rebirth is explored in Ernest Lee Tuveson, *Redeemer Nation: The Idea of America's Millennial Role* (Chicago, 1968), and Nathan O. Hatch, *The Sacred Cause of Liberty: Republican Thought and the Millennium in Revolutionary New England* (New Haven, 1977). The illustrative quotation from Thomas Paine comes from *Common Sense* (1776; reprint, New York, 1986). Lincoln's observation about the ambiguity of "liberty" (which I first heard in a paper delivered by James M. McPherson) is quoted from Roy P. Basler, ed., *The Collected Works of Abraham Lincoln*, 8 vols. (New Brunswick, 1953). So are many other citations from Lincoln scattered throughout the text.

The broadening of political democracy in the free states and its significance deserves a reexamination in the light of the historiography of the last twenty years. Until then, see Elisha P. Douglass, *Rebels and Democrats: The Struggle for Equal Political Rights and Majority Rule During the American Revolution* (1955; reprint, Chicago, 1965); Chilton Williamson, *American Suffrage: From Property to Democracy, 1760–1860* (Princeton, 1960); Walter Dean Burnham, "The Changing Shape of the American Political Universe," *American Political Science Review,* 59 (1965): 7–28; idem, "Those High Nineteenth-Century American Voting Turnouts: Fact or Fiction?" *Journal of Interdisciplinary History,* 16 (1986): 613–44; Lynn L. Marshall, "The Strange Stillbirth of the Whig Party," *American Historical Review,* 72 (1966–67): 445–68; and Harry L. Watson, *Liberty and Power: The Politics of Jacksonian America* (New York, 1990). A restudy of the expansion of political democracy in most of the North would also shed light on the Dorr War, the most accessible studies of which remain Arthur May Mowry, *The Dorr War: The Constitutional Struggle in Rhode Island* (1901; reprint, New York, 1970); Marvin E. Gettleman, *The Dorr Rebellion: A Study in American Radicalism, 1833–1849* (New York, 1973); and George M. Dennison, *The Dorr Warr: Republicanism on Trial, 1831–1861* (Lexington, Ky., 1976).

For material bearing on the meaning of republicanism and the debate over economic rights in the North, see Robert E. Shalhope, "Republicanism and Early American Historiography," *William and Mary Quarterly,* 39 (1982): 334–56; J. E. Crowley, *This Sheba, Self: The Conceptualization of Economic Life in Eighteenth-Century America* (Baltimore, 1974); Gordon S. Wood, *The Creation of the American Republic, 1776–1787* (New York, 1969); Joyce Appleby, *Capitalism and a New Social Order: The Republican Vision of the 1790s* (New York, 1984); John R. Nelson, Jr., *Liberty and Property: Political Economy and Policymaking in the New Nation, 1789–1812* (Baltimore, 1987); Paul E. Conkin, *Prophets of Prosperity: America's First Political Economists* (Bloomington, 1980); John K. Alexander, *Render Them Submissive: Responses to Poverty in Philadelphia, 1760–1800* (Amherst, 1980); Joseph Dorfman, *The Economic Mind in American Civilization, 1606–1685,* 5 vols. (1946; reprint, New York, 1966); Eric Foner, *Tom Paine and Revolutionary America* (New

York, 1976); Ronald Schultz, "The Small-Producer Tradition and the Moral Origins of Artisan Radicalism in Philadelphia, 1720–1810," *Past & Present*, No. 127 (1990): 84–116; Irving Mark and Eugene L. Schwaab, eds., *The Faith of Our Fathers: An Anthology Expressing the Aspirations of the American Common Man, 1790–1860* (New York, 1952); Philip S. Foner, ed., *We, the Other People: Alternative Declarations of Independence by Labor Groups, Farmers, Woman's Rights Advocates, Socialists, and Blacks, 1829–1975* (Urbana, 1976); John R. Commons et al., eds., *Documentary History of American Industrial Society* (Cleveland, 1910–11); idem, *A History of Labour in the United States*, 4 vols. (1918; reprint, New York, 1966); Folsom and Lubar, *eds., The Philosophy of Manufactures* (cited earlier); Joseph L. Blau, ed., *Social Theories of Jacksonian Democracy: Representative Writers of the Period 1825–1850* (Indianapolis, 1954); and a number of the studies in labor history cited above. The quotations from Francis Lieber are taken from Frank Freidel, *Francis Lieber: Nineteenth-Century Liberal* (1947; reprint, Gloucester, Mass., 1968), and Thomas Sergeant Perry, ed., *The Life and Letters of Francis Lieber* (Boston, 1882). "Communitarianism" has been examined many times. I have made greatest use of Charles Nordhoff, *The Communistic Societies of the United States, from Personal Visit and Observation* (1875; reprint, New York, 1965); and J. F. C. Harrison, *Quest for the New Moral World: Robert Owen and the Owenites in Britain and America* (New York, 1969).

The literature on land reform is thinner than the subject deserves. The principal work on the subject is still Helene S. Zahler, *Eastern Workingmen and National Land Policy, 1829–1862* (New York, 1941), an excellent study that, a half century later, needs updating. Local studies of labor and social reform have added only incrementally to Zahler's portrait. Mark A. Lause is presently at work on a modern interpretation. In the meantime, see contextual information contained in George M. Stephenson, *The Political History of the Public Lands, from 1840 to 1862* (Boston, 1917); Benjamin Horace Hibbard, *A History of the Public Land Policies* (Madison, 1965); Vernon Carstensen, ed., *The*

Public Lands: Studies in the History of the Public Domain (Madison, 1968); and Malcolm J. Rohrbough, *The Land Office Business: The Settlement and Administration of American Public Lands, 1789–1837* (New York, 1968).

The white South's discussions of slavery can be examined in a number of reprints and documentary collections. In addition to some already cited, see Thomas R. Dew, *Review of the Debate in the Virginia Legislature of 1831 and 1832* (1832; reprint, Westport, Conn., 1970); Eric L. McKitrick, ed., *Slavery Defended: The Views of the Old South* (Englewood Cliffs, N.J., 1963); *The Proslavery Argument; As Maintained by the Most Distinguished Writers of the Southern States, Containing the Several Essays, on the Subject, of Chancellor Harper, Governor Hammond, Dr. Simms, and Professor Dew* (1852; reprint, New York, 1968); Drew Gilpin Faust, ed., *The Ideology of Slavery: Proslavery Thought in the Antebellum South, 1830–1860* (Baton Rouge, 1981); and Harvey Wish, ed., *Ante-Bellum: Writings of George Fitzhugh and Hinton Rowan Helper on Slavery* (New York, 1960). I have supplemented these sources with selections from Clyde N. Wilson, ed., *The Papers of John C. Calhoun* (Columbia, S.C., 1959–   ); and Richard K. Crallé, ed., *The Works of John C. Calhoun*, 6 vols. (New York, 1855).

The terms of this discussion have been evaluated in Clement Eaton, *The Mind of the Old South* (1964; rev. ed., Baton Rouge, 1967); Harvey Wish, *George Fitzhugh: Propagandist of the Old South* (Baton Rouge, 1943); Eugene D. Genovese, "The Logical Outcome of the Slaveholder's Philosophy," in *The World the Slaveholders Made* (already cited); Winthrop D. Jordan, *White over Black: American Attitudes Toward the Negro, 1550–1812* (1968; reprint, New York, 1977); George M. Fredrickson, *The Black Image in the White Mind: The Debate on Afro-American Character and Destiny, 1817–1914* (New York, 1971); Allen Kaufman, *Capitalism, Slavery, and Republican Values: American Political Economists, 1819–1848* (Austin, Tex., 1982); William W. Freehling, *Prelude to Civil War: The Nullification Controversy in South Carolina, 1816–1836* (New York, 1965);

William J. Cooper, Jr., *The South and the Politics of Slavery, 1826–1856* (Baton Rouge, 1978); Alison Goodyear Freehling, *Drift Toward Dissolution: The Virginia Slavery Debate of 1831–1832* (Baton Rouge, 1982); and Larry E. Tise, *Proslavery: A History of the Defense of Slavery in America, 1701–1840* (Baton Rouge, 1987). A powerful general argument rooting American racial doctrine in the ideological requirements of slavery is presented in Barbara Jeanne Fields, "Slavery, Race and Ideology in the United States of America," *New Left Review,* 181 (1990): 95–118. The newest contribution on this subject is the most comprehensive, subtle, convincing, and (with the possible exception of Tise's book) the most stylistically eccentric—William W. Freehling, *The Road to Disunion: Secessionists at Bay,* 1776–1854 (New York, 1990). Freehling's principal contribution is to relate political differences over slavery within the white South to intraregional variations in geography, climate, land tenure, economic development, and social relations. See also John Niven, *John C. Calhoun and the Price of Union: A Biography* (Baton Rouge, 1988).

The outlook and political influence of the South's smallholding white population are addressed in a number of the studies of the southern up-country cited in the bibliography to Chapter 1. See also Fletcher M. Green, *Constitutional Development in the South Atlantic States, 1776–1860* (Chapel Hill, 1930); idem, "Democracy in the Old South," *Journal of Southern History,* 12 (1946): 3–23; Harry L. Watson, "Conflict and Collaboration: Yeomen, Slaveholders, and Politics in the Antebellum South," *Social History,* 10 (1985): 273–98; J. Mills Thornton, *Politics and Power in a Slave Society: Alabama, 1800–1860* (Baton Rouge, 1978); and Cooper, *The South and the Politics of Slavery* (already cited). The Missouri conflict is analyzed in Davis's *Problem of Slavery in the Age of Revolution* (already cited) and referred to in virtually every study of the roots of the Civil War. Remarkably, however, Glover Moore's brief work, *The Missouri Controversy, 1819–1821* (Nashville, 1937), remains the essential reference. (Here is another subject long overdue for review.)

The attraction of Democrats and Whigs for different electoral constituencies in antebellum America, North and South, is suggested in the following works: Marvin Meyers, *The Jacksonian Persuasion: Politics and Belief* (Stanford, 1957); James Roger Sharp, *The Jacksonians versus the Banks: Politics in the States after the Panic of 1837* (New York, 1970); John Ashworth, *"Agrarians" and "Aristocrats": Party Political Ideology in the United States, 1837–1846* (London, 1983); Daniel Walker Howe, *The Political Culture of the American Whigs* (Chicago, 1979); Jean H. Baker, *Affairs of Party: The Political Culture of Northern Democrats in the Mid-Nineteenth Century* (Ithaca, 1983); Robert Ernst, "The One and Only Mike Walsh," *New-York Historical Society Quarterly*, 36 (1952): 43–65; Amy Bridges, *A City in the Republic: Antebellum New York and the Origins of Machine Politics* (Cambridge, Eng., 1984); Harry L. Watson, *Jacksonian Politics and Community Conflict: The Emergence of the Second American Party System in Cumberland County, North Carolina* (Baton Rouge, 1981); and Freehling, *Road to Disunion* (already cited).

6. To *"Fight Against the Serpent"*: Antislavery and Its Early Progress

On slave revolts and attempted revolts, see Herbert Aptheker, *American Negro Slave Revolts: Nat Turner, Denmark Vesey, Gabriel, and Others* (1943; reprint, New York, 1969); Eric Foner, ed., *Nat Turner* (Englewood Cliffs, N.J., 1971); Michael [Gerald W.] Mullin, *Flight and Rebellion: Slave Resistance in Eighteenth-Century Virginia* (New York, 1972); Stephen B. Oates, *The Fires of Jubilee: Nat Turner's Fierce Rebellion* (New York, 1975); and Harvey Wish, "The Slave Insurrection Panic of 1856," *Journal of Southern History*, 5 (1939): 206–22. The most fertile general analysis to date is presented in Eugene D. Genovese, *From Rebellion to Revolution: Afro-American Slave Revolts in the Making of the Modern World* (Baton Rouge, 1979).

The evolution of the organized antislavery movement can be

traced with the aid of James Brewer Stewart's fine survey, *Holy Warriors: The Abolitionists and American Slavery* (New York, 1976); Aileen S. Kraditor, *Means and Ends in American Abolitionism: Garrison and His Critics on Strategy and Tactics, 1834–1850* (New York, 1967); Russel B. Nye, *William Lloyd Garrison and the Humanitarian Reformers* (Boston, 1955); John L. Thomas, *The Liberator: William Lloyd Garrison* (Boston, 1963); the essays in Martin Duberman, ed., *The Antislavery Vanguard: New Essays on the Abolitionists* (Princeton, 1965); Lewis Perry and Michael Fellman, eds., *Antislavery Reconsidered: New Perspectives on the Abolitionists* (Baton Rouge, 1979); Bertram Wyatt-Brown, *Lewis Tappan and Evangelical War against Slavery* (Cleveland, 1969); Robert H. Abzug, *Passionate Liberator: Theodore Dwight Weld and the Dilemma of Reform* (New York, 1980). Ronald G. Walters presents a valuable thematic analysis in *The Antislavery Appeal: American Abolitionism after 1830* (New York, 1978). Gordon E. Finnie explores an important aspect of the subject in "The Antislavery Movement in the Upper South before 1840," *Journal of Southern History*, 35 (1969): 319–42.

Organized opposition to slavery among northern blacks is discussed in Benjamin Quarles, *Black Abolitionists* (New York, 1969); Jane H. Pease and William H. Pease, *They Who Would be Free: Blacks' Search for Freedom, 1830–1861* (Urbana, 1974); Vincent Harding, *There Is a River: The Black Struggle for Freedom in America* (New York, 1981); and Roy E. Finbine, Michael F. Hembree, and Donald Yacovne, eds., *The Black Abolitionist Papers*. Vol. 3: *The United States, 1830–1846* (Chapel Hill, 1991). David Walker is quoted from William Loren Katz, ed., *Walker's Appeal* (New York, 1969). The quoted 1813 speech by George Lawrence is taken from Dorothy Porter, ed., *Early Negro Writing, 1760–1837* (Boston, 1971); for the 1799 appeal of Philadelphia free blacks, see Herbert Aptheker, ed., *A Documentary History of the Negro People in the United States*. Vol. 1: *From Colonial Times through the Civil War* (New York, 1951). Thomas L. Haskell recently sparked a lively and wide-ranging discussion of the social-intellectual sources of abolitionism in his critique of

Davis's *Problem of Slavery in the Age of Revolution*, entitled "Capitalism and the Origins of the Humanitarian Sensibility." *American Historical Review*, 90 (1985): 339–61, 457–566. Davis replied in "Reflections on Abolitionism and Ideological Hegemony," *American Historical Review*, 92 (1987): 797–812. John Ashworth joined the discussion in "The Relationship between Capitalism and Humanitarianism," *American Historical Review*, 92 (1987): 813–28; and Haskell's rejoinder can be found in "Convention and Hegemonic Interest in the Debate over Antislavery: A Reply to Davis and Ashworth," *American Historical Review*, 92 (1987): 829–78. The debate might have advanced the discussion further but for Haskell's apparent misunderstanding of Davis's basic argument.

The northern working class's response to slavery and abolitionism has been analyzed in Hermann Schlüter, *Lincoln, Labor, and Slavery: A Chapter from the Social History of America* (1913; reprint, New York, 1965); Joseph G. Rayback, "The American Workingman and the Antislavery Crusade," *Journal of Economic History*, 3 (1943): 152–63; Williston Lofton, "Abolition and Labor," *Journal of Negro History*, 33 (1948): 249–83; Philip S. Foner, *History of the Labor Movement in the United States*. Vol. 1: *From Colonial Times to the Founding of the American Federation of Labor* (New York, 1947); Bernard Mandel, *Labor: Free and Slave—Workingmen and the Anti-Slavery Movement in the United States* (New York, 1955); John Barkley Jentz, "Artisans, Evangelicals, and the City: A Social History of Abolition and Labor Reform in Jacksonian New York," Ph.D. dissertation, City University of New York, 1977; Jonathan A. Glickstein, " 'Poverty Is Not Slavery': American Abolitionists and the Competitive Labor Market," in Perry and Fellman, *Antislavery Reconsidered* (already cited); Eric Foner, "Abolitionism and the Labor Movement in Ante-Bellum America," in his *Politics and Ideology in the Age of the Civil War* (New York, 1980); and Edward Magdol, *The Antislavery Rank and File: A Social Profile of the Abolitionist Constituency* (New York, 1986). Also relevant are Gilbert Osofsky, "Abolitionism, Irish Immigrants, and the Dilemmas of Romantic Nationalism," *American Historical Review,* 80 (1985): 889–912, and Daniel J. McInerney, "'A State of Commerce': Market Power and Slave Power in Abolitionist Political Economy," *Civil War History,* 37 (1991): 101–19; Leonard L. Richards, *"Gentlemen of Property and Standing": Anti-Abolition Mobs in Jacksonian America* (New York, 1970); and Levine, *The Spirit of 1848* (already cited).

7. *"A Firebell in the Night":* The Struggle Escalates

The now classic study of nullification is William Freehling's *Prelude to Civil War* (already cited). But see also Richard H. Brown, "The Missouri Crisis, Slavery, and the Politics of Jacksonianism," *South Atlantic Quarterly,* 65 (1966): 55–72; Richard Ellis, *The Union at Risk: Jacksonian Democracy, States' Rights, and the Nullification Crisis* (New York, 1987); and Freehling's recent *Road to Disunion* (already cited). The planter response to slave rebellions, abolitionism, and other threats to the peculiar institution is discussed in Clement Eaton, *The Freedom-of-Thought Struggle in the Old South* (1940; rev. ed., New York, 1964); idem, *Mind of the Old South* (already cited); Charles Sydnor, *The Development of Southern Sectionalism* (Baton Rouge, 1948); Russel B. Nye, *Fettered Freedom: Civil Liberties and the Slavery Controversy, 1830–1860* (East Lansing, Mich., 1949); Ira Berlin's *Slaves without Masters* (already cited).

The response of the northern business elite to the deepening of sectional conflict is traced in Richards, *"Gentlemen of Property and Standing"* (already cited); Kinley J. Brauer, *Cotton versus Conscience: Massachusetts Whig Politics and Southwestern Expansion, 1843–1848* (Lexington, Ky., 1967); Thomas H. O'Connor, *Lords of the Loom: The Cotton Whigs and the Coming of the Civil War* (New York, 1968); and Philip S. Foner, *Business & Slavery: The New York Merchants and the Irrepressible Conflict* (1941; reprint, New York, 1968).

My discussion of abolitionism's popular constituency, the

northern reaction to planter repression (including the gag rule), and the reflection of the early antislavery struggle in electoral politics draws upon Nye's *Fettered Freedom*; Gerald Sorin, *The New York Abolitionists: A Case Study of Political Radicalism* (Westport, Conn., 1971); Reinhard O. Johnson, "The Liberty Party in Massachusetts, 1840–1848: Antislavery Third Party Politics in the Bay State," *Civil War History*, 28 (1982): 237–65; Alan M. Kraut, ed., *Crusaders and Compromisers: Essays on the Relationship of the Antislavery Struggle to the Antebellum Party System* (Westport Conn., 1983); James Brewer Stewart, *Joshua R. Giddings and the Tactics of Radical Politics* (Cleveland, 1970); and Richard H. Sewell, *Ballots for Freedom: Antislavery Politics in the United States, 1837–1860* (New York, 1976). On the Mexican War and the northern reaction to it, see especially John H. Schroeder, *Mr. Polk's War: American Opposition and Dissent, 1846–1848* (Madison, 1973).

8. *"Keep It Within Limits"*: *Western Lands and Free Soil*

For general guidance through the political developments of the 1840s and 1850s I have looked to Allan Nevins, *Ordeal of the Union*, 2 vols. (New York, 1947); and idem, *The Emergence of Lincoln*, 2 vols. (New York, 1950); David M. Potter, *The Impending Crisis: 1848–1861*, ed. Don E. Fehrenbacher (New York, 1976); Cooper, *The South and The Politics of Slavery* (already cited); James M. McPherson's *Ordeal by Fire: The Civil War and Reconstruction* (New York, 1982) and his *Battle Cry of Freedom: The Civil War Era* (New York, 1988). A number of essays in Kenneth Stampp's *The Imperiled Union: Essays on the Background of the Civil War* (New York, 1980) are unmatched in value. Also of great use, despite the passage of time, is Arthur C. Cole, *The Irrepressible Conflict: 1850–1865* (1934; reprint, Chicago, 1971). Major statements of party policy can be found in Kirk H. Porter and Donald Bruce Johnson, eds., *National Party Platforms, 1840–1960* (Urbana, 1961). Kenneth M. Stampp, ed., *The*

Causes of the Civil War (1959; rev. ed., Englewood Cliffs, N.J., 1975), contains many illuminating contemporary documents and editorial comments of major interpretive value.

The genesis of the Wilmot Proviso is uncovered in Chaplain W. Morrison, *Democratic Politics and Sectionalism: The Wilmot Proviso Controversy* (Chapel Hill, 1967), and Eric Foner, "The Wilmot Proviso Revisited," *Journal of American History*, 56 (1969): 262–79. On the racist admixture in northern free-soil sentiment, see Eugene H. Berwanger, *The Frontier Against Slavery: Western Anti-Negro Prejudices and the Slavery Extension Controversy* (Urbana, 1967). Fissures within the Whig party are lucidly analyzed in Brauer, *Cotton versus Conscience* (already cited). On the eruption of the Free Soil party, see Herbert D. A. Donovan, *The Barnburners: A Study of the Internal Movements in the Political History of New York State and of the Resulting Changes in Political Affiliation, 1830–1852* (New York, 1925); Joseph G. Rayback, *The Election of 1848* (Lexington, Ky., 1970); Frederick J. Blue, *The Free Soilers: Third Party Politics, 1848–54* (Urbana, 1973); and Sewell's *Ballots for Freedom* (already cited). The escape of slaves to the North and the impact on sectional politics are examined from various angles in Larry Gara, *The Liberty Line: The Legend of the Underground Railroad* (Lexington, Ky., 1961); Thomas D. Morris, *Free Men All: The Personal Liberty Laws of the North, 1780–1861* (Baltimore, 1974); Paul Finkelman, *An Imperfect Union: Slavery, Federalism, and Comity* (Chapel Hill, 1981); and Stanley W. Campbell, *The Slave Catchers: Enforcement of the Fugitive Slave Law, 1850–1860* (Chapel Hill, 1968).

On the Kansas-Nebraska Act and its immediate aftermath, see Roy F. Nichols, "The Kansas-Nebraska Act: A Century of Historiography," *Mississippi Valley Historical Review*, 43 (1956): 187–212; James C. Malin, *The Nebraska Question, 1852–1854* (Lawrence, Kan., 1953); James P. Rawley, *Race and Politics: "Bleeding Kansas" and the Coming of the Civil War* (New York, 1969); and Gerald W. Wolff, *The Kansas-Nebraska Bill: Party, Section, and the Coming of the Civil War* (New York, 1978). On John Brown's life and role in Kansas (and later at Harpers Ferry), see W. E. B. Du Bois, *John Brown* (1919; reprint New York, 1972); Louis Ruchames, ed., *John Brown: The Making of a Revolutionary* (New York, 1959); F. B. Sanborn, ed., *The Life and Letters of John Brown* (1885; reprint, New York, 1969); Benjamin Quarles, *Allies for Freedom: Blacks and John Brown* (New York, 1974); and Stephen B. Oates, *To Purge This Land with Blood: A Biography of John Brown* (Amherst, Mass., 1984). The letter sent to Brown by a free black woman is taken from James Redpath, ed., *Echoes of Harper's Ferry* (1860; reprint, Westport, Conn., 1970). The dismissal of Brown as "a psychopathic ne'er-do-well" can be found in William E. Gienapp, *The Origins of the Republican Party, 1852–1856* (New York, 1987).

9. *"Anti Nebraska Feeling Is Too Deep":* *Origins and Triumph of Republicanism*

The disintegration of the Whigs (and therewith the "second party system") and the rise of the American and Republican parties have been analyzed in a large number of studies, including Michael Fitzgibbon Holt, *Forging a Majority: The Formation of the Republican Party in Pittsburgh, 1848–1860* (New Haven, 1969); idem, *The Political Crisis of the 1850's* (New York, 1978); Ronald P. Formisano, *The Birth of Mass Political Parties: Michigan, 1827–1861* (Princeton, 1971); Robert Kelley, *The Cultural Pattern in American Politics: The First Century* (New York, 1979); Paul Kleppner, *The Third Electoral System, 1853–1892: Parties, Voters, and Political Cultures* (Chapel Hill, 1979); Stephen L. Hansen, *The Making of the Third Party System: Voters and Parties in Illinois, 1850–1876* (Ann Arbor, 1980); Stephen E. Maizlish, *The Triumph of Sectionalism: The Transformation of Ohio Politics, 1844–1856* (Kent, Ohio, 1983); Dale Baum, *The Civil War Party System: The Case of Massachusetts, 1848–1876* (Chapel Hill, 1984). All contain invaluable data. The most recent contribution is the most ambitious and deeply researched— William E. Gienapp's *The Origins of the Republican Party* (already cited).

Some (though by no means all) of these scholars identify with the so-called ethnocultural school of voting analysis. The most ardent exponents of this school minimize the importance (in the 1850s and in general) of both class identities and substantive political issues to the formation of party loyalties. Such considerations mattered, they argue, only to a numerically tiny elite. "Political notables," said Paul Kleppner, responded politically to specific issues because they were "active, well informed, and articulate. Theirs wcrc political worlds of principles and policy, information and issues" (7). But "most people generally lacked the levels of contextual information that are common among the elite. As a consequence, mass belief systems are more loosely constrained, they encompass a narrower range of relevant ideas, and the character of those elements central to the mass systems is typically less generic or abstract than in elite belief systems" (8). The voting decisions of most people, he explained, were determined not by their feelings about slavery, its expansion, or related issues but by their response to "irreconcilably conflicting values emanating from divergent ethnic and religious subcultures" (144). The squaring-off between the North and South, Kleppner concluded, represented a conflict "bctwecn Yankee moralist subculture and white southern subculture," paralleled (within the North) by a division between "pietistic [i.e., evangelical Protestant] and antipietistic subcultures" (58). Robert Kelley's *Cultural Pattern in American Politics* made the distinction between political issues and ethnic culture even sharper, arguing that "the Republican party was not primarily an antislavery party; rather, it was anti-Southern and pro-Yankee" (208). In *Forging a Majority* Michael Holt went further still, arguing that many members of distinct religious groups voted differently principally to express their hostility for one another. While conceding that "Protestants and Catholics probably took different views on nonreligious issues such as slavery extension" (217), Holt's explanation of popular political alignments minimized the significance of such issues. He asserted, instead, that "a large number of Protestants voted Republican out of a negative reflex response to the Catholics in the Democratic party. Simply because Catholics were Democrats, and not necessarily for any positive reasons, many Protestants voted Republican" (218n). In this respect (as Kenneth Stampp pointed out some time ago), the ethnoculturalist argument belongs to a long tradition of "revisionist" interpretations that attribute the coming of the Civil War to popular hostilities divorced from (or that exaggerated) actual conflicts of interest between North and South. My own approach to the subject departs from such reasoning not by denying cultural clashes but by trying to reconnect such conflicts to the socioeconomic and political forces at work in the larger society.

William Gienapp disassociates himself from some of the most extreme of the ethnoculturalist tenets. He acknowledges, for example, that the mass of voters were very much interested in the issues explicitly advanced in party platforms. (His earlier essay, "Politics Seem to Enter into Everything," in Stephen E. Maizlish, ed., *Essays on American Antebellum Politics, 1840–1860* [College Station, Tex., 1982], is filled with important insights about and documentation of popular interest in the substance of electoral contests.) Gienapp also recognizes that the triumph of the Republicans and the shattering of the Know-Nothings demonstrated the salience of free soil over nativism as a political issue in the North. Indeed, his account of the Know-Nothing party's fracturing is the most satisfactory one thus far in print. (I have supplemented it with the account contained in Henry Wilson, *History of the Rise and Fall of the Slave Power in America*, 3 vols. [1872–77; reprint, New York, 1969].)

Nonetheless, Gienapp's *Origins of the Republican Party* conveys the impression that much northern hostility to slave owners and their political representatives was artificially whipped up (by what Stephen Douglas would have called the "designing politicians" of the Republican party). Moreover (and even more problematically), Gienapp adheres to the original ethnocultural argument by explaining the crisis of the Whig party in the early 1850s—which opened the breach into which both Know-Nothings and Republicans stepped—almost exclusively in terms of the divisive effects of nativism. In the process, Gienapp severely slights the tensions generated within the Whig organization by the slavery question. He sees the destruction of the second party system and the creation of the third as resulting from distinct forces, almost as though their proximity in time were purely fortuitous.

Nativism was, of course, a real force in American life and politics and remained such even after the collapse of Know-Nothingism. Indeed Gienapp convincingly demonstrates (in "Nativism and the Creation of a Republican Majority in the North before the Civil War," *Journal of American History*, 12 [1985]: 529–59) the virulence of nativism in many state Republican organizations. The standard study of antebellum nativism remains Ray Allen Billington, *The Protestant Crusade, 1800–1860: A Study of the Origins of American Nativism* (1938; reprint, Chicago, 1964). Though the work contains a wealth of useful information, its analysis is often superficial and trails off into retrospective moralizing. W. Darrell Overdyke, *The Know-Nothing Party in the South* (Baton Rouge, 1950), attempts to resituate the American party in the era's deepening sectional crisis and the attempt by old Whigs and others to muffle it. I have suggested the nature and appeal of popular nativism in the text. In doing so, I have made use of the most widely circulated nativist tracts of the day, including J. Wayne Laurens, *The Crisis:, or, The Enemies of America Unmasked* (Philadelphia, 1855); Thomas R. Whitney, *A Defence of the American Policy, As Opposed to the Encroachments of Foreign Influence, and Especially to the Interference of the Papacy in the Political Interests and Affairs of the United States* (New York, 1856); Samuel S. Busey, *Immigration: Its Evils and Consequences* (New York, 1856); and John P. Sanderson, *Republican Landmarks: The Views and Opinions of American Statesmen on Foreign Immigration* (Philadelphia, 1856). Madeleine Hooke Rice, *American Catholic Opinion in the Slavery Controversy* (1944; Gloucester, Mass., 1964), examines the opinions expressed by the Catholic Church hierarchy on the subject of slavery, in the process helping to explain how so many opponents of slavery could see the papacy and the Slave Power as twin evils. A brief but suggestive glimpse into working-class nativism during the 1840s is offered in David Montgomery, "The Shuttle and the

Cross: Weavers and Artisans in the Kensington Riots of 1844," *Journal of Social History*, 5 (1972): 411–46.

The surest single study of the antebellum Republican party remains Eric Foner, *Free Soil, Free Labor, Free Men: The Ideology of the Republican Party Before the Civil War* (New York, 1970). Abraham Lincoln's place in the political crisis of the 1850s is treated in David Donald, *Lincoln Reconsidered: Essays on the Civil War Era* (2nd ed., New York, 1961); Stephen B. Oates, *With Malice Toward None: The Life of Abraham Lincoln* (New York, 1977); idem, *Abraham Lincoln: The Man Behind the Myths* (New York, 1984); Benjamin P. Thomas, *Abraham Lincoln: A Biography* (New York, 1952); and Don E. Fehrenbacher, *Prelude to Greatness: Lincoln in the 1850's* (Stanford, 1962). Harry V. Jaffa explored the themes raised in Lincoln's 1858 senatorial bid in his *Crisis of the House Divided: An Interpretation of the Issues in the Lincoln-Douglas Debates* (Chicago, 1959). Don E. Fehrenbacher, *The Dred Scott Case: Its Significance in American Law and Politics* (New York, 1978), is the definitive work on that subject. Kenneth M. Stampp's *America in 1857: A Nation on the Brink* (New York, 1990) surveys the key political events of 1857–58. James L. Huston, *The Panic of 1857 and the Coming of the Civil War* (Baton Rouge, 1987), discusses the impact that economic crisis had on sectional and party politics. Deepening fissures within the Democratic party in the years between Kansas-Nebraska and Lincoln's election can be examined in Roy Franklin Nichols, *The Disruption of American Democracy* (New York, 1948)—which should be reprinted—and two biographies of the Little Giant: Gerald M. Capers, *Stephen A. Douglas: Defender of the Union* (Boston, 1959), and Robert W. Johannsen's exhaustive *Stephen A. Douglas* (New York, 1973). James L. Huston's "Facing an Angry Labor: The American Public Interprets the Shoemakers' Strike of 1860," *Civil War History*, 28 (1982): 197–212, examines that conflict in the light of the looming presidential election. Reinhard H. Luthin, *The First Lincoln Campaign* (1944; reprint, Gloucester, Mass., 1964), remains useful in studying that election, as does Frederick C. Luebke, ed., *Ethnic Voters and the Election of Lincoln* (Lincoln, Neb., 1971).

10. *"The Inexorable Logic of Events":*
Secession, War, and Emancipation

The secession crisis can be examined in a number of studies, notably Steven A. Channing, *Crisis of Fear: Secession in South Carolina* (New York, 1970); Michael P. Johnson, *Toward a Patriarchal Republic: The Secession of Georgia* (Baton Rouge, 1977); William L. Barney, *The Secessionist Impulse: Alabama and Mississippi in 1860* (Princeton, 1974); and Daniel W. Crofts, *Reluctant Confederates: Upper South Unionists in the Secession Crisis* (Chapel Hill, 1989). Especially relevant to the argument advanced in this chapter is Peyton McCrary, Clark Miller, and Dale Baum, "Class and Party in the Secession Crisis: Voting Behavior in the Deep South," *Journal of Interdisciplinary History*, 8 (1978): 429–57. See also Fred Siegel, "Artisans and Immigrants in the Politics of Late Antebellum Georgia," *Civil War History*, 27 (1981): 221–31.

My treatment of the northern response to secession and the outbreak of war draws upon Kenneth Stampp, *And the War Came: The North and the Secession Crisis, 1860–61* (1950; reprint, Chicago, 1964); David M. Potter, *Lincoln and His Party in the Secession Crisis* (rev. ed., New York, 1962); Phillip Shaw Paludan, *"A People's Contest": The Union and the Civil War, 1861–1865* (New York, 1988); LaWanda Cox, *Lincoln and Black Freedom: A Study in Presidential Leadership* (Columbia, S.C., 1981); David Herbert Donald, *Charles Sumner and the Coming of the Civil War* (1960; reprint, Chicago, 1981); and Joel H. Silbey, *A Respectable Minority: The Democratic Party in the Civil War Era, 1860–1868* (New York, 1977).

On the Confederacy and its internal stresses, see (in addition to general works already cited) Ella Lonn, *Desertion during the Civil War* (New York, 1928); Georgia L. Tatum, *Disloyalty in the Confederacy* (Chapel Hill, 1934); Carl N. Degler, *The Other South: Southern Dissenters in the Nineteenth Century* (New York, 1974); James L. Roark, *Masters without Slaves: Southern Planters in the Civil War and Reconstruction* (New York, 1977); Emory M. Thomas, *The Confederate Nation: 1861–1865* (New York, 1979);

Paul Escott, *After Secession: Jefferson Davis and the Failure of Confederate Nationalism* (Baton Rouge, 1978); Drew Gilpin Faust, *The Creation of Confederate Nationalism: Ideology and Identity in the Civil War South* (Baton Rouge, 1988); and Wayne K. Durrill, *War of Another Kind: A Southern Community and the Great Rebellion* (New York, 1990). Ira Berlin years ago supplied me with the text of the report from escaped Union POWs quoted in this chapter.

Much modern discussion of the role played by slaves in the Civil War and the evolution of Republican policy regarding emancipation and black troops derives from W. E. B. Du Bois, *Black Reconstruction in America, 1860–1880: An Essay toward a History of the Part Which Black Folk Played in the Attempt to Reconstruct Democracy in America, 1860–1880* (1935; reprint, Cleveland, 1968). See Benjamin Quarles, *The Negro in the Civil War* (1953; reprint, New York, 1968); James M. McPherson, *The Negro's Civil War: How American Negroes Felt and Acted during the War for the Union* (1965; reprint, Urbana, 1982); Ira Berlin, Barbara J. Fields, Thavolia Glymph, Joseph P. Reidy, and Leslie Rowland, eds., *Freedom: A Documentary History of Emancipation, 1861–1867.* Series I, vol. 1: *The Destruction of Slavery* (Cambridge, Eng., 1985), and Series II: *The Black Military Experience* (New York, 1982); Eric Foner, *Reconstruction: America's Unfinished Revolution, 1863–1877* (New York, 1988); Dudley Taylor Cornish, *The Sable Arm: Negro Troops in the Union Army, 1861–1865* (New York, 1966); Joseph T. Glatthaar, *Forged in Battle: The Civil War Alliance of Black Soldiers and White Officers* (New York, 1991). See also Thomas Wentworth Higginson, *Army Life in a Black Regiment* (1869; reprint, Boston, 1962). Many of the vignettes that conclude my chapter are drawn from Leon F. Litwack's magnificent volume, *Been in the Storm So Long: The Aftermath of Slavery* (New York, 1979). I have also made use of Frank Moore, ed., *The Rebellion Record: A Diary of American Events, with Documents, Narratives, Illustrative Incidents, Poetry, Etc.*, 12 vols. (New York, 1861).

INDEX